THEOLOGICAL
OF COUNSELING

By

Thomas J. Edgington, Ph.D.
and
Linda K. Edgington

Copyright 2014

Thomas J. Edgington, Ph.D. and Linda K. Edgington

All rights reserved. No part of this book may be reproduced in any form or by any means without written permission of the author.

ISBN: 978-1-304-54578-7

Edgington Publications: Leesburg, IN

Printed in the U.S.A. by Lulu

DEDICATION

A number of years ago, Dr. Dave Plaster (who was the Academic Dean of Grace College and Seminary and the Systematic Theology professor) sat in on my master's level counseling class which had the same title as this book -- *Theological Foundations of Counseling*. He had asked if he could do so because he was interested in co-authoring a book with me by this same title. He knew of my interest in theology and I was well aware of his heart for counseling and helping those who hurt. As a prelude, Dave and I did a seminar together with some of the basic material we wanted to write about; but before we had a chance to work on this book, Dave went to be with the Lord unexpectedly. I think about him often and wish he were still here on earth. I also wish we could have collaborated on this book, but I am grateful for the time we had together, the seminar we did together, and for the time he spent in my class.

Dave, I miss you and dedicate this book to you. God used you powerfully in my life and in the lives of many people. Your godly impact has become a part of this book.

TABLE OF CONTENTS

Introduction..6

Chapter 1 – Presuppositions...12

Chapter 2 – Integration..42

Chapter 3 – Image of God..86

Chapter 4 – Social Capacity...90

Chapter 5 – Existential Capacity..100

Chapter 6 – Longings and Strategies..108

Chapter 7 – The Rational Capacity..182

Chapter 8 – The Teleological Capacity....................................202

Chapter 9 – The Volitional Capacity..218

Chapter 10 – The Behavioral Capacity 230

Chapter 11 – The Emotional Capacity.....................................240

Conclusion..276

Scriptural Index According to Page Number...........................278

Scriptural Index in Biblical Order..282

References..288

INTRODUCTION

In this text, we want to look at (as the title says) a theological foundation of counseling. What does the Bible have to say about how we help people? It has a great deal to say. So what this text will present is a biblical theory of personality, an understanding of what it means to be in the image of God – and basically, an understanding of how God made us, what goes wrong, and how to get back to His design.

So, if you think about those three steps, if you can figure out what He intended, and what goes wrong, then you can determine how to make things right and get back to what He intended. That is a very simple process -- at least on paper. And yet doing it (the counseling part), is often a difficult process-- especially when people say, "I don't want to get back to His design. I want to do it my way."

So really, that is the book -- those 3 things. But, the theory of personality in and of itself will take some in-depth study. We will try to answer several theological questions like: What does it mean to be made in the image and likeness of God? What is sin and how does it affect our personalities? Once we have come to an understanding about a biblical theory of personality, then we can better understand how to help people get back to the design that God intended. So this course will give you a comprehensive theory of personality, based upon a biblical anthropology. (That biblical anthropology can be found in another book I have written entitled, *Biblical Psychology [Edgington, 2013]*.)

We will start with presuppositions. What are the basic beliefs that must be present as a foundation for understanding this work? Our starting point is crucial to our final conclusions.

We will then look at the topic of integration. I do not like the term, but we will consider how one can put psychology and counseling together with the Bible. Are there better ways of describing that, than using the term, "integration?" An explanation will be given as to why I do not like the term, "integration." Then a phrase will be proposed that gives a better understanding of this term; however, the term could be legitimate if properly understood.

Much of this course is going to require thinking. I want you to think in ways that you may have never thought before. The main thing is, not to divorce yourself from the material – making it a theological discussion apart from who you are, rather than looking at what is inside of you. Because what we are going to be looking at is not just what is going on inside people, but what's going on inside of ourselves, as counselors – realizing what we bring to the table. And what we bring, inside of us, is going to determine, many times, what we do in counseling. So we are going to discuss not only theological topics, but personal topics.

God's design works. We want to know that design so that we can do the kind of things God intended -- not only to live fully and godly, but in a healthy way as well. We need help as we look to do this in our own lives, -- in learning and applying these things. When we do so, we can help others in a more effective way, giving to them what God has given to us. I hope you will be able to think about these things and incorporate them and use them for God's good. Ask for God's guidance as you look into his Word and attempt to assess how God made us, what goes wrong, how to get back what God intended, and how to implement what you have learned.

What are some of the global questions we ought to be asking in counseling? When you think of somebody coming in with a problem, if the first question is: "What do I do?" you are probably starting at the wrong place. In order to know what to do, you need to know some things first. What do you need know?

Why do we do what we do? This text will talk about motivations. What drives us? Why do we do the things we do?

What is the goal for counseling? Why did the client come in for counseling? We will look at "goals" versus "desires" and a stated goal versus the REAL goal. Sometimes people come in and say, "I really want help with my marriage," but what they are really saying is, "I'm here to change my spouse." Sometimes a man will sound like he wants to be a better husband when he is really saying, "Can you work on my wife a bit?" or "Can you help me, so I can go home and change her?" It's important to know the real goal of counseling because you may "block" it and they may not like you.

Where does victimization end and responsibility begin? When does something happen that I do not have any control of versus something I do have control of? How much of it is that "I am a personal agent? How much of it is, "I have a choice here. And if I don't do it, it's my responsibility"? And how much of it is "I'm a victim, and there's nothing I can do about it"? These are important questions because sometimes it is hard to distinguish between where one stops and another begins. We have all been victimized and some things I am naturally going to react to . . . I do not want to . . . but I am going to react because of what has happened to me in the past. Then I have some choices about what to do with those reactions that are based on how I have been victimized. Now we are talking about agency (responsibility). How do I put victimization and agency together?

What is my worldview? That is important too, because the way I look at the Bible affects my worldview. Do these biblical concepts apply to every culture? When I presented this material in Korea, I was amazed at the number of people who asked, "How did you know?" The answer: Because it is true for all people. It is not Korean, or German, or African, or Brazilian. It is not American. It is true for everyone.

Though there are some cultural issues that affect counseling, God's truths apply to everyone. The concepts taught in this book will be the ones that are more universal.

So to go beyond the first question of "What do I do?" you must ask a second question: "What is wrong?" Why is it important to know what is wrong? It is pretty tough to know what to do if we do not know what the problem is.

If your client says, "I'm depressed, I just can't get out of bed, I've been struggling, I'm just really been depressed and 'weepy,' I meet 8 out of the 9 criteria in DSM 5, so major depression is true for me, Please help me," what should the counselor do? Well, what is wrong?

What causes depression? Why do people get depressed? It could be a choice: "I'm choosing to be depressed." Maybe it is not a conscious choice, but a choice on some level. Maybe it is my thinking. Maybe it is my thyroid. It is bad thinking, bad choices, or a bad thyroid. Which is it?

The one you pick will determine what you do. Correct? Because if you believe your client has a thyroid problem, you are thinking: "Don't talk to me. Talk therapy isn't going to do anything for a thyroid problem. See your physician. Get some medication."

If it is bad thinking, as a counselor you do not want to look at your client's choices necessarily. Now choices might be part of it, but it is not that your client is choosing to be depressed. He/She could be choosing to think in the wrong way -- those two can go together. Maybe he/she doesn't even know he/she is making choices. So how can we help clients to think differently if they are just thinking the way they think? Maybe there is trauma in their background and they have never worked through that trauma, so their depression stems from the past trauma. If you do not get to the trauma, are you going to help alleviate it? You had better know what is wrong.

But be careful of thinking that you know for sure -- "I know what your problem is." Maybe as a counselor you think, "You are not trusting God. You need to read your Bible more and pray more." Well, if that is the problem, then maybe you have got the right solution.

Has anyone ever given you that advice? Has anyone ever diagnosed your problem as a "spiritual" one when you felt they were "missing" your heart or what the true problem was? And could it be a "spiritual" problem and yet not so simply resolved by simply reading the Scriptures and praying without clear guidance as to where the focus should be? And could the method of a counselor's delivery – sounding cold and judgmental, warm and concerned, or caring, yet confrontational – affect the healing process? You had better know what is wrong.

Yet sometimes you do not know right away. You can start by sending the client to their physician and ruling out the thyroid. But, you still may not know for sure. The tests could be wrong.

Or the problem could be serotonin levels. How do you detect that? There is presently no instrument now that measures serotonin levels. Do you know how they find out if you have got a serotonin problem? They give you medication. They say, "Let's see if this helps." It helped. Then the physician can say, "We think you've got a serotonin problem." Or you may say, "It didn't help." Well then, that must not be it. Or maybe it is combination of serotonin and norepinephrin. Or maybe it's dopamine.

Does the physician know for sure? NO! But, the more experience the physician & counselor have, the more they can say, "I think we can rule some of this out and we'll try this," but they do not know. It could still be bad choices. It could be past trauma. Be careful of, "I KNOW what's wrong with you."

I will call that the "I know syndrome." Many counselors, psychologists, psychiatrists, and physicians struggle with this syndrome. They think they know. They want to be the authority. And if you do not get better, it is because of you, not them. Be careful, as counselors, not to do this. Have strong convictions, but have humility and be willing to be wrong. Gather a great deal of data before jumping to conclusions and then trying to prove you are right. This will do damage to clients.

The question of "What's wrong?" is very important as you begin the counseling process. You do not know until you take more time to assess the situation, and even then you may not know. To know what is wrong, we had better know what is right!

I probably wash my hands 8 times a day. Is that a problem? Some may say, "Yes, that's a problem." Do you think that's a problem?

If I wash my hands 10 times a day, is that a problem? Well, you may say it depends on why I am doing it. If I am a doctor and I am working with patients and doing surgery, I would wash my hands more.

So let's say I am a professor. Is 10 times a day a problem? How about 15? 20? 40? When is it a problem? Well, I do not know it is a problem until I know what the proper or appropriate amount is. Right? If we say 10 is the standard, then 20 is a problem. If the line is that 20 is legitimate, then if I am washing my hands 40 times, it is a problem. But, if I'm a doctor/physician, I may wash more and that is legitimate. Or rather than setting a numerical limit, what if the criteria was: It is not a problem unless it is interfering with my life. Now, there is another criterion. I could be washing them 40-50 times a day and say, "I like washing my hands a lot." I could say, "I like to be clean."

So, how do I know if it is a problem? I have got to know what is RIGHT – what is proper functioning. What did God intend? What is normal?

The world has one view of what is normal. Does that fit with what the Bible teaches? This is a very important question since we are trying to help people get to a proper level of functioning -- what we will call "normal."

To know what is right (or proper functioning), we need a sound theory of personality. That is the purpose of this book – to look at a biblical theory of personality. With this kind of theory or model, we can better know what goes wrong and how to help others (and often ourselves) get back to what God originally intended.

But to know what is right and wrong (and how to help) we have to start with our presuppositions. Where we begin will determine where we land. If we begin with wrong presuppositions about life and humanity, we cannot help in the best way possible. That is why the next chapter begins with presuppositions. From there we will look at the topic of "integration," and then move on to a theory of personality. That theory will come from an understanding of what it means to be made in the image and likeness of God.

CHAPTER 1

PRESUPPOSITIONS

Everyone believes in something. Even if we believe that there is nothing to believe in, that is a belief. We all build our thinking and live our lives according to those beliefs or set of assumptions. And many of those beliefs or assumptions cannot be proven. We simply believe them. In order to develop a biblical theory of personality, we must start with a set of assumptions that will be termed "presuppositions."

1) There is Transcendence and There is Immanence

DEFINITIONS

As Christians we assume two important things: 1. We believe that there is another world outside of our own. 2. We believe that this world, our present world, is created. We believe in **Transcendence and Immanence**.

"Transcendence," in the strictest sense of the term, means that "non-created" world that "transcends" all time and creation. That could only include God.

"Immanence," in the strictest sense of the term, means "all that God created." This would include man, animals, earth, the universe, etc., along with heaven, angels, Satan (a fallen angel), spirits, etc. Typically however, most people and most theologians do not use these terms in their strictest senses.

The more common usage of the word "transcendence" refers to things that we *cannot* physically experience -- see, touch, hear, smell, or taste -- at this time. One designation is that the term "transcendence" denotes things that are "unseen" (broadly used to indicate things that are not physically experienced through man's five senses). *As typically used, transcendence includes God, along with Heaven, angels, Satan, spirits, demons, etc.*

When we think of "immanence," we tend to think more commonly about that which is "immanent" to us -- those things that we *can* see, touch, or physically "sense" in some way. *Immanence can be distinguished as those things which are "seen"* (or those things physically acknowledgeable by earthly man through his five senses) -- *including the earth, stars, man, animals, etc.* For the intent of this book, the more common reference to the terms "transcendence" and "immanence" will be used.

Whether the distinction is termed "Unseen vs. Seen" or "Transcendent vs. Immanent," as Christians we believe that a world exists that is outside of our current physical experience. God created a world that we cannot see, a world we cannot get to this side of the grave. We cannot take a bus trip today to Heaven. We cannot see it, yet we still believe that there is a vast, other world. It is an accepted belief, a "presupposition," for us. We "presuppose" it to be true. We assume that God and Heaven exist, without a need to be convinced, because God and Heaven are part of our belief system. They are part of a world that is "unseen" for us. The Bible talks about this in Hebrews 11:1 – "Now faith is being sure of what we hope for and certain of what we do not see."

THERE EXISTS ANOTHER WORLD

But are there people who do not believe in God, that also believe this presupposition -- that there is a world that we cannot see? During the months following the terror attacks of September 11, 2001, photos surfaced which observers claimed revealed spirits or "evil." Many were heard proclaiming verbally or in emails that

(Source: Public Domain)

they could see the shape of "the devil," "a demon," "evil personified," in the images of smoke rising from the twin towers. The people were talking about evil. They were talking about something Satanic.

Many of those imaginings came from people who did not even go to church. And though church was not a part of their lives, they were talking about demons and guardian angels -- supposing that there were angels there to help the distressed or deceased people. Pictures were created with angels superimposed who were holding, comforting, or directing victims of the attack. Those considering such things were not necessarily believers. Many certainly did not follow a conservative theology.

I was once invited into the office of a clinician and noticed crystals hanging up on the window. So I asked the clinician, "What are those?"

She responded, "Oh, those crystals give me power."

Becoming even more curious, I asked her to tell me more. She explained that there was energy in the crystals. Sometimes she would stare at them. Sometimes she would rub them. Sometimes she had clients also do those same things. The crystals would then empower her or empower her clients, she said.

She had put her belief in crystals. She presupposed that they had an energy that was important to acquire.

IMPLICATIONS FOR COUNSELING

If that presupposition is true, what are the implications for counseling? Our presuppositions will affect how we counsel others. If there is another world other than our own, that will affect how we counsel.

And if you say, "This world is it. This is all there is. We are here simply by time and chance -- evolutionary forces"; that presupposition is HUGE! Because if "this is it," then how would I do counseling?

"Seize the day?"[1] Seek personal happiness? Learn to cope and adapt?

What about morality? As a counselor who follows evolutionary thinking,[2] are you going to teach morality? Does morality make any sense if you follow that thinking? Only if it helps us survive, cope better, give us a better quality of life, or bring personal happiness. Why do we help people? I hope it is more than symptom relief, coping and adapting, better and greater happiness. I think there is more.

What if we believe "there *is* another world"? -- proposed in Presupposition 1. And what if we believe "there *is* a God"? -- Presupposition 2 (which will be discussed in the next section). Just add those two: 1) another world and 2) God. How will that affect how I do counseling? Does morality now make sense? Maybe it is not all about personal happiness. A presupposition of a spiritual world (transcendent) has many implications.

One of the divisions in the American Psychological Association is "Spirituality." It is interesting that an organization that uses General Revelation (research) as its base for knowledge would include a division that pertains to spirituality.

---

[1] Translated "Seize the day," from the Latin phrase, "Carpe Diem," used by the ancient philosopher and poet, Horace (65 BC - 8 BC), and popularized contemporarily by the 1986 movie, "Dead Poets Society."

[2] There is an aspect of "evolution" that is true – known as "microevolution." This has to do with variation within species. Creationists agree with this. The problem is with "macroevolution" in which one species gradually evolved into another species. This involves mutation and natural selection. Creationists do not agree with this. When I use the term, "evolution," I am referring to "macroevolution."

Why? Could it be that they know there is more? Ecclesiastes 3:11 says that God has "set eternity in the hearts of men."[3] We know there is more!

How many times have people said, "There's got to be more than this"? They are right.

That has huge implications for counseling. When we assume that there is another world out there -- a transcendent world, it will affect us psychologically and it will affect how we do counseling.

2) There Exists a "Personal" God

The second presupposition follows the first: There is a God, a PERSONAL (key word here) being, who is transcendent and who dwells in transcendence.

Genesis 1:1, "In the beginning <u>God</u> created . . ."

Where did He come from? How did he get there? Had He been planning? When did He start planning? How long did it take Him to plan?

These are things that children often ask their parents. "Where did God come from?" "How old is He?" "How could someone just always be?"

All the Bible says is, "In the beginning, GOD. . ." The Bible assumes His presence. It says that He is eternally present in the past. That is all we know. We just have to believe it (or better said, we *choose* to believe it).

Exodus 3:14, "I am, who I am." What is He trying to say?

Moses: "Who should I say sent me?"

"Tell them, 'I am' sent you."

"What is your name?"

"I am that I am"

What is God trying to say? He is trying to say something about His name. His name is important. His name is trying to say, "I'm the self-sufficient one," "I'm it," "I'm what it's all about," ". . . I am." Christ came along and said, "I am the bread of life., I am the living water . . . I am."

Now here is the important part: God is a personal being. He is not a blob. He is not a "force" (like that referred to in the *Star Wars*

---

[3] Unless otherwise indicated all Bible references in this book are quoted from the New International Version.

movies --"May the *force* be with you"). He is a PERSONAL being who is really out there.

And not only is He "out there," but He is everywhere -- omnipresent. He is not IN everything; that would be Pantheism. But everything is within His grasp. He is omnipresent.

So right now God sees us and He can take hold of us if He needs to. That probably does not mean that He is flowing through the room necessarily, but He is saying, "I see you. I can take hold of you at any moment."

So what are the implications for counseling? Remember God is personal. What makes that different from being "the force"? How is that different from a God who is a "blob"? Or how is that different from a belief that there is just some "force of good and/or evil" out there?

Accountability would be a natural consequence of our belief in God. If God is personal, if He is a person, then we are accountable to someone. All other persons are accountable to the Supreme Person.

That belief could also impact our thinking in negative ways. We could think, "Where was He? If He is personal and He loves me and He could have been there, why wasn't He?"

Now we could speculate that He started all of this but then said, "You guys do whatever you want. I'm going to be in heaven. Whatever you do is up to you.'"

But, that is not what the Bible tells us. The Bible says we are accountable to Him. We are going to give an account. We are going to answer to Him.

Now think about it. If God created personal beings, it only makes sense that He would think, "I've invested something in you. I made you like me. I want to know that you are doing things that I want you to do." Does that change how we do counseling?

And IF we believe that we are personally accountable to a God and one day we will have to give an answer for how we lived our lives, does that change how we live our lives and how we work with people? I think so.

GOD IS A GOOD GOD

This brings us to a sub-point: The person we are accountable to, is a GOOD God. So a sub-point to Presupposition number 2 is the presupposition that "God is good."

We are accountable to someone who has our best interests in mind. That is different from a God who is a tyrant, a God who is like Zeus -- who is fickle and leaves us never knowing what is going to happen or what we can depend on. We have a God who is perfectly righteous. He always does what is right and good, even if it may not appear so. This is an important sub-point to our presupposition.

IMPLICATIONS FOR COUNSELING

So the question then is: "What makes Christian counseling different?" This is an important question that follows our presuppositions. If there is a personal God who is transcendent and dwells in transcendence, what is the goal of counseling (if done from that perspective)?

The primary difference between Christian and secular counseling has to do with our goals and the theology that we base those goals upon. One thing that makes Christian counseling different is the GOAL. It is not just the Bible, though our counseling should be biblical. We need to have theologically driven goals. Our theology (based on the Bible) drives what we do. Because of that theology, the goals of a Christian counselor are very different from those of the secular world.

My goal as a Christian counselor is to help people find God, know God, and serve God. If you do not know God, I want to help you find Him. If you have found Him, I want to help you know Him better. And if you know Him, I want to help you serve Him.

In the secular world, the goal is not to help people find God, know God, and serve God. Typically the secular counselor's goal is helping people cope, adapt, and be happier. But that is also kind of a "skyhook" -- "I want to be happy." And what are you grounding your happiness in? "Whatever makes me happy."

But, what is interesting is that the existentialists will say, "That's the way it is, There is no ground." Their word is "groundlessness." There is no ultimate rock. There is no ultimate hope. There is nothing. The existentialist would say that you are out there on your own, BUT you are small "g" god and you can create meaning and purpose -- therefore, that is what life is all about.

I once went to hear Irvin Yalom – an incredible existential therapist who has done a great deal of in-depth thinking and writing. What I find interesting is that he said, "When I do counseling, this is what I do. I help people with their problems . . . help them be a little less depressed, less anxious, have better relationships. I do all of that, but that's not what I really want to do. What I really want to do is teach existentialism. I want to talk about the universal concerns of life which include depth, meaning, and relationships. But really," he said, "the ultimate concern is 'aloneness.' Ultimately, we do this life alone. We do relationships, but ultimately it comes down to having to face the world alone." He talked about 4 pillars of existentialism and said that is what he really wanted to discuss in counseling. "I'll do other things to help people live a better life and help them feel better," he said, "but what I really want to do is teach what I'm passionate about." And I thought, if existentialists can do that, why can't we Christians do that as well (even in secular settings)?

But, I do not want to push my agenda onto my clients. I do not want to force anyone into my belief system, but I do hope and pray that when I am working with someone, helping them to better manage their lives, what I really want to do is talk to them about God. My primary goal is to help them find God, know God, and serve God. That is what drives me. That is what makes Christian counseling different.

If we do not have the first two presuppositions -- "There is another world" and "There is a personal God" -- then we are not going to be driven to know God better and to serve God because that would not make any sense. There would be no transcendence. There would be no God. So personal happiness or coping and adapting would be what life is all about. That is what would make sense.

But even Christians have said, "Isn't happiness what it's all about? Doesn't God want us to be happy?" Not necessarily.
It is clear that God likes happiness. The Bible demonstrates that in numerous places. It talks about having a happy/cheerful heart" in Proverbs 15:13 and 17:22. Psalms is filled with verses describing joy as a positive experience desired by God. David "danced before the Lord" (2 Sam. 6:14) -- an indication that this "man after God's own heart" enjoyed events in his life. In Luke 2:11, the shepherds were told by an angel, "I bring you good news of great joy. . ." God does not want us to be "overwhelmed by excessive sorrow" (2 Cor. 2:7). And ultimately (meaning -- in heaven), God wants us to be happy.

But in this present world, to be in some kind of constant "euphoric state" is not what God seems to have in mind. And sometimes, the best way to understand joy is to have something to compare it with -- pain.

Christ felt deep sadness and was known as a "Man of Sorrows" (Isa. 53:3); yet Paul talks about contentment in spite of his trials (Phil. 4:11). So something seems to be even more important than a perpetual state of happiness in response to our world and events in our lives, and that is godliness. True godliness will lead to contentment.

Contentment is a deeper form of happiness. Contentment says, "I'm okay, even if my circumstances aren't. I have hope, even when it seems hopeless. I have enough, even if it seems like there is not enough to go on."

We can actually use life's difficulties to find God. We can learn to know deeper peace when we go through trials and problems. But is that something that comes easily for a Christian?

Even Paul asked God not once, but THREE TIMES, to remove a particular "thorn in his flesh" (2 Cor. 12:9)! Yet what was God's answer? ". . . My power is made perfect in weakness." We can find God in a deeper way and display His grace with more power when we are confronted with life's difficulties.

Yet, some attempt to USE God to solve their problems. If we USE God to solve our problems, then who is God? When we try to manipulate God to give us what we want or to get us out of pain or to change a situation, who is trying to be in control? We are.

We sometimes approach God like He is a cosmic Santa Claus who will give us what we want, whenever we ask for it; rather than saying, "Maybe God is allowing me to go through this depression, or this anxiety, or this marital/family problem, or this sleep problem, or this illness, or whatever it is . . . Maybe He is allowing that, so that I can find Him in a new way." Many times it is when we have really struggled with life's difficulties that we are able to understand God in a new way. And maybe He also allows those we care about -- a friend or a child or a family member -- to have difficulty so that they can know Him better as well.

So if that is true, as a counselor, do I want people out of the "pit" right now? I do not like to see people struggle. I want to see good things happen. But, maybe the ultimate goal is not to "get them out of the pit." Maybe in the pit, they are going to find God. And when that happens, they will eventually get out of the pit, yet be better because of the time spent there. Maybe they found God. Or maybe they found Him in a new way. Or they know Him a little bit better. Or they want to serve Him more.

I have worked with a number of people who I have asked, "Before this happened to you or before your depression or before you struggled the way you did, what would you have told people who were in your situation?" Many of those strong, devout believers said something to the effect that, "I would have told them, 'You're not trusting God enough.' 'You need to read the Bible more.' 'Quit feeling sorry for yourself and get on with your life!' 'Go out and help somebody! Your problem is selfishness and you need to quit thinking about yourself and go help someone else!'" Yet after battling through the same difficult situation -- maybe it was the loss of a child or a job or maybe it was a disease or cancer or rape, the response often changes to something like this: "I'd tell them, 'Let's talk. Can we talk?'"

We do not want to have struggles. We want to have joy, comfort, pleasure, and good circumstances. But maybe the ultimate goal is not for us to have all of our desires fulfilled. Maybe through difficult times we are going to find God; and when that happens, we will actually enjoy our lives more!

Because of our pain, sometimes we become better "lovers." God often uses our pain as a way of helping us to love people better. And pain often bonds us to others. We feel a connection; and it can also be an avenue of leading a fellow sufferer to Christ. God, in His infinite wisdom, knows what we need in order to enjoy life more -- and sometimes that is pain that appears to make no sense to us.

The following poem by Bob Perks is written as a wish from a parent to a daughter. Maybe that is what a good parents should wish for their children. Maybe that is what God desires for us.

ENOUGH

I wish you enough sun to keep your attitude bright.
I wish you enough rain to appreciate the sun more.
I wish you enough happiness to keep your spirit alive.
I wish you enough pain so that the smallest joys in life
    appear much bigger.
I wish you enough gain to satisfy your wanting.
I wish you enough loss to appreciate all that you possess.
I wish you enough "Hello's" to get you through the final
    "Good-bye."[4]

Now, do we want to struggle or to see those we care about struggle? No! Not at all! But in the "pit," sometimes something can happen that is bigger than not being depressed or being healthy, or making lots of money, or being treated fairly all the time, etc., because the two greatest commandments are: "Love God with your heart, soul, and mind," and "Love your neighbor as yourself."

Through pain, we can learn how to love a neighbor better. We can even learn to love God more. We can appreciate His comfort, and His mercy, and His grace. Before loss, we often do not see the NEED for any of that.

So one may not feel the need to stay very close to God when comfortable and "having it all together." But, when someone is in the

---

[4]Bob Perks, "I Wish You Enough," http://www.motivateus.com/stories/iwish2.htm, Copyright © 2001. Bob has also published a book with the same name -- *I Wish You Enough!* – published by Thomas Nelson Publishers, based on the "Eight Wishes" given in the poem. Permission to use poem granted by Bob Parks, 10/5/10.

"pit" and when all that can be said is, "Help!" that is often when God does His greatest work. And sometimes God wants us there because dependency is more important than feeling good and immediate personal happiness.

Believing in a personal God causes us to focus on Him and His ultimate purpose. We realize we are dependent beings and when we struggle and have pain, we understand God is in control and wants to accomplish something in and/or through us. That dependency on God gives us a rock for our foundation, which provides us the strength and determination to carry on.

3) Everything Reflects God

Presupposition number 3: "There is a God who is the creator and sustainer of everything; therefore, everything reflects God."

If you have ever created something -- drawn something, painted something, sculpted something, built something, decorated something, invented something -- you realize that your creation says something about you. If someone were to examine your product, what might that person learn about you? That person might learn that you are very detailed. He/she may learn that you take pride in what you do. Maybe the examiner would learn that you are a very bold person, that you have a sense of humor, or that you care about others. You cannot create without your creation reflecting you, because it is YOU coming out onto that piece of paper or in that building or whatever it is that you have created.

It is the same with God. When He created the world, the world said, "I reflect God." It was telling us something about its creator. The creation cannot help but do that.

Everything in the world that God created, reflects God -- including us. We reflect God. We illustrate who He is.

So does it make sense to study psychology? If psychology is: "The study of mental and behavioral processes" and God created those mental and behavioral processes, does it make sense that we can get to know God better by studying His creation -- which involves mental and behavioral processes?

This point is important because some Christian people have said that psychology is sinful, "of the devil," and should not be studied. But, if psychology is something that God created (Psychology must be defined correctly -- as the study of our thinking and behavior -- because if one starts with a faulty definition of psychology, the result will be a faulty conclusion as to whether we should study it or not), then does it not make sense that studying it will help us know God better? (Psalm 111:2).

If God created psychology -- mental and behavioral processes, if that is true, does psychology reflect God? Would Biology reflect God? How about Philosophy? Mathematics?

How does math reflect God? There are laws that make sense. With math there is order; and importantly, with math comes an understanding of infinity.

Most of us remember some childhood experience that involved infinity. The conversation probably went something like this: "I'm going to do this one hundred million zillion, times" to which the friend responds, "I'm going to do it one hundred million zillion and one!" which is countered with, "I'm going to do it one hundred million zillion and two." And this could keep going on and on with each one trying to "better" the other's statement. There is no end to how far it could go. With math, we understand something about infinity.

IMPLICATIONS FOR COUNSELING

Everything in this world reflects God -- including us. So what are the implications for counseling?

First of all, the whole idea of "Creation versus Evolution" comes to the forefront of our consideration. Could all of this have happened by chance, without some sort of plan or design?

But if God created everything, then it makes sense that we ought to know the Creator and understand His design. And life works better if we take the time to know and understand our Creator and His design for this world and for us.

A number of years ago when our children were small, I put together a swing set. As I unpacked the materials, I quickly set aside the paper that was included in the box with a list of steps on how it was to be assembled.

"Instructions?" I thought, "I'm a man; I don't need instructions. I can do this."

I laid it all out. "It's simple! It's a swing set. There's nothing hard about this!"

But I found it was a tedious job. There were lots of nuts and bolts and pieces to screw together.

When I got to the second-to-the-last step, I was ready to attach the swing to the rod that went through the hollow pole at the top. I looked at the ground and there was the rod! Everything else on the swing set was put together.

As I stared at the rod and then at the hollow pole, I came to a sobering realization, "Hmmm, that was probably supposed to be in there, so I could attach the swing to that." My heart sank.

Realizing I had made a mistake, I dismally began unscrewing the pieces. I ended up taking the WHOLE swing set apart, because when I looked at the instructions I noticed that it said, (in clear, bold letters) to make sure to put the rod in BEFORE proceeding. Needless to say, I was NOT a "happy camper."

After I got it all apart, I put the rod in, put the whole thing back together, and attached the swings. But what should have been a two-hour job turned out to be about a six-hour job. If I had just looked at the instructions first, I could have saved myself a lot of trouble!

Do you think maybe God is saying that? "If you would just take a look at how I created things and understand what I intended, it would make life go a lot better than your trying to do it on your own."

The evolutionist says, "There is no God; therefore . . ." What? "Cope. Adapt. Find personal happiness. That is what it is all about." I believe there is more.

The study of psychology reflects God. It is the same as biology, chemistry, physics, math, and philosophy; it all reflects God and it is all worth studying.

After learning about amoebas, a Christian college student was struck with their intricacy in her biology class. "I don't know how people cannot believe there is a God," she shared. "There are thousands of detailed characteristics to this one-celled creature. How do you not believe in God?"

Yes! Look what God did with amoebas! Incredible! Compare that to the biggest star. He is big God! It is pretty awesome to try to fathom what God is all about. And that reflection of God has huge implications for counseling!

We want to help others reflect God's design and as counselors, we want to reflect God in our words and in our work. Why? Because we believe God's way works!

4) "God Has Revealed Himself to Us"

Presupposition Number 4: Not only is God's creation a reflection of Him, but it is a revelation of Him as well. It does not just demonstrate to us what God is like, but it is also one way He communicates to us about Himself. In essence, God says, "I'm going to tell you about me." The following are five ways that God tells us about Himself.

GOD HAS REVEALED HIMSELF THROUGH NATURE

When you experience a storm or when you see anything -- the beauty of mountains or trees, God is being revealed. In fact, Psalm 19:1 says, "The heavens declare the glory of God."

Those who have never visited the Grand Canyon still usually have a preconceived opinion of what it looks like. But those who have visited it describe an astounding "masterpiece" that cannot be comprehended unless actually experienced personally.

Before I saw the Grand Canyon I thought, "Yeah, yeah! It's a big hole in the ground." But, when I stepped off of the tour bus and began to take in its beauty and immensity, it literally took my breath away. I did not realize that nature could have that effect on me. I remember thinking, "Wow! This is incredible!"

And the Grand Canyon is simply a big hole! But there is just something about nature that says, "Look at God!" "Look what He can do!" "Look what He made!"

What an extraordinary experience it must be {Source: Lawlor, O. (2004)} to travel in space. What an amazing encounter with God's creation! It makes sense why scientists at NASA become so excited when observing the stars, the galaxies, and all of the formations and interactions in the entirety of outer space -- that HUGE expanse of infinite proportions!

So, that which is observed and experienced in God's created world tells about Him. Therefore, *Nature* is certainly a way that God has revealed Himself to us. We call this "general revelation." God has also used other methods to reveal Himself.

GOD HAS REVEALED HIMSELF THROUGH HIS SON

(Source: Public Domain)

When God sent His Son, Christ Jesus, to Earth, God told us more about Himself. He provided us with a tangible figure that could be observed interacting with all of man's natural activities. He furnished us with a glimpse of what perfection in manhood looks like and another evidence of what God is like. Since Christ is God, Christ revealed God to man.

This is why it is so important to study the life of Christ. It tells us how God would respond in a particular situation. It tells us how God thinks, acts, and feels as a human being. In counseling, it is helpful to direct our clients to the 4 Gospels to see how Christ dealt with difficult situations.

GOD HAS REVEALED HIMSELF THROUGH MIRACLES

We also presuppose another method of revelation in miracles! Christ raised Lazarus (John 11). He changed water into wine (John 2). He healed many sick and afflicted people. God used miracles to tell us about Himself -- His awesome power, His caring nature, etc.

GOD HAS REVEALED HIMSELF THROUGH DIRECT CONVERSATION -- SPEAKING

{Source: Clipart.com (2011)}

Sometimes God the Father has *talked* directly to man or through His angels to man. When God spoke to Moses through the burning bush, He was using direct communication (Exod. 3, 4). Both through the words that He spoke and through His method, God was saying, "Moses, let me tell you who I am and what I want you to do!" God also spoke directly to Abraham (Gen. 17), to Saul/Paul (Acts 9) and others. He used direct conversation to tell man about Himself.

GOD HAS REVEALED HIMSELF THROUGH THE BIBLE – HIS WORD

The last of God's revelations of Himself is through His Word -- the Bible. As Christians, we accept that fact. If we want to get to know God better, we need to know what His Word says about Him. The Reverend John MacArthur said, "If I can't trust the Bible fully, then I can't trust what it says about God" (MacArthur, 2009). So we have to start with that belief because it is upon an inerrant word that the rest of our faith is learned and built.

{Source: Clipart.com (2011)}

"All scripture is God-breathed and is useful for teaching, rebuking, correcting and training in righteousness..." (2 Tim. 3:16). What are the implications of that belief?

THE BIBLE DEALS WITH REAL PEOPLE WITH REAL FEELINGS AND ACTIONS!

It is remarkable how pertinent the Bible is to our everyday lives. It has something to say about life's most important issues -- relationships, marriage, depression, anxiety. It is all in there -- even though we often forget to look there for help with those issues. Or sometimes, we do not have the eyes to see the answers given. We may read a particular passage without thinking, "Wait a minute! What is it that Hezekiah was feeling at that moment?"

When God went to Moses and said, "I want you to go to Egypt and lead my people out," what did Moses do (Exod. 3, 4)? He argued with God! "Uhhh...You really don't want me. You see, I'm not a good public speaker. I don't do that real well. So . . . uh . . . You probably want somebody else" (my paraphrase).

So God went into a lengthy discourse and said, "No, Moses, I want you and I'm going to give you what you need. I made you. I made your mouth. I know what you are capable of."

And Moses continued, "Okay, I hear you God. But, there's another problem. Nobody's going to believe me! They're going to say, 'Who are you?' and 'Who sent you?' and 'How do we know that?'"

What you hear is *self-contempt*! And yet GOD is talking to him! Begin taking apart that story. What an amazing story! God is talking to him. Moses is looking at a miracle -- the burning bush, and he is ARGUING with God based on his self-contempt!

"You don't want me! I tried that 40 years ago. It didn't work out so well! I've been in the desert now. It's pretty comfortable. And, I just wondered if it would be okay if I could just stay here" (my paraphrase).

Rather than confront Moses's self-contempt (which He would have been justified to do), God decided to send Aaron with Moses to provide some help and "security." With that, Moses finally agreed.

You can see numerous examples of psychology in there! God's word is FULL of people, <u>real</u> people, who are struggling, and trying to figure things out, and making a mess of their lives, and then trying to find the right way to go!

And then, look at David. The story of his life provides ALL kinds of psychological data -- unfair treatment, success, failures, family problems, highs and lows, etc. But, you have to have eyes to see it and to look at Scripture and say, "I think there's something more there than simply a systematic theology or simply a story. There is a lot going on there." They were REAL people that felt just like we do!

THE BIBLE IS A THE ULTIMATE COUNSELING GUIDEBOOK

And notice what the rest of 2 Timothy 3:16 says: The Bible is profitable "for doctrine, for reproof, for correction, and for instruction" (KJV). It is a great book for counseling! AND it tells us something about God's design. So we ought to learn the Bible to know God's design.

IMPLICATIONS FOR COUNSELING

If God has revealed Himself through nature (including the nature of man), we want to use that general revelation to help us in counseling. If He has revealed Himself in the Bible, which talks about psychology and counseling, we want to discover what it says. The Bible tells us about God's design for us, what went wrong (and what goes wrong), and how to get back to His design. The intention of this book is to study those various revelations of God.

5) God Made People in His Image and Likeness

Not only did God create us, but the Bible says that God created us in His image and in His likeness (Gen. 1:26, 27). We are going to try

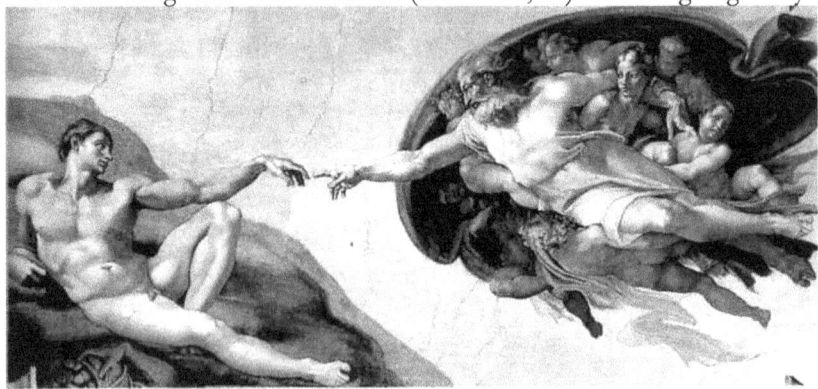

{Source: Michelangelo (1511)}

to figure out what that means because we have a problem: God told us in six different passages that we are made in His image and likeness, yet He never tells us specifically what that means.

Nowhere in the Bible are we given a definition for the "image" and "likeness" of God, so numerous theologians have given varied ideas of what those words mean. Different views of "image" and "likeness" will be examined in Chapter 3 along with the effect that being created in God's "image" and "likeness" has on "personality"; but for now, "image" and "likeness" will be assumed -- even though we may not fully understand what that means. We are like God in some way.

IMPLICATIONS FOR COUNSELING

Our view of the image and likeness of God influences our thinking and behavior. One way that happens is that we have a respect for human beings -- ALL human beings, no matter how "bad" they are. We have an intrinsic respect for people. So even though we do not think highly of criminals, as sincere Christians, we can choose to love them and pray for them.

Taking the time to do something that may benefit the wicked goes against man's natural inclination. The tendency is to just want to hate evil people! It is easy for people sometimes to look at certain others and think, "I don't respect you. There's no intrinsic value to you. This has HUGE implications for counseling -- how we look at a perpetrator of abuse, addicts who have destroyed their families, or perverts who have severely neglected their children.

The desire is to see evil people punished! And though the Bible does demonstrate that there is a time for punishment of and/or separation from unrepentant sinners, there is something about being in the image and likeness of God that gives us a respect for human beings. That respect says, "I want your salvation. I want you to know God. I want you to receive His forgiveness." Shouldn't we pray for those people and desire to see them change?

I have heard, "I could never work with perpetrators. I just can't work with that type of person." Some say, "I can't work with somebody who's a cocaine addict. I couldn't work with that!" I think we need t to be careful about believing that some types of people are a little "lower" than we are.

Now if one is thinking, "I don't know a lot about that area and because I'm not an expert I wouldn't be of much help," that is different. There is a time to say, "I'm not good with that particular problem" or I am still working on some of my own issues and I am not ready quite yet for that particular population."

But sometimes the belief is: "I can't work with THOSE people." I wonder if it is because we think we are a little better and they are a little less valuable. We have to be careful of that in counseling.

Other implications for counseling will be discussed in chapters 3-11. It will become clear in those chapters that there are many implications.

6) We Represent God – Though Sinfully/Imperfectly

Now we move to Presupposition number 6. Part of what it means to be in the image and likeness of God is that God says, "You are to represent Me. You are my ambassadors here on Earth. You are to represent Me and to represent Me well."

After God created man, a problem entered in. That problem is called "sin." It changed how man represented God. People no longer have the FULL capacity to represent God well.

Sin has to do with not going God's way. We have chosen to go our own way and we think that there will be no negative consequences when we do so. The Bible makes it clear that there are divine consequences (Prov. 14:16).

Now some say, "Sin MARRED the image of God." Though that is commonly used terminology -- especially among theologians, it is not always clear what that means. We may know what it means to "mar" a statue. -- Someone or something breaks off the nose or the arm, etc. But, what does it mean to "mar" the image and likeness of God?

The problem could be summarized by saying: We do not represent God well. We do not have the full capacity to represent God well, the way we used to.

Because of sin, we are now corrupted. We are "depraved." But what does that mean?

Depravity is a concept that is sometimes misunderstood. Depravity, or being fully depraved, does not mean you are as sinful as you can be.

Even Hitler had days where he chose to do "nice" things. He had a female companion. He must have treated her well enough that she decided to stay with him. He picked up children and hugged them. He put food on people's tables! He had seemingly good moments! The horrific, evil things that he did are well known, but he wasn't as BAD as he could have been!

Depravity simply means, "We're as BAD OFF as we can be" (Eph. 2:1, Rom. 6:23). In the sight of God, we are in deep trouble -- and all it takes is ONE sin! Every human being misses the mark of perfection (Jer. 17:9; Rom. 3:23). So it does not mean we are as BAD as we can be; but it does mean we are as BAD OFF as we can be. Some major consequences of sin keep us from a relationship with God and keep us from following His design. Yet we still have characteristics that represent God, though those characteristics can "bend" in sinful directions. As Christians, we have the opportunity to use those characteristics for good as we strive to represent God well.

IMPLICATIONS FOR COUNSELING

As counselors, we will represent God. We can represent Him in good ways or in sinful ways. If we want to represent Him well as counselors, it will be important to understand His design for us.

7) People Are Held Accountable to God.
We Are Personally Responsible for Our Sins.

Sometimes we think we are pretty good people and we can become proud of our accomplishments. That is not to say that we should not feel good about being productive and useful; but what does our righteousness without Christ look like to God?

Isaiah 64:6 paints an abhorrent mental picture for us. It says,

"Our righteousness is as . . . filthy rags." The passage is actually comparing our righteousness to menstrual rags.

The context of the passage refers specifically to the Israelites in Isaiah's time who were not following God. It is interesting to note that Isaiah includes himself in this passage, showing that this truth could be applied to the entire human race.

All of us are declared "unclean" and our righteous acts (even the best of them) have "become like a garment stained with menstrual discharge" (Keil & Delitzsche, 1975, p. 470). This passage is quite strong. It compares righteousness to a soiled, feminine hygiene product that is repulsive to God. This is the best we can do without God.

Even as Christians, our righteousness can look like that. We have the capability to be righteous, but we will still struggle with sin (Rom. 7:7-25). Thanks be to Christ that He is the answer (not us) and in Him there is no condemnation (Rom. 8:1). So, even as Christians we struggle with sin and sometimes our sin can be very ugly.

PEOPLE WHO SEEM TO BE "NICE" ARE NOT ALWAYS GOOD CHRISTIANS

There are people -- Christians, people claiming to be Christians, and non-Christians -- who are very "nice-looking" people. Some of them may also lead us to believe that they are really "good" -- not possessing that filthy core -- and to us they may look "good." But remember Christ's words concerning the Pharisees in Matthew 23 and other passages? What about motive? What about thinking? What about things that are under the surface -- they look good on the outside, but maybe underneath is there something else going on? Proverbs 20:5 addresses the fact that knowing "the purposes of a man's heart" can be difficult because they are "deep waters." Yet the Bible says that "a man of understanding draws them out."

When living our lives as Christians in this world, we need to be aware that though we all have a filthy core and are dependent on God's grace for entrance to heaven, there are some who lead us to believe that they do not possess that filthiness. They may even be very convincing as they cite their attainment of high Christian values without acknowledging fault. Those are the ones that Christ warns us about. When you understand the "psychology" of what is going on (of which the entire Bible cites specific incidences over and over again), then you can be "armed" with the weapons (Eph. 6:10-18) to recognize and attack the evil that may be intent on "sucking" you in. When you are in relationship with those who never acknowledge specific sins -- who rationalize away the wrong that they do and seem to be intent on "selling" themselves as godly – beware! When people promote themselves, reluctant to humbly acknowledge their failures to others, the Bible says of that type in Mark 8:15, "Be careful . . . Watch out for the yeast of the Pharisees . . ." (All of us have a desire to overlook our own faults, so having that tendency is not what is being referred to here. The godly person will "catch" himself many times and humble himself by acknowledging his sin. The ungodly person refuses to look at his wrongdoing when directly confronted or even over time, and tends to find convincing ways to rationalize his sin away.)

As believers, we want to try to find out, "How do I keep myself from being that kind of Christian?" and "What do I do when somebody comes in to me for counseling and that person is living with someone who is full of arrogance and pretense, but he/she can make it look so good (and even look godly)?" What if a client is living with somebody who's sinful in that way? How does one help that person when his/her family member looks good and others buy into the "persona?" That is a difficult situation!

If I do not have eyes to see that in counseling, I may just "buy" what looks good on the outside, and respond, "What are you talking about? He/she is wonderful!" That, obviously, would be very detrimental to the client if his or her counselor did not realize that he/she was aware of something, that is true. Sometimes people do live with what we sometimes call "crazy-makers."

Or what if one's client is the "Pharisee?" Sometimes counselors get "sucked in" to the lies and do not give the appropriate feedback. These clients can look and sound so good!

So what we need to realize and assume as Christians and as counselors is that we all DO have a filthy core and we are responsible for that sin. Everyone has that "rotten," "grimy" core. We all need forgiveness by confessing our sin and humbly offer our wretched selves to God. We all need to take responsibility for what is ours. Sin is there in everyone. Realizing that we all have a filthy core helps us avoid being "fooled" by those who can present a convincing "front" and helps us keep from developing those dishonest traits as well.

Ezekiel 18 is a passage that points out responsibility. In this passage, it is saying, "No, it is not what your father or your grandfather did. It is you." You are going to be held accountable only for you. The Bible says that each one is accountable for his/her own sins (Jer. 31:30). Though it is true that other generations can cause you problems and, because of their sin, they can do things that damage you that can go on or have gone on for several generations; but YOU can break the cycle. Why? Because we are responsible for our own lives and we can make godly choices in the present, no matter what has happened to us in the past. As counselors, we want to remind our clients of this important truth.

IMPLICATONS FOR COUNSELING

So what are the implications for counseling? And how should Christians respond to their own victimization or the "victim" mentality of someone else?

THE "VICTIM" MENTALITY

If we were victimized as children, does that take away our responsibility as Christians? Can we blame any of our present condition on that victimization?

First of all, we all have been victimized -- some much worse than others. Some have been victimized in dreadful ways and that should not be overlooked or minimized. But, the fact of the matter is that all of us have gone through some sort of victimization. If we did not receive it at home, we probably did at school. All of us can tell stories of ways we were hurt by other children . . . ways we were hurt by other adults . . . by people who were supposed to be leading, who were supposed to be caring for us, looking after us . . . even by people in the church – sometimes "spiritual" people. We can all tell stories of how we have been victimized.

We are not responsible for that. We are not responsible for what our parents did to us . . . what a teacher did to us . . . what the Boy Scout leader did to us. We are not responsible for people who victimized us. We are not responsible for our victimization and how we were treated by others.

But we ARE responsible for how we respond to our victimization. How will we think about that? What choices will we make around that? How will we behave given that? We may not be able to control certain emotions that come up, but what do we choose to do with those emotions? Now, we are talking about responsibility!

This is so important because counseling often stops with victimization. And if that is the case, some are very drawn to counseling because they get to talk about their victimization. As the counselee, it becomes a chance for me to talk about people who have hurt me and how I have been damaged by them. I like it when my counselor empathizes with and feels for me. But do not ask me to do anything about it! Do not ask me to be different. And that type of counseling that allows victimization as an endpoint, also allows me to BLAME a lot of things, including my current situation, upon my victimization.

"The reason I perpetrated abuse is because I was abused." Is that true? No. But I even hear counselors say this sometimes: "Well, my client abused others because he was abused."

That is not true! Our past can contribute certain pieces to the puzzle, but we choose our own actions. Anyone who has abused others <u>chose</u> to do so regardless of what happened in the past. How do we know that? Because some who were abused do not go out and abuse others. Why? They chose to respond to their past in a different way. That past is a major part of who we are today, but we still have control over our present choices and behavior. This is a very important concept for counselors to remember.

Sinfulness is deep in the core of all of us, and one of the ways it emerges is in deferring responsibility and "playing the victim." We like "playing the victim" and avoiding responsibility because taking responsibility exposes us to the possibility of consequences that may be uncomfortable or even painful. So where we need to be focused, as Christians, is going to a place that is hard for us to go -- taking time to look at our sin, taking responsibility, and saying, "Will you please forgive me?"

That can be a tough thing to do. But taking responsibility and acknowledging personal sin is something that we must do and is the basis for the Christian life (1 John 1:9).

The lack of responsibility is also something that drives away the non-Christian community faster than anything else. No one likes a hypocrite, and non-Christians become especially disillusioned and angered by people who claim to be Christians and yet do not take responsibility when they are wrong or defend themselves in an attempt to appear "faultless." As Christians, it is paramount for our growth and for our impact in our community that we take responsibility for our sin and seek forgiveness.

8) There is Salvation from Sin

But God provided a solution to the devastating sin problem: He provided salvation from sin. We are powerless to bring about our own salvation. We need a Savior. Christ, our Savior, died for us (Rom.5:6-8). Because of Christ dying on the cross, all we have to do is accept his work on our behalf, and the burden of our sin is gone (John 3:16).

When Christ died for us, He justified us (declared to be righteous) and sanctified us (set apart from sin) (1 Cor. 6:11). Those two words explain what Christ did and what He continues to do for us. Those effects of Christ's death are extremely important aspects of our salvation and of the Christian life.

IMPLICATIONS FOR COUNSELING

Counseling is more than helping people find personal happiness, lessen negative symptoms, and acquire better coping skills. People need God, and we want to help them find Him. There is nothing more satisfying in counseling than to lead a client to a saving knowledge of our Lord.

9) New Life in Christ

And after salvation, there is new life in Christ. Take a look at the photo of Mount St. Helens in Washington State. Though the volcano caused severe devastation to the countryside after its eruption in 1980, it did not take long for new life to appear. New life came out of destruction! Out of all of the ash and devastation, look at what happened. Though the pinks and greens are not shown here, do you see what is growing up out of all of that mess? It is hard to fathom the transformation to a beautiful landscape and the return of animal life after such ruin.

{Source: Topinka, L. (1984)}

The same is true in our lives. As we deal with sin and all of its consequences, a beauty can emerge -- as Joseph said, "What you meant for evil, God meant for good" (Gen. 50:20). And look what happened! Look at what God did and continues to do!

IMPLICATIONS FOR COUNSELING

That is what we try to do in counseling – help people see the good that can come. "With what you meant for evil, parents, teacher, coach, other adults, other kids, God can do something good."

You can always start anew. You can always learn from your sins, mistakes, or hurts of the past and allow God to make something new and better. You can "help" because you know what "hurt" looks like. You can say, "Look at what God did!" There is hope? There is new life?

So we want to offer that to people, that there is hope, even in your depression. There is hope in your anxiety. There is hope in your divorce. No matter what it is, there is hope and a new life is possible.

I do not know if that means your symptoms will all go away. But I do know there is hope. And something beautiful can come out of it. There are many people who have been able to use horrendous circumstances for God's glory. Some counselors are working with other people who are looking for hope as they once were. I have heard them say, "I'm so glad now, for what God has brought me through. For awhile, all I could do was question God and ask "Why?!" "Why me?!"

The goal is to bring clients into the understanding of what Christ did for them so each can say, "I thank God for bringing me through those hard times and those sinful times. Without my realization of that sin and/or without those hurts, I would not have the ability to understand others in the way that I do now. I could not touch those people's lives without that. Not that I don't still struggle sometimes, but I would not have the joy of living in Christ that I have now, had I not had a need and seen how Christ could fulfill it."

10) Life Has One Fundamental Purpose: To Please God

Lastly, life has one fundamental purpose, and that is to please God. "Whatever you eat, or drink, or whatever you do, do all to the glory of God" (1 Corinthians 10:31).

As Christians, we always know why we are here. We always know our purpose -- to please God. We were "built" to please Him.

IMPLICATIONS FOR COUNSELING

I can offer that to people in counseling. I can offer a solution to their needs and what their purpose is. I can say, "I know what you need. – and as a Christian, you have it. You have what you need. You have eternal relationship with God. He will never leave you or forsake you. He will always love you. AND, you know why you are here? -- To please Him and to glorify Him in whatever you do."

Whether we sell insurance, teach school, counsel, work in a factory, farm land, raise children, etc., it doesn't matter; whatever we do as Christians, our purpose is to please God. Some of the ways we can do that are by working hard, praying, and loving people well. If we realize that our one purpose is to please God, we always have a reason for living and a goal to strive for. That purpose can be accomplished through each of our unique personalities in various ways. And it is true in every situation that we find ourselves. We can always make a choice to please God. As counselors, we can please God by loving our clients well, giving them biblical information, and praying for them.

Final Thoughts

WHAT WE BRING TO THE TABLE

Now that the foundation of presuppositions has been laid, here are a few final thoughts to ponder.

If you are a Christian, you probably held to most of the previously discussed presuppositions even before you ever began reading this material. It could be that you would alter the wording a bit. You may add a few more presuppositions to the ones mentioned. But probably, you would be willing to say with conviction that, "I believe there is a God," "I believe that He has given us the Bible as His revelation," and "I believe that the Bible ought provide our guidelines for life."

It is important for us as Christian counselors to understand what we bring to the table. That is what we believe. That will affect how we think and how we live our lives. It will affect our goals for counseling with people, what we are going to say to them, and what we are going to do in the counseling session. But it is also important to understand that others bring their own presuppositions to the table as well.

THE END OF EVERY ARGUMENT

We base our beliefs on faith. Our faith makes sense to us because God has revealed it to us. Yet others may not accept what seems to be so clearly evident to us. Though it may seem that we can "convince" others, it may be helpful to realize that our presuppositions are the end of every argument or discussion that we encounter.

Presuppositions are not only the BEGINNING of every argument even though they are "pre" suppositions. Presuppositions are the END of every argument. Why might that be true?

If someone who believed in evolution[5] came to you right now and said, "Here is all of the data we have as to why we believe evolution to be true" . . . if he presented a compelling case for evolution and determined that there was NO supernatural force behind it at all, would you believe it? If you espouse to the previous ten presuppositions, you would say, "No!"

Why not? Maybe he has good data and compelling arguments. Why wouldn't you believe it?

You would probably respond with something like this, "I know what you are telling me. I hear it. You have got some strong arguments. But, I don't believe it."

Have you ever had an argument with someone like that . . . when you knew you were right!? Maybe you had done some research. Maybe you saw something on TV. Maybe you witnessed the event in person, and yet your observation was discounted.

Some people still believe that the earth is flat. In fact, there is a "Flat Earth Society." People in that society believe that the earth is not a sphere. It is not circular. It is flat ("Flat Earth Society," 2009).

---

[5] Reference is to Darwinian Evolution – the theory that we all came from one common ancestor and as changes occurred over time we have what we have today. Most Christians would say that God created specific kinds (multiple ancestors) – one being human. An evolution that involves small-scale changes and not a common ancestor could be a part of a Creationist view, but typically when people think of Evolution, they think of the Darwinian Evolution.

If you spoke with someone in that group, he may say to you, "Just go outside and look. There's no curvature!" He may walk for miles in his effort to prove it to you and continue to declare, "It's flat!"

In the early 1960s, when the Mercury spaceships were sent into space; astronauts took pictures which showed that the earth was ROUND! However, some STILL denied that fact!

One such naysayer asked, "What kind of camera did they use?"

The answer, "Well, just a regular camera."

He continued, "What kind of lens did it have on it?"

"Well, you know, a round lens."

"Okay! There you have it!" he said.

That was his argument for why the earth looked round in the pictures. He thought the 'round' lens produced the 'illusion' that the earth was round! And so, he was still convinced and steadfastly maintained his belief that the earth was flat.

You may have heard the story of the guy who thought he was dead. So someone poked his skin with a needle until he bled and then said, "See, you're bleeding!" But, the guy responded, "Oh, I guess dead people DO bleed."

Now, whether that story is true or not, it still illustrates the point very well. Presuppositions are the end of every argument. When all is said and done, when it comes right down to it, the most important question is, "What do you believe?"

The question is not who has the most compelling data. Though at times we run across compelling data and change our beliefs, many times our beliefs are just our beliefs. There are certain things that we simply believe.

It is important for us to be aware of this -- that sometimes in counseling we are going to say, "Here is what the Bible says," or "Here is what I learned in my experience," and our client will say, "I don't believe that. I think my way is right." If that is what he or she believes, that is what he/she is most likely going to believe.

Be aware of what you "bring to the table" and that some of the people that you deal with may not bring the same presuppositions. And, you may give profound information to them, but they may say, "I don't buy that! I'm not interested."

Does that mean we cannot work with those with whom we disagree or have a positive impact on them? No. We are just going to have two different sets of presuppositions, and need to be aware of that while we work with them. Hopefully one day they will say, "I'd like to hear more about your beliefs." Then we have a chance to tell them. That can be our prayer and our hope for those who are unsaved. But it is important to understand that our presuppositions will not always align with those of our clients. But we can still love them well and interact with them in a way that reflects Christ.

Presuppositions are powerful! They will determine our eternal destination! Think about that. What you believe will determine where you spend eternal life -- heaven or hell. That is how powerful they are. That is why I believe in cognitive therapy, because beliefs are so powerful. Good cognitive therapists will say, "What you believe will determine how you behave and how you feel." Presuppositions are that powerful.

This brings us to the next section which is entitled, "Integration." We will be looking to answer the question: "Can we take anything from secular psychology?" Can we take anything from secular theorists -- who do not believe in our presuppositions, who do not believe in the Bible, and who do not believe in God? We need to understand that there are intelligent people whom God has gifted in many ways, who may draw faulty conclusions from observed data because of their presuppositions. But can we take information from those astute, secular theorists who have made observations, yet who have different presuppositions than we do? The next chapter, entitled "Integration," will attempt to address those questions as they pertain to Christians and our Christian belief system.

CHAPTER 2

INTEGRATION

We now focus on the questions that concluded the previous chapter: Can we take anything from secular psychology? Can we take anything from secular theorists who do not believe in our presuppositions, who do not believe in the Bible, and who do not believe in God?

There are a number of people in the Christian community who would say that integration is not appropriate for the Christian when it comes to the subject of psychology. Much of their determination regarding integration is based on good reasoning. Teachings of some in the field of psychology do not match up with biblical principles and Christian beliefs.

How do you bring together the view that the Bible is the inerrant, inspired word of God and the belief of one who says, "The book has some relevance, but is not all that important," or "It's just a book and has no importance," or "It's a group of myths -- put together over the years. People invented it and invented the religion that came out of it"? How does one put those viewpoints together and say, "We're going to integrate that"? The two concepts are mutually exclusive.

"There is a God. God created. The world is His design. His design works."

"No, there is no God. We are here due to evolutionary forces. It is just time and chance.

How does one integrate those positions? If the intention is to put those two ideas together, obviously, it is impossible. The ideas are not compatible.

Integration of Theology and Psychology

Integration: Not a Good Term

Christian	Secular
Inerrant, Inspired Word of God	**Book with Some or No Relevance**
Creation: **God's Design**	**Evolution:** **Time Chance**
Life Goal: **Glorifying God** **(I Cor. 10:31)**	**Life Goal:** **Coping and Adapting**

For the Christian, 1 Corinthians 10:31 defines our purpose for living. Life is all about glorifying God, "Whether you eat or drink or whatever you do, do it all for the glory of God." This is a foundational belief.

What is life all about in the secular world? Without God, it is all about *survival* -- "coping and adapting." Survival is the goal and in order to survive, you have to cope and adapt to your environment. That is the essence of the evolutionary-based belief of our secular world.

If *integration* means bringing together two opposing sets of beliefs and trying to make them become one perspective, then that is not a suitable approach for the Christian. It is not something that can happen. It makes sense then why some Christians say it should not be done. But what some then conclude is: "Let's throw out psychology."

This conclusion often seems to stem from an underlying belief that psychology consists of the *theories* that have been produced by psychologists, rather than the true definition of psychology. Psychology is merely the study of mind and behavior. Psychology involves the study of those things connected with the mind. In addition to the biology of the brain, psychology involves thought processes, emotions, learning, memory, worry, stress, and the behavior that results from the workings of the mind. If one starts with that as a definition of psychology, it will be easier to understand the basis for the concepts developed in this book.

The intention of this book is to build a platform for understanding the thinking and behavior of man and to reveal what the Bible has to say about those faculties.

Can You Throw Psychology Out of the Bible?

If we look at psychology as thinking and behavior, is it possible to take psychology out of the Bible? That would be like taking out all of the nouns in the Bible or taking out all of the history in the Bible or taking out all of the lessons in the Bible? The nouns and the history and the lessons are all important parts of the Bible message. Without them, the Bible does not exist. They are all needed to communicate the message that God has intended for us to get. In fact, one may think that he has "thrown out" psychology from the Bible; but if he still believes what is written, he has only discarded the *label*, "psychology," not the existence of psychology.

You cannot take the psychology out of the Bible. You cannot discard all of the thinking and behavior, just like cannot discard the nouns in the Bible and still communicate the message. You can change the label "nouns" to something else, but they are still nouns. They still name persons, places, or things. The same is true with the "psychology" in the Bible. Psychology (mind and behavior) is inherent in the Bible message.

Are All Secularists' Teachings Wrong?

But that is only one of the issues that needs to be dealt with in regard to psychology and the Christian. Even though we may be aware that a psychology of the Bible exists, what do we do about all of the "psychology" apart from the Bible? What do we do about all of those theories and secular psychologists that address different psychological topics?

Take a minute and return to the idea held by some that psychology is the *theories* that psychologists have proposed and assume that those theories were proposed by secular theorists. Or suppose that psychology is the research that secular psychologists have conducted. Would that now mean that we should throw out all of psychology because the information came from a secular psychologist?

And even though we know that psychology is not the theories or research, we still must address the question of what to do with the information that is dispersed from secular psychologists. Can Christians learn anything from secular psychologists? Is everything learned and reported or theorized by secular psychologists wrong?

"Let's throw out anything that is secular, because somehow it's bad. It's tainted. It's not what God wants." Is that what Christians need to conclude? -- Probably not.

But, it does bring up some important questions. First of all, if the presuppositions of Christians and non-Christians are mutually exclusive, does secular psychology have anything *good* to offer?

Or consider this: Can secular psychologists and theorists stumble upon biblical truth? Could they observe the world and find truth? That is worth pondering.

If they can (and the Bible seems to indicate that they can -- Prov. 29:13, 1 Cor. 15:33), is it legitimate for us to borrow from them? Can we use their material? Is it legitimate to acknowledge the truths that they have found?

Cognitive Therapy emphasizes that thinking is vitally important. Could the cognitive therapist have stumbled on truth when choosing to look into man's thinking? Could he have stumbled on truth while seeking to know what the source of man's emotions and behavior is? Proverbs 23:7 says, "For as he thinketh in his heart/*soul* (translated in NASB "within himself"), so is he" (KJV). Did the cognitive therapist happen to learn something that the Bible teaches? If you are familiar with Freud's "Defense Mechanisms," you realize that Freud made a keen observation that makes sense. Looking at Freud's explanation of defense mechanisms and then going to Scripture, one may be surprised to realize that some can be found there. Though unregenerate (and many of his theories reflect that unregenerate mindset), Freud was also able to notice things that were true. Yet it was the same person, Freud, who came up with the Oedipal Complex and other theories that contradict Christian teaching.

Did Freud create defense mechanisms? No. Defense mechanisms have been around since sin entered the human race. But Freud drew attention to them and noticed what techniques people use to make themselves look good and hid their real selves. He put a label on them so that we could study them and think through what they are accomplishing for us in life. Could those "defense mechanisms" have been found if one had not read Freud? -- Maybe. -- But maybe not. -- Maybe not to the same degree to which Freud described them.

So studying psychology and then checking out that information with Scripture, can cause us to think in ways that we have not thought before and find things that we may not have found otherwise. Can we reclaim those things and say, "Freud stumbled upon some biblical truths"?

Freud labeled one of his defense mechanisms, "projection." It is not called that in the Bible, but could it still it be a real mechanism employed by people to hide what is going on inside? And could one use Freud's material on "projection" to understand human nature a little bit better?

An attentive Christian may find that there are many pieces of information that secularists have "stumbled upon" through God's enlightenment that are very true and quite useful. And Scripture even supports the fact that unbelievers can come up with truth -- as demonstrated in the verses previously mentioned -- Proverbs 29:13 and I Corinthians 15:33 (where Paul quotes the philosopher/poet, Menander).

Dangerous?

However, can taking information from secularists be dangerous? Can we be led astray by unbelieving theorists?

Well, can Christians be led astray by the world? Of course! The Bible makes it clear that we can be misled. (That is part of the psychology of how our minds work and how things can influence us for evil.) That is why the Bible gives us parameters for dealing with our world. God wants us to maintain our relationships with Christians (by not "forsaking the assembling of ourselves together," Heb. 10:25). God wants us to "think about such things" that are true, noble, right, pure, lovely, and admirable (Phil. 4: 8). God wants us to meditate on His laws "day and night" (Ps. 1). God's Word warns us about forming "chummy" relationships with non-Christians where we allow them to lead us into sinful behaviors -- "Bad company corrupts good morals" (I Cor. 15:33), and it communicates to us that a steady diet of sinful exposure can influence us in negative ways in Proverbs and other passages. The Bible warns over and over of lurking temptation, teachings, and evil people who are waiting to "devour us" with their wickedness.

Immersing ourselves in any secular teachings alone without a firm biblical base can be dangerous. If we have not equipped ourselves with the "armor of God" (Ephesians 6), it becomes more difficult to ward off the evil teachings and to make wise decisions. That is why we need a firm biblical base in order to function in our world at all. That is why we need to understand the advice that Paul gives in order to "stand firm" (Phil. 4:1). No matter what we do, no matter what profession we pursue, no matter what activities we get involved in, we need to know what God teaches and how to deal with ourselves and our world (2 Tim. 2:15).

So is it dangerous to go to a baseball game? Could I learn bad habits from a player or someone in the stands? Yes, possibly. Is it dangerous to watch TV? It could be. Is it dangerous to listen to music? -

- Maybe. Is it dangerous to read theories proposed by a secularist based on his/her research? -- Perhaps.

But could we also learn something from a secularist that would be helpful to our lives? Yes, it is possible! Is it not within the realm of God's ability to use secularists to actually help us know God better and serve God better? Yes!

Most Christians agree that contributions by secularists in the medical world have merit and are worth studying -- even though the medical world can also promote things that Christians often oppose such as abortion, embryonic stem cell research, and euthanasia. But some of the very same Christians that accept information from the medical world are opposed to studying psychology.

So what makes the difference in our thinking? Whether we are studying medicine or psychology, how do we know what information and approaches we should accept and which ones we should oppose? In order to make the best judgments to discern what is appropriate and in order to make the best use of the secularists' teachings, we need to have a good biblical understanding.

Better Word than Integration?

If we accept the idea that there *are* things that secularists can contribute to the Christian life, how would we define our use of that material? Does the word "integration" fit?

Integration is the most commonly used word, yet it implies different things to different people. The discussions in this chapter will focus on the varying views that are implicated by the word "integration."

But, before looking at those views, it might be important here to consider the appropriateness of the term "integration" when it comes to discussing psychology and the Bible. Is "integration" the best word to describe what the Christian should do with information discovered by secularists? Or is there a better way to communicate what we mean when we speak of including the truths of secular teachings?

Integration is a word that conjures up connotations of our previous discussion of combining truth and non-truth which, it was determined, cannot be done. So, maybe it is not the best word to use. But, if "integration" is not a good term, what wording could be used to describe the usefulness of some secular teachings without accepting those pieces of information that are untrue and sometimes against what God's word teaches?

It could be that no *one* word can accurately describe the procedure that is involved when the Christian attempts to incorporate the truths found in the secular world (as they relate to psychology) into his own thinking. There may not be one word that can summarize what he is trying to do.

Proposed in this book is a group of words to describe the best method for Christians to use when taking truths discovered by secularists and using them. The group of words proposed in this book is: "Scriptural Foundation, Secular Nuggets." That wordage will be explained in the last of the five views examined next.

Five Views of Integration

What are the different views of "integration" -- if that term is going to be used? When people think of integration, what are the views that are most commonly assumed? In this textbook, views of integration are divided into five categories: 1) Facts, Not Faith; 2) The Word, Not Worldly Wisdom; 3) Accept Both, Integrate Neither; 4) The Two-Book View; and 5) Scriptural Foundation, Secular Nuggets.

1) FACTS, NOT FAITH

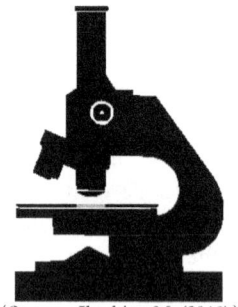

{Source: Ibrahim, M. (2010)}

In the first view, one is looking for scientific facts. That inquiry alone for "facts" tends to eliminate this as a true view of integration. The view basically says: "Theology isn't scientific. Throw it out." Only scientific psychology can be trusted, not theology, because theology is based on faith, a "non-trustable entity."

The view assumes that psychology is built upon empiricism. (The main pillar of science is empiricism: We bring things through our senses and make sense of those things.) Theology (they say) is built upon "non-science" (some would say "nonsense"). They say, "It's built upon 'faith';

therefore, theology ought to be rejected." Whatever is "nonscientific" is rejected, because "We're looking for *facts*!"

So the next question is: "Are there facts?" Do true "facts" exist? Can I say, "I know this to be 100% true and there is NOTHING that could disprove it?!" (That is how "fact" is being defined here.) Can anyone know things to be 100% true?

OUR SENSES CAN DECEIVE US

Consider the information that comes through our senses. Is that information 100% fool-proof? Are any or all of those things that come through our senses, facts? That is the concept that the "Scientific Method" is based upon -- bringing things through our senses and making sense of those things. But can we trust our senses? Take a look at the following diagram.

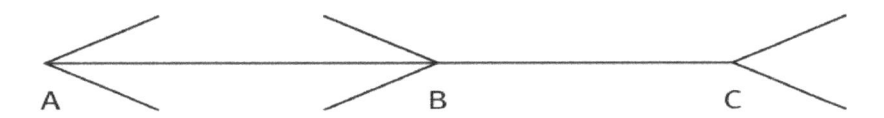

>---< >---<
A   B   C

Which line appears to be longer? A to B or B to C?

The answer that your senses will usually tell you is: B to C is longer. But if you measure the lines; you would find that your senses were wrong! Your senses deceived you!

(Source: Public Domain)

This is also true with airline pilots. (Source: Public Domain)
They are trained to use instruments to fly because sometimes their sense of position and motion fails to be accurate. They can have the illusion of being straight and level when almost nearly inverted or tumbling end over end when actually straight and level. It is called "spatial disorientation"

{www.aopa.org (2009)} and is caused by visual references being unclear or by the disturbance of fluid in the inner ear due to the Coriolus Effect (Seaman, 2009).

Another example is when you are stopped at a traffic light and car beside you inches forward. It can cause you to feel like you are going backwards.

Sometimes our senses deceive us. What looks like truth is not always truth. In looking at the two lines, one looks longer. When considering what direction we are going or how level we are in an airplane, we can feel convinced that we are in one position when we are actually in another. Our senses can "play tricks" on us.

The 1999 movie, *The Matrix*, based its entire plot on such deception. The premise of the movie is that what looks like reality is really a software program and the true reality is outside the Matrix. Of course, we do not believe we are part of the Matrix; but can we prove that absolutely? No, just like we cannot prove Heaven to an unbeliever. Sometimes even empiricism fails us. Because it cannot be proven through what they can currently see or touch, the idea of Heaven and Hell seem as ludicrous to the unbeliever as being in the Matrix seems to us. [6]

Those who believe that truth can be proven through empiricism need to be careful. Sometimes our senses deceive us and we assume truth that is not necessarily truth. And yet other times we are aware of things that other people are not aware of, that might be true.

In studies involving witnesses to a crime, research has shown that eyewitnesses can even disagree on what actually happened, and they can be convinced that their perspective is the correct one. (Source: Cutler & Penrod, 1988). Documentaries on the John F. Kennedy assassination that evaluate the angles of the bullet holes show that the shots could have only come from the Texas Depository Building. But some witnesses were convinced that shots were fired from a "grassy knoll." What is the truth and could it be that people's senses were deceived? How do we know?

What point is being made here? The point is that sometimes our senses can deceive us; yet, many times we can trust them. But we put our faith in our senses (we trust them) even though we cannot prove that they are accurate. In other words, faith is involved.

---

[6] Author's note: It may be misconstrued by this discussion that this author does not believe in absolute truth. This author does believe in absolute truth, but notice that he has said, "He believes in absolute truth." He just can't absolutely prove it here on Earth.

OUR RATIONALITY SOMETIMES DECEIVES US

If that is not compelling, we have other problems. Our rationality sometimes deceives us. Sometimes we have good data, but we draw the wrong conclusions from that data.

In one of the Monty Python movies that emerged in the 1970s, there is a discussion about whether a particular woman is a witch. The characters go through various aspects of evaluating the reality of that claim, such as the fact that you burn witches and wood also burns, so witches must be made of wood. Wood floats and so does a duck; so if she weighs the same as a duck, she must be a witch.

Now, is that scientific? Did you catch that logic? Why did we know she was a witch?
-- Because she weighed the same as a duck. Now we laugh at that, but how many times do we get good data and draw those kinds of conclusions in the scientific world?

A search on the Internet will produce a number of articles telling of fish fossils or sea life fossils found in places where water creatures and plants were not likely to be found -- such as at the top of a mountain. Even Charles Darwin found fish fossils on tops of mountains. How do you think they got there? What would be your theory?

As Christians, some of us immediately think that that is evidence of the Great Flood. But that is not the conclusion that was drawn by Charles Darwin when he observed that phenomenon (Edmondstone, 2009) or by numerous others.

Though investigators can go into great lengths to present very elaborate data of the type of fossils and the type of fish and how it would have been highly unlikely for them to have inhabited that area at any time, and though the researchers can demonstrate detailed ways to measure the time and age of the fossils, the primary conclusion of some of the articles could be summarized like this: A meteor hit the ocean. It splashed the water up to the mountain. As a result of the "splashing," fish were thrust up to that remote, dry area at the top of the mountain. The fish flopped around, and they died.[7]

---

[7] Articles on the Internet regarding fish fossils on mountains and meteors causing fish fossils are numerous. Two such articles of fish fossils on mountains are: www.natureandscience.org/research/wyoming.asp and www.yellowstonetreasures.com/fish_fossils.htm Other sites promoting the idea of meteors causing fish extinction are:
www.nsf.gov/news/news_summ.jsp?cntn_id=100836&org=NSF&from=news and school.discoveryeducation.com/lessonplans/programs/livingfossils/ where a study unit is designed for students to discuss the various theories including the idea of a meteor causing the extinction of creatures such as fish and causing fish fossils.

Could that have happened? Or could it have been the Great Flood? Could it be that the mountain rose up from the ocean and brought the fish with them? What could have happened? How do we know? We weren't there. The conclusions drawn from that data can vary greatly -- especially from that of the Christian.

So that is the problem that can happen, even with collecting good data. The conclusion that seems rational to us based on our data may not be accurate. Our rationality can deceive us.

But in order for science to work, we have to put some trust in our thinking, because some or all of it could be correct. We have to put faith in our rationality, because we cannot prove that it is 100% accurate. So again, faith is involved.

WHO IS GOING TO INTERPRET THE DATA?

But, if our rationality can deceive us, then how do we know if the interpretation of the data is accurate? Do we have someone that we know can evaluate the data correctly? Who is going to interpret the data for us? Are you going to interpret the data? Are you "trustable"? What about the leading scientists? Can we trust them? Might they have their biases and prejudices and backgrounds that influence and "slant" their interpretations?

So who is going to do it? Ultimately it comes down to "Me." Why? "Well, I trust me."

That is where we are in the post-modern world. "I trust me, therefore my belief is right. And you have to respect that."

Now, treating others with respect is a godly way of behaving. And respecting others' beliefs can be considerate. But, just because you think you are right and they think they are right, does it follow that both of you are right? -- Obviously not.

---

http://www.cps.org.yu/Innerpeace/Creation/noah.html. Paragraph 6, documents "marine" fossils on mountains. (Footnote continued on next page.)

Quote from Chapter 5, "The Hovind Theory," cs.joensuu.fi/~vtenhu/hovind/CHP-5.htm "Maybe it all happened because of the meteor hitting the earth. If hot water came shooting out of the earth's crust, it would cause some problems on earth. If you dumped a million gallons into a lake what would happen to the fish? It would kill them in an instance, wouldn't it? The reason would be due to a condition known as thermal shock. Fish have a certain temperature change that they can withstand per minute. If the temperature changes too quickly, it will kill them. Thermal shock would take place if hot water from beneath the ocean came shooting up into the ocean and it would kill things in the immediate vicinity."

If one answer is right and it excludes the other, then the other cannot also be right. If two people have opposing opinions, then it could be that one of them is right and one is wrong, or both could be wrong. But the idea that opposing opinions (opinions that are diametrically opposed to each other) could both be right, obviously, is impossible. If one says, "There is no God," and the other says, "There is a God," they both may think they are right; but in reality, they cannot both be right. At least one of the answers always has to be wrong.

So my senses can deceive me. My rationality can deceive me. The scientific method cannot assure me with certainty that what the scientists promote is right. They cannot prove their "facts" with absolute certainty and they cannot prove their interpretations either.

But, some put their faith in leading scientists. They agree with the scientists' interpretations. Can the scientists prove those interpretations with absolute certainty? No. Therefore, faith is involved.

YOU CAN'T GET ALL OF THE DATA

Then there is another problem: You can't get all of the data. Even if we have the best methods in the world for gathering data, how do we know for sure that we have all of the data?

At one time, we thought that the table that we ate off of was totally solid. Our senses told us that and we trusted them. Now, with research and electron microscopes, we know that the table is made up of atoms, and atoms are mostly space. It is the speed of the electrons around the nucleus that makes the table appear solid. With more data, we realized that our perception was wrong.

At one time, people thought that everything revolved around the Earth; but with research, we found that the planets revolve around the sun. Again, our senses deceived us, and new data discredited the old theory.

We can never be sure that we have all of the data! And even though we have added much more data and know a great deal more about the subject, there is always the possibility of new data. We can't get all of the data. We can't get all of the NEW data because tomorrow there is going to be more new data.

Some have said, "To put our faith in research is like a spider building his house on the hands of a clock. As time passes, his house is continually destroyed." As time passes, we always have new data, new theories, and those new theories sometimes discredit the old theories. So am I going to put my faith in theories that 20 years from now we may consider obsolete?

HOW DO YOU PROVE THE "PROVER"?

And lastly, how do you prove the "prover"? Assume that we have a method that proves a particular piece of information to be true. Now we have to prove that the method for proving that is true. Well, how do we prove that the method is true? Whatever technique we employ to prove that the method is true, needs now to be proven to be true. So how do you prove the "prover"? You can't.

Those who believe in the Scientific Method are still building their belief upon faith! "I have faith in my senses. I have faith in my rationality. I have faith in this method, but I cannot prove the method to be true." The Scientific Method is a philosophy. The Scientific Method is a good method for ascertaining data and learning about our world, but it does not absolutely prove anything.

So if you were asked, "Which of the following is based on faith: philosophy, chemistry, physics, psychology, sociology, science, or theology?" what would be the correct answer? The answer is all of the above. They are all based on faith. Everything is based on faith. (We are talking at a presupposition level.)

If we accept the Scientific Method as a good method, then we seek "facts" that are testable, measurable. We want to make observations and weed out old ideas. It is a good method; but one of the drawbacks of the Scientific Method is that it is only good for that which is observable. When we consider subjects such as heavenly angels or the existence of God, the Scientific Method does not help us much with our analysis and our study. So what do we do with that?[8]

SUMMARY OF "FACTS, NOT FAITH"

"Facts, not Faith" is not a valid concept, first, because it is not "integrating" psychology and theology at all and, secondly, because we cannot prove "facts" (in the absolute sense). There is faith in what we believe to be facts. But faith is the key element to all of the "facts." I must have faith in my senses, my rationality, the scientific method, or in someone who will interpret the data for me. It is the same kind of faith that we Christians have when we believe in God and His Word.

---

[8] Again, to reiterate, this author believes in absolute truth, but as stated earlier, he <u>believes</u> it, but cannot absolutely prove it. What is BELIEVED can be true, yet cannot always be <u>proven</u> scientifically here on earth.

2) THE WORD, NOT WORLDLY WISDOM

ELIMINATE PSYCHOLOGY

The first view says that scientific psychology is the only way to go -- the Bible should be discarded. The second view says just the opposite: "Discard psychology and only use the Bible." Proponents of this view would say that psychology is of the world and follows worldly wisdom. Therefore, the second view is "The Word, not Worldly Wisdom."

It is apparent that neither this view nor the previous one is really a view of integration. Those who hold to the first two views look at psychology and theology and discard one of them. In the first view, they eliminated theology entirely. In this view, psychology is eliminated entirely.

Those who advocate this view say, "Only the Bible." "The only wisdom that can be found is in the Bible." "The only way to understand our thinking and beliefs is through studying the Bible."

Now, what is wrong with that? Don't we want the Bible to be the core of our thinking? Certainly! The Bible is the basis for the Christian life. So what could possibly be wrong with this view from the Christian perspective?

Proponents of this view suggest that psychology was built upon a humanistic philosophy or "Secular Humanism." Today the philosophy that is in vogue is termed "Post-Modernism." Given that theology is built upon God's Word and not a secular philosophy, those holding this view therefore reject psychology.

As a result of this pairing of psychology with humanistic philosophy, the Christian psychologist is then confronted by advocates of this view with inquiries such as, "How can you be a psychologist and be a Christian?" In the mind of many who are supporters of this view, psychology is "of Satan" and "evil," and theology is of God. Their biggest question is: "How can you put these two together?"

Obviously, if they presuppose those two opposing ideas of Satan versus God, then their questions are very legitimate. This was discussed earlier in this chapter and also in the chapter entitled, "Presuppositions." You *cannot* put those two opposing views together.

Others who hold to this view have said, "Moses and Paul did not need psychology. Why do WE need psychology?"

What is the answer to those questions? Did Moses need psychology? Did Paul need psychology? Why is it that, today, we "need" psychology?

ONE EXAMPLE OF PSYCHOLOGY IN THE BIBLE -- JETHRO COUNSELS MOSES

{Source: Clipart (2011)}

Exodus 18 sheds some light on this question. Jethro, Moses' father-in-law, came for a visit at the time that Moses was leading the nation of Israel. The day following the first day's greetings, Moses went to work while his father-in-law looked on.

As Jethro was observing Moses, he noted that Moses was not applying the best plan as he cared for the people's problems. Jethro realized that Moses's *behavior* was not going to be helpful to his own well-being. Moses was not *thinking* correctly when it came to addressing so many people's problems. So Jethro *counseled* Moses concerning his flawed approach.

Jethro said to Moses (in essence), "What you're doing is not good." He said, "Why are you trying to do all this alone? You are going to wear yourself out -- and the people too." He then counseled Moses to get help, having other honest and capable men handle the little problems and Moses handle the most difficult ones. "That will make your load lighter, because they will share it with you. If you do this and God so commands, you will be able to stand the strain, and all these people will go home satisfied," he concluded (Ex. 18:23).

That is both counseling and psychology. In psychological terms, we call this "self-care" or "self-management." In other words, Moses did need psychology (if properly defined).

As a Christian, challenge yourself while reading the Bible to search for the places where that kind of psychology and counseling is present. You may be amazed to find how much psychology is there.

Now here is an important point to consider. Could application of such psychological principles help those Christians who go too far with their need to be spiritual and/or push other Christians to overwork for the apparent sake of godliness? Could psychology such as this point out the fallacies of those who say, "Hey, burn out for Jesus!" "Just keep working and if you burn out, at least you burn out doing the right thing." Why didn't Jethro say that? Wouldn't that sound more spiritual? Just because something sounds more spiritual does not mean that it *is* more spiritual.

Jethro applied psychology by observing what was happening (the detriment that Moses was potentially doing to himself) and counseling Moses to change his approach. Jethro wanted Moses to be able to preserve his ability to be useful. He suggested that Moses *think* differently about how he was going about his work and encouraged him to *change his behavior*. That is what is often missed by those who do not think that psychology and the Bible can be together. The stories of the Bible have psychology woven all through them.

So those who propose the idea that Moses and others did not need psychology are missing something. How are they defining psychology? Are they some of the ones who are saying that "Psychology equals Freud, Skinner, and Rogers"? That is an important distinction to be made and realized about those who adamantly oppose psychology. Sometimes what they are against is *not* the essence of psychology. It is an *aspect* of psychology.

SUMMARY OF "THE WORD, NOT WORLDLY WISDOM"

Psychology is *not* Freud, Skinner, and Rogers. Psychology did not begin in 1879 with Wilhelm Wundt, who set up the first "laboratory" for psychology and began putting the focus on some of the more scientific aspects of psychology. (He pioneered the *science* of psychology, not psychology itself.) Psychology (thinking and behavior) has been around forever. It did not start with Wundt or Freud. Thinking and behavior and decisions made to influence or react to thinking and behavior have been a part of man's world since creation. Psychology is the study of thinking and behavior, and the Bible has much to say about it.

3) ACCEPT BOTH, INTEGRATE NEITHER

The third view is not really a view of integration either because it does not try to bring psychology and the Bible together. It sees both as equally valid disciplines that should be kept separate.

There are Christian people and Christian schools that believe that the disciplines of theology and psychology are totally separate and should not be brought together and, yet, both are useful. In some schools, the two disciplines are housed in totally separate buildings with rare interaction. There is a deliberate intention NOT to bring them together. Those who hold this view of "integration" are convinced that this is the best way to approach the subject, and it would be unwise, otherwise, to bring them together. This view is held with conviction by some godly Christians. "Accept Both, Integrate Neither" assumes that both are equally valid and, yet, should not be integrated.

So is this the best approach -- that we should not try to bring the two disciplines together? What if there is overlap? If there is overlap, how do we separate the two?

HOW DO YOU PUT CERTAIN PROBLEMS IN A PARTICULAR CAMP?

Consider the psychological manifestation of anxiety. Everyone has anxiety from time to time -- all people! None of us are exempt from worry or concern about something. Whether Christians or non-Christians, we are all bombarded with things that can consume our thoughts.

So, in theology, can it be said that the topic of anxiety does not come up? What about "Do not be anxious about anything, but in everything, by prayer and petition, with thanksgiving, present your requests to God" (Phil. 4:6) or "Do not worry about tomorrow" (Matt. 6:34)? So the question then is: "Is anxiety a spiritual problem or a psychological problem?"

Do you see the dilemma? How do you put anxiety in a camp?

"Well, if I'm worried about spiritual things, then it is a spiritual problem and if I am having anxiety about my world, then is it a psychological problem." Is that a good distinction?

"When I'm not really trusting God, I get anxious." According to the above explanation, it sounds like that is a spiritual problem. The Bible says not to be anxious about anything. But, if I am having panic attacks, then that must be a psychological problem? -- Not a spiritual problem? How do you separate the psychological aspect of anxiety from the spiritual aspect? How do you discuss the inclination that anyone has (including Christians) to worry or be concerned, without viewing the *thinking* that is behind the emotion or activity and using a *biblical* approach to determine the cause and treatment?

What about "fear"? Why were the shepherds afraid when the angels came to them (Luke 2:8-9)? What was going on inside them?

Or why did the angels think that their announcement would bring the shepherds joy (Luke 2:10-20)? Joy is another emotion. How could the angels anticipate that emotion? Are those spiritual feelings or psychological feelings? Are they spiritual because angels are involved?

What if I am afraid to fly? Is that a psychological problem because it concerns aircraft, or is it a spiritual problem because I am not trusting God?

FALSE DICHOTOMY

Another problem with this approach is that many times, in order to promote this way of thinking, one has to create a "false dichotomy" between "soul" and "spirit." Depending on the context, the words can convey different aspects, but many times, the words are used synonymously. {See Chapter 3 in *Biblical Psychology* (Edgington, 2013)} for how the terms are used in the Bible).

If these words are often used synonymously, then the concepts can be the same. Our anxiety problems are psychology/spiritual problems, not one or the other. Our "psychological past" is our "spiritual past" (that part of us that is not the body.). The same is true for depression. It can be a psychological/spiritual problem, rather than one or the other.

There are those who do try to categorize such previously mentioned problems and make clear distinctions that cause tremendous damage because they try to guide people without a proper understanding of all of the inner-workings and complexities of those problems. They may use wrong Scriptures to try to help because they misunderstand what is wrong. Or they may use improper techniques because they do not understand the spiritual depth of the difficulty being presented and/or the ramifications of their techniques and advice.

SUMMARY OF "ACCEPT BOTH, INTEGRATE NEITHER"

So, to summarize this section, a hard and fast designation that "This is your 'psyche' or your 'psychological part,' which is distinct from your 'spiritual part,'" does not exist. It is therefore the conclusion of this writer that using a false dichotomy to separate the psychological and the spiritual part is not a proper approach to viewing the problems that confront man. No clear distinction can be drawn to specify one problem as being totally psychological and another problem as being totally spiritual.

4) THE TWO-BOOK VIEW

We will now move to the most common view of integration -- the "Two-Book View." In most Christian circles, when the topic of integrating psychology and theology is discussed, this view tends to represent what is endorsed.

The two-book view was originated by the philosopher, Francis Bacon, in the 17th century, who believed that there were two types of revelation: the Bible -- "Special Revelation" and the created universe -- "General Revelation." (Kulikovsky, 2005). Bacon wanted to give credence to scientific study among the religious world (Hutchinson, 1998).

(Souce: Public Domain)

The idea was renewed in the 1970s by Kirk Farnsworth (1974), who included psychology under the heading of "General Revelation" (what God has given the world). "General Revelation," in this view, includes scientific study through empiricism and observation. The goal is to find out, through science, what is true in the world. (Psychology -- especially scientific psychology -- would be a part of that.) General Revelation assumes that there is truth to be found in the world that God has revealed because God has made a world that has truth in it.

The second "book" of the Two-Book View, involves "Special Revelation." Special Revelation is where the Bible is the central focus. Hermeneutics -- or how you interpret the Bible -- is an important part of that study. The languages of the Bible -- primarily Greek and Hebrew -- are also an important part of that "Special Revelation." From those and other aspects of study, one develops his "theology."

The Two-Book View

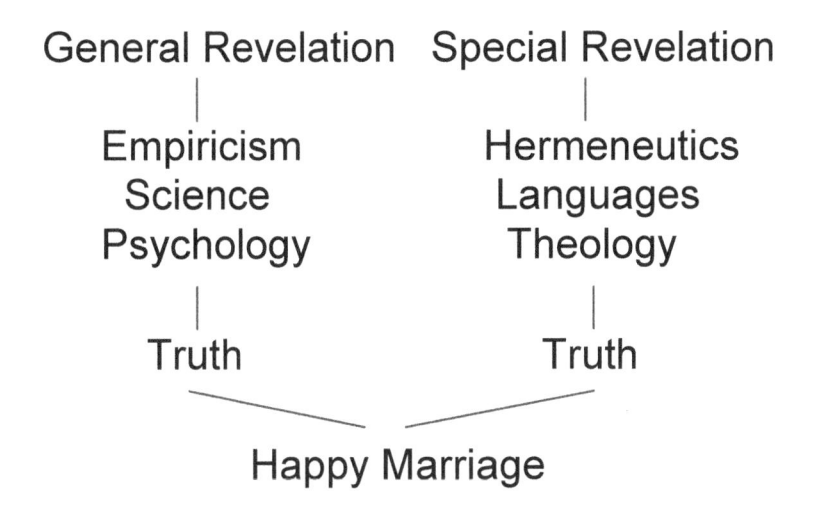

General Revelation   Special Revelation
| |

Empiricism   Hermeneutics
Science   Languages
Psychology   Theology

Truth   Truth

Happy Marriage

(Source: Crabb, 1987)

So the goal is to put together the truths of General Revelation and the truths of Special Revelation. It is assumed that if the two are put together, then there could be a "happy marriage." Now, what could be wrong with that?

It makes a nice chart, but is it biblical? What do we do if those who interpret the truths do not agree? The real world is not always so neatly divided. And who is making the decisions on what the "truths" are and how are those decisions being made? On what are those decisions based?

PROBLEM #1 -- WHAT IF THEY DO NOT AGREE?

When they do not agree, what typically happens is that those who hold to this view tend to "fall off" on the scientific side. The thinking goes something like this: "Well, the Bible was written 2,000 years ago and we know a lot more now. We have more and better data."

This is especially true with topics like homosexuality. Some believe that the data we have today "proves" that the homosexual lifestyle is not sinful. They conclude that what was written in the Bible was simply the belief (a wrong one) of that time or that our interpretation of what appears to be a clear teaching is inaccurate. In other words, science dictates how we interpret Scripture.

The problem with the "Two-Book View" is that if there is a discrepancy and there is indecision as to which "book" to go with, then, all of a sudden, the Bible tends to get "explained away" with the assertion that man is much more knowledgeable now than he was 2,000 years ago. That thinking brings with it many problems. A major one is our belief in an inspired, inerrant word.

C.S. Lewis (1955) wrote of "Chronological Snobbery" -- "the uncritical acceptance of the intellectual climate common to our own age and the assumption that whatever has gone out of date is on that account discredited" (pp. 207-208). The idea is that "our" generation is the "smart bunch." Are we really smarter than those who God ordained to pen the words of Scripture? Or are we now putting ourselves above God? Christians need to take a careful look at the implications of this type of thinking.

Isaiah 55:8-9 says, "For my thoughts are not your thoughts, neither are your ways my ways . . . my ways (are) higher than your ways and my thoughts (are higher) than your thoughts."

Proverbs 3:5 says, "Trust in the Lord with all your heart and lean not on your own understanding."

God is trying to communicate to us that our minds are never fully able to comprehend Him and His world. We must rely on Him and His Word to give us the only enduring truths that are to be known. To rely on our own wisdom apart from God and His word is foolishness.

PROBLEM #2 -- THEY HAVE DIFFERENT PURPOSES

The next problem: What is the purpose of each one? What is the purpose of General Revelation and the purpose of Special Revelation? Take a look at the two passages regarding General and Special Revelation in this section.

General Revelation:

Psalm 19:1 – The heavens declare the glory of God; the skies proclaim the work of his hands.

(Source: Public Domain)

The Bible tells us that the creations of God demonstrated in our world (General Revelation), declare God and His glory. If that is true, when we observe or study anything in the world, including psychology, we are saying, "Wow, look at God! Look at what He made. This is incredible!"

But, the purpose of General Revelation was not necessarily to teach me how to live life. The purpose was not to help me with my marriage or to learn how to love my roommate or my sibling better. When I go out at night and look at the stars, I do not come back in and say, "I think I know what I need to do now." When I spend time with the trees, I do not say, "I now know what is moral and what is not."

It does tell me: "Look at God!! He is an awesome, incredible God. He is the One to worship."

When we study the intricacies of our world, we see that they reveal a great deal about Him. But is General Revelation going to tell me how to live a fulfilling and moral life? -- Probably not.

The purpose of Special Revelation is quite different from that of General Revelation. "All Scripture is God-breathed and profitable for teaching, rebuking, correcting, and training in righteousness" (2 Tim. 3:16). When I go to God's word -- "Special Revelation" -- I find principles to live my life by. I find the answers to the way I need to think and what I need to do. I find a reason for my existence.

So to put them (General Revelation and Special Revelation) on the same level and say they are equal in terms of purpose does not seem to fit God's intention. Although the stars and trees and plant life certainly declare God's glory and tell a lot about Him, they fall short of giving us what we need to know in order to "find God, know God, and serve God." The difference in purposes is important to consider because God's creation is not intended to be a "teacher" of morality, only a demonstrator of an awesome God!

PROBLEM #3 -- CLARITY

And yet another problem exists: What is the clarity of each? How clear is General Revelation in terms of how we are to live our lives? We have already concluded that General Revelation is not very clear when it comes to morality and finding answers to life's important questions..

When looking at Special Revelation, Scripture is clear in some cases and unclear in others. Of those instances where Scripture is not as clear, a study of our world can help try to discover what God intended. But one problem that often surfaces with many conservative, fundamentalistic Christians, is an intentional "forcing of clarity" where clarity is not found. There is a tendency to twist the intended message and follow the idea that, "Where the Scripture is clear, be clear; where Scripture is vague, be clear; and where Scripture is silent, be clear." Those who feel that specific answers are always there to be found in Scripture, often "force" those specific answers for problems when they are not given -- where only "parameters" are given. "Manufacturing" answers to promote clarity in Scripture does not seem be what God intended when those Scriptures were penned.

Does the Bible say anything about Multiple Personality Disorder (renamed Dissociative Identity Disorder)? A person once insisted to this author, "Yeah. It has to, because that disorder is out there. If it exists, then the Bible HAS to say something about it." Does it?

The following "proof" was given: "The double-minded man is unstable in all his ways" (James 1:8). Is that verse talking about Multiple Personality Disorder? It is improbable that James is talking about Multiple Personality Disorder when it refers to a "double-minded man."

How about Nebuchadnezzar grazing in the pasture (Dan. 4:28-33)? That was God's curse on him, but would you call that Schizophrenia? Does the Bible really tell us about Schizophrenia? Not really. There is no clear reference to Schizophrenia or Multiple Personality Disorder in the Bible. We need to be very careful when we make proclamations about biblical clarity that may not really be there.

Sometimes Christian speakers will declare that Multiple Personality Disorder/Dissociative Identity Disorder equals demon possession. As Christians, we should cautiously evaluate such assertions. There is no scriptural evidence to support the idea that Multiple Personality Disorder is demon possession.

Could there be spiritual influences? -- Absolutely. But there could also be spiritual influences in the very room where you sit as you read this book. There could be spiritual influences present with depression and anxiety. Negative spiritual influences or demonic influences may even affect people who look spiritual and well put-together.

How do we know that to be true? The Pharisees looked great. But, in speaking to them, Christ made reference to "Your father, the devil" (John 8:44). So even those who look good on the outside – who look "spiritual" to us, can have demonic influences affecting their lives.

We need to be very careful when we make proclamations about biblical clarity that may not really be there. The Bible does not speak specifically to every life event, issue, or circumstance; nor does our world teach us the correct view of morality and godly living.

PROBLEM #4 -- ON THE SAME LEVEL?

(Source clker.com)

Since General Revelation and Special Revelation have different purposes and because there is a difference in clarity, it would be erroneous to see them as being on the same plane or on the same level. If one of the types of revelation were to be put above the other, then it would only make sense that Special Revelation would be viewed as more important and the grid through which all other information should be processed. General Revelation would then be positioned below Special Revelation. If an error were to be made, it would seem to be "safer" to err on the side of evaluating everything through Scripture than to leave those important evaluations to human assessments. Though General Revelation is helpful to us (especially in the "hard" sciences such as Biology and Chemistry), it is limited when it comes to things like morality, spirituality, angels, God, and important questions about life.

SUMMARY OF THE TWO-BOOK VIEW

Though putting the two types of revelation together seems like a good system in theory, the view brings dilemmas regarding agreement, differences in purpose, clarity, and inequality. Since God's thoughts are far superior to ours (Isa. 55:8-9), Scripture needs to be our solid foundation and any structure we build using data from the world needs to be constructed on that.

5) SCRIPTURAL FOUNDATION, SECULAR NUGGETS

INTRODUCTION – 4 DEFINITIONS OF PSYCHOLOGY

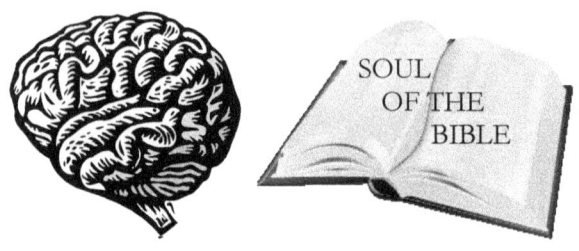

(Soure: Microsoft Word 7 Clipart)   (Source: Public Domain)

Take a look again now at the question that is under consideration: "Does psychology have anything good to offer?" Before answering that question, our terms must be defined. We have previously concluded that the accepted definition of psychology used in this book is "the study of mind and behavior" and all that that entails. It was noted how faulty presuppositions -- "underlying beliefs"[9] -- can affect one's viewpoint. But consider now a more in-depth look at a few of the popular definitions of psychology.

Though there are many definitions of psychology floating around in various circles, four will be examined here: 1) The Study of Mind and Behavior. 2) The "Scientific" Study of Mindand Behavior. 3) The Study of the "Soul" (psuche) in Scripture. 4) Theories of Psychology such as those of Freud, Skinner, and Rogers.

The first definition is more philosophical in nature. The second one is based more on observations and experiments that provide data which lead to theories. The third refers to the study of the "soul" in the Bible. (The term "psuche" – psyche, which is the Greek term for "soul" -- or sometimes translated "heart" -- is studied. This word is different from "pneuma" -- spirit.) And the fourth definition revolves around the theories of psychologists, such as: Freud, Skinner, and Rogers.

So to answer the question: "Does psychology have anything good to offer?" we have to first ask: "What do you mean by 'psychology'?" To which of those four are we referring?

---

[9] Refer to page 34 of this document.

The Study of Mind and Behavior

If you are a believer in the first definition, then you accept that psychology is "The Study of Mental and Behavioral Processes." Here, psychology is simply a neutral term. It is not sinful. It is like Biology, Chemistry, and Physics. It is simply a term denoting the study of something -- mind and behavior. And the study of something is not sinful. Now, one's conclusions could be sinful. The results could differ from what God wants. But the study of something is neutral. And it has been stated previously in this book: psychology reflects God, just like all of the other subjects reflect God. Math reflects God. Biology reflects God. Chemistry reflects God . . . Philosophy . . . Physics. They all reflect God. He is the inventor of them. And anything that reflects God is worth studying. "Great are the works of the Lord; They are studied by all who delight in them," says Psalm 111:2 (KJV).

The "Scientific" Study of Mind and Behavior

What about the "Scientific" Study of Mental and Behavioral Processes? Could adding the scientific component make it bad?

To answer that, remember that science is neutral. That has already been discussed. Simply bringing things through our senses and trying to make sense of them is a philosophical way of finding truth, and that is also neutral. So you have "neutral" on top of "neutral" -- nothing sinful yet.

In fact, science is biblical. What does Genesis 1:28 say? What are we supposed to do with our world? We are to subdue it and have dominion over it as a representation of God here on the Earth. How can that be done without studying it? How do I subdue anything and have dominion over it without studying it, knowing it, and understanding how it functions best? So science is biblical and psychology is biblical. Therefore scientific psychology is biblical (the enterprise, not necessarily the conclusion).

But science, as important as it is, is limited. It is helpful for that which is "immanent." Science is not so helpful for that which is "transcendent." We are back to that presupposition again.

So science is limited to that which is immanent – the things that can be seen, the created domain. Science is very helpful for those things. We are very thankful for the medical community and what it has found for us, but it is limited.

It cannot help much with that which is transcendent. Science will not and cannot prove God. Science will not prove that there are angels.

Science will not prove that there is a heaven or hell or demonic forces. It does not have the capability to do that -- at least not yet.

One day we will all be good scientists. How do we know that? The Bible says that one day every tongue will confess and every knee shall bow (Phil. 2:10) and we will all be good empiricists and say, "There He is." Every tongue! Every knee! Everyone will say: "There is a God and I now believe." Why? "I see it." One day, we will all be empiricists. On this side of heaven, however, we have to take things by faith.

In his book, *Disappointment with God*, Philip Yancey shares an analogy told by C. S. Lewis regarding a beam of light in a dark took shed. He says, "When he first entered the shed, he saw a beam and looked at the luminous band of brightness filled with floating specks of dust.

(Source: Pagella from dreamstine.com, 2011)

But, when he moved over to the beam and looked *along* it, he gained a very different perspective. Suddenly, he saw, not the beam, but framed in the window of the shed, green leaves, moving on the branches of a tree outside and beyond that, 93 million miles away, the sun. Looking *at* the beam and looking *along* the beam are quite different." (Yancy, 1988, p. 218)

What is the point? Science is an effective instrument for studying the beam. You can measure how long the beam is. You can count how many specks of dust there are in the beam. You can study what the light is made up of and note that light, itself, is made up of particles (photons). You can observe the contrast of the beam of light to the darkness -- which is simply the absence of light. However, science cannot look *along* the beam, to the source beyond. It cannot tell us the source of the beam. Faith is

(Source: Pheoktistov from dreamstime.com)

68

required to look along the beam. Science is a tremendous instrument for looking at the beam; however, science is limited.

The Study of the "Soul" (psuche) in Scripture

How about the study of the soul, "psuche," in Scripture? God created mental and behavioral processes; therefore, those processes reflect God. The word "soul," or "psuche," is often used in Scripture to describe those deep inner-workings of man's beliefs and thinking. The important point to remember when looking at the idea of integrating psychology and theology (which was stated earlier in this chapter) is: Psychology is a part of the Bible message. There is an inherent psychology in our theology.

When we study the Greek word "psuche" or "soul" (and sometimes translated "heart") in Scripture, we see a wealth of psychology. In fact, that word alone sheds light on the makeup of man, dealing with all of his thoughts, emotions, and what drives his behaviors.

Proverbs 23:7 ". . . as he thinketh in his heart/soul (translated in NASB "within himself"), so is he" (KJV). In the secular approach of Cognitive Therapy, thinking is vitally important to understanding the person and the Cognitive Therapist bases his theory on that truth. But understanding the "soul" seems to be stressed in biblical references for the Christian as well, and this psychology is part of our theology.

Two Greek words make up our word psychology: "psuche' " -- psych, and "logos" -- ology. "Psuche" is the Greek word for "soul." When we study the soul and see how it is referred to in Scripture, we are learning about how man is made up -- how he thinks and how that thinking is the basis for his behavior. My soul or mind is the center for my thinking, action, emotions, etc.

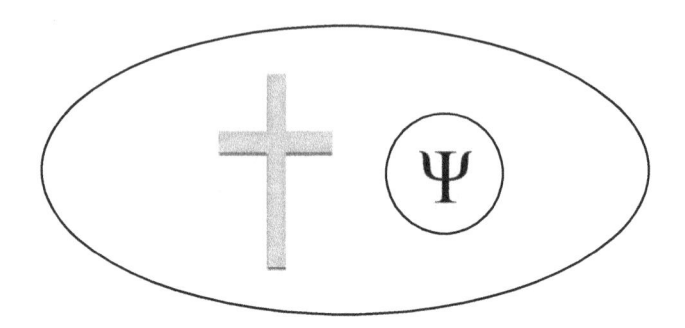

The large oval that surrounds the cross in the preceding diagram[10] represents theology and psychology is represented by the encircled Greek symbol, "ψ".[11] The diagram illustrates the point that inside of our theology is a psychology. God made our minds which dictate our behaviors and they are part of our theology. A person's mental state (thinking) and the behaviors that emerge based from that thinking are discussed in the Bible. So any time someone looks into Scripture and finds the word "mind" or behavior, or how people emoted, or the word "soul" and then processes what is being communicated in that passage, that person is discovering something about theology. That "psychology" is part of our "theology."

Our theology is not a sterile thing. Our theology does not consist of simply knowing the five points of Calvinism. That is *part* of theology; but, that is not the full embodiment of our theology. Our theology is demonstrated in the way we treat people. The way we behave toward others is theology. Did God have anything to say about how we treat people? Yes!

Our theology begins with our thinking and is demonstrated by how we live our lives. And yet, many find themselves sometimes believing that theology is simply rational and conceptual. The often omit the practical nature.

The way we treat people *is* part of our theology! In fact, it is a very important part of our theology. It demonstrates our theology. And

---

[10] Diagram by author, Thomas J. Edgington, Ph.D.
[11] A subpoint can be added while on this topic. Psychology can be symbolized by the Greek letter "ψ" --"psy." There are people who have said, "Ah, that's the devil's pitchfork!" There are a couple of problems with that. Number one, it is the Greek letter, not a pitchfork. It is neutral. The same letter is used in many other words that could not even be "stretched" to mean something evil. To put that kind of pronouncement upon the letter, just because it is the beginning of the word "psychology," seems a bit forced.

Secondly, the Devil doesn't have a pitchfork. He's not red and he does not have a big long tail. That is not Satan.

the way we hold our theology is as much theology as the theology to which we hold. If I try to control people and damage people with my interpretation of theology, God has something to say about that. It is a part of theology – a vital part!

The study of the word "soul" alone provides much evidence of that deep inner part of man -- the part that consists of the beliefs that influence how we think and how we live our lives. And when the evidences of the word "soul" are combined with the remaining teachings of the Bible, we find even more material that enlightens us and instructs our thinking and behavior. The entire Bible contains a wealth of material for the field of psychology.

Theories of Psychology such as those of Freud, Skinner, and Rogers

The last definition that some attribute to psychology is that psychology consists of the theories of famous psychologists such as Sigmund Freud, B. F. Skinner, and Carl Rogers. Though they were

(Source: Public Domain)   (Source: PsychArt, 2011)   Source: Public Domain)

psychologists that contributed to the field of psychology, they were men who held wrong presuppositions. Therefore, aspects of their theories are wrong. Obviously, they did not believe their presuppositions were faulty, but many of them contradict biblical teachings. And what is interesting about each of their theories is that all of them reacted against religion on some level.

Sigmund Freud was raised by Jewish parents while living in the Roman Catholic town of Freiburg, Moravia. He wrote a number of books interpreting the religious influences he encountered.[12] "Religion is comparable to a childhood neurosis," {(Freud (1927)} he wrote in *The*

---

[12] Books directed toward religion included *Totem and Taboo* (Mineola, New York: Dover Publications, Inc., 1913), *The Future of an Illusion* (London: Hogarth Press, 1927), *Civilization and Its Discontents* (London: Hogarth Press, 1930), and *Moses and Monotheism* (1938).

Future of an Illusion (p. 53). "The different religions have never overlooked the part played by the sense of guilt in civilization. What is more, they come forward with a claim...to save mankind from this sense of guilt, which they call sin" (pp. 82-83), was written in *Civilization and Its Discontents (Freud, 1930).*

Skinner attended a Protestant Sunday School as a child. As a man, he contemplated the ideas he had been taught, which included the fear he had acquired of Hell -- enhanced by his grandmother's warning that children who told lies would go there. He felt that religion had negatively influenced his behavior, causing him to withdraw from others because of his shame over his sexual desires (Skinner, 1976).

After trying religion, he seemed to come to the conclusion that it was a type of crutch that people needed to control behavior and explain baffling situations. "Physics and biology soon abandoned explanations of this sort," he said, "and turned to more useful kinds of causes, but the step has not been decisively taken in the field of human behavior" (Skinner, 2002, p. 7). When speaking of those who believe in "indwelling agents," he stated, "Although physics soon stopped personifying things in this way, it continued for a long time to speak as if they (people) had wills, impulses, feelings, purposes, and other fragmentary attributes of an indwelling agent. . . . Careless references to purpose are still to be found in both physics and biology, but good practice has no place for them" (Skinner, 2002, p. 8).

Rogers came from a fundamentalist background. Two beliefs that he was taught very strongly at home when he was growing up, were: 1) People are depraved and 2) Do not mix with worldly people (Rogers, 1961).

But, as a psychologist, two of his main tenets could be summarized as: "People are basically good" (Rogers, 1961) and we should get together and share with one another. (He was a strong proponent of group counseling/"encounter" groups).[13] He greatly reacted against some of his religious upbringing even going so far as to say, "Neither the Bible nor the prophets -- neither Freud nor research -- neither the revelations of God nor man -- can take precedence over my own direct experience" (Rogers, 1961, p. 24). Yet, even though he

---

[13] "In an intensive group with much freedom and little structure, the individual will gradually feel safe enough to drop some of his defenses and facades; he will relate more directly on a feeling basis (come into a basic encounter) with other members of the group; he will come to understand himself and his relationship to others more accurately; he will change in his personal attitudes and behavior; and he will subsequently relate more effectively to others in his everyday life situation." Carl Rogers, "The Process of the Basic Encounter Group," in K. Roy MacKenzie's, *Classics in Group Psychotherapy* (New York: The Guilford Press, 1992), p. 217.

asserted presuppositions that were false, or in some cases, fell short of total accuracy, during his years as a psychologist, he *did* stumble on some truth -- due to the common grace of God.

God allowed all three of the previously mentioned psychologists to be brilliant and allowed them to find some truth. A number of those truths are mentioned throughout this book.

So is psychology basically the theories of Freud, Skinners, and Rogers? No. We have already demonstrated that. But did Freud, Skinner, and Rogers make important contributions to psychology? Yes. Can other non-Christians make contributions that can enlighten us in regard to our understanding of our world? Yes.

And we need to remember that all three of the men previously mentioned were image-bearers. Secularists are still image-bearers. They are made in God's image and gifted with rationality, just as Christians are. Non-Christians can be brilliant people who can think deeply and make accurate observations of their world.

Summary of Definitions

So which of the four definitions is correct? They all are correct in some way because they all include an aspect of psychology -- though they are not all complete. The first definition encompasses all of the other three aspects and is the most comprehensive. It will be the one that can be assumed as you read on to the next pages and chapters of this book. So as you read, assume that psychology means, "The Study of Mind and Behavior" and the various aspects involved in that study.

5) SCRIPTURAL FOUNDATION, SECULAR NUGGETS

WHAT DO WE TAKE FROM PSYCHOLOGY?

All of this leads to the discussion of the fifth view of integration, which is the view that is held by the writer of this book -- "Scriptural Foundation, Secular Nuggets."

What does that mean? It means that secularists *do* have something to offer that can be of value to the Christian.

If integration is defined that way, this author would be an "integrationist" (though not on a presuppositional level -- since the assumed belief is that psychology is inherent in theology and does not need to be integrated). Yes, those who assume the teachings of this text would be "integrationists" – meaning that it is believed that secularists have something positive to offer; but NO, we are not "integrationists" on a presuppositional level because the presuppositions are mutually exclusive and secular theorists have faulty presuppositions.

So what we want to look at is: "How do we use some of those truths that secularists have found?" Jay Adams (1973) put it very adeptly in his book, *The Christian Counselor's Manual*. In spite of the fact that Adams has been known to have a strong view against psychology (though possibly because his definition of "psychology" is different from the one espoused in this book), even he realizes the importance of some of the contributions of others in the secular world.

He said, "From the vantage point of his biblical foundation, the Christian counselor may take note of, and evaluate, and *reclaim the truth, dimly reflected by the unbeliever* so long as he does so in a manner that is consistent with biblical principles and methodology" (p. 92). What Adams was saying is that there *is* truth from the secular world that is available to be reclaimed by the Christian. But most importantly, the reclaiming process is preempted by a strong biblical base through which the believer evaluates that truth.

Adams (1973) further stated: "On our foundation of biblical presuppositions, there must be built a fuller methodology that grows out of them and that is appropriate to them at every point. The methodology must be oriented biblically and remain in the framework of scriptural principles. When you have constructed a platform like that, then you are able to stand upon it. . ." (That's your foundation.) ". . . look around at what is happening elsewhere, and you can pick and choose and adapt from that perspective, whatever *nuggets* that an unbeliever (in the common grace of God) has unearthed" (p. 93)

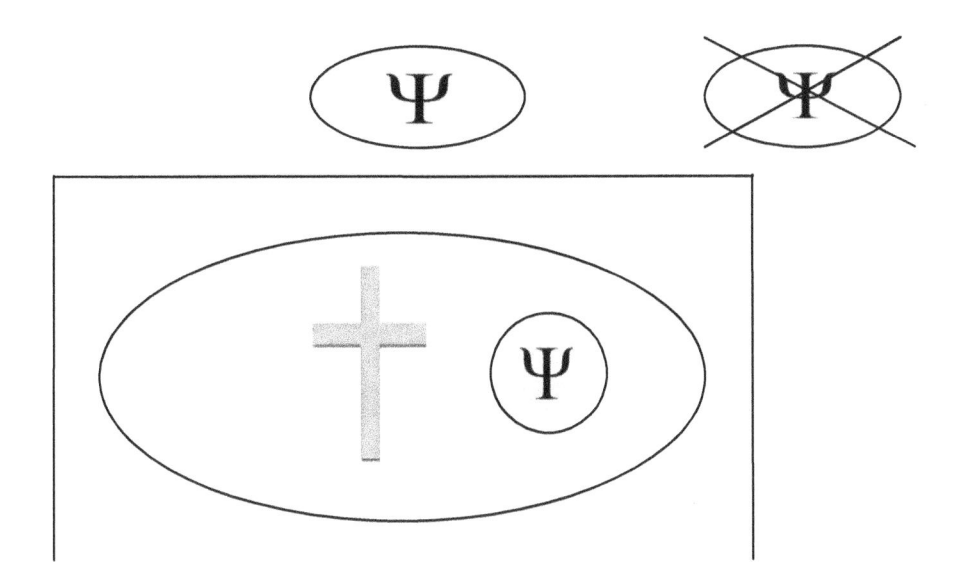

Our theology is our foundation. Yet, within that theology, is a psychology. We do not have to integrate that. It is already *in* our theology. Mind, behavior, how we treat people, relationships, marriage, depression, anxiety -- they are all there. But once we have that foundation, then we can build upon it.

In the secular world, we can pick and choose and adapt what secularists have unearthed. They stumbled upon truth. God allowed them to be intelligent people who observed their world, gathered data, and developed theories (which contained some truth and some error). As Christians, we can reclaim the true information (that they discovered through His enlightenment) for His glory. But if parts of their theories contradict Scripture, we need to discard those parts. In other words: Accept what is complementary. Reject what is contradictory.

Accept what is complementary -- what complements Scripture. But if it does not complement Scripture, if it is saying that Scripture is wrong, we should reject that. We only accept the "nuggets" that complement and guild upon the truths found in our foundation: God's Word.

EXAMPLES OF HELPFUL NUGGETS

(Source: Dreamstime.com)

So what are some examples of helpful nuggets? Some who question this view of integration may want to know what contributions psychology can make that would be helpful to the Christian. The following are examples of helpful nuggets.

Example 1

What is the best mechanism to lessen prejudice? Gordon Allport (1954) wrote a book entitled *The Nature of Prejudice* which espoused the "Contact Hypothesis." He said that *under certain conditions*, direct contact between members of opposing groups would reduce prejudice. (The conditions were important since just putting them together could actually increase prejudice, as one study showed {Stephan 1986}.) The conditions were: equal status, no competition, contact being sanctioned by authority, and common goals (also known as "superordinate goals").

The movie, *Remember the Titans*, is a great example of common or "superordinate goals." The football players were not simply combined. The two prejudiced sides were put together with a common goal. As was shown in the movie, when two sides are joined with a cooperative goal that they have to work together to meet, the prejudice dissipates.

Now, is that in the Bible? No, not directly. But the Bible does tell us not to be prejudiced and not to lift one above another. We should not give the best seat to the rich and cast aside the poor (James 2:1-4). The Bible gives us parameters. But it did not directly give superordinate goals as a way to lessen prejudice.

So some people who do not claim to be Christians have discovered things that are very useful in terms of what will help reduce prejudice. Though traditional teaching or preaching can be effective, other methods can sometimes teach lessons even better.

Example 2

Another example involves studies that were conducted to discover better ways to help girls learn math. Anita Li and Georgina Adamson found that the type of classroom environment affected girls' interest. The idea of competitiveness seemed to be a hindrance to girls' enthusiasm and thus their learning of math (Li & Adamson, 1992). Judy Diamond and Deborah Bono (1994) also found gender differences, each claiming that cooperative environments (group learning) were helpful to girls learning math.

In a typical math class, what often happens? A typical math class is visual -- diagrams are put on the board. And how are students arranged in the classroom? Often, all are in individual seats and work on problems individually. Or sometimes the environment is competitive, where the "fastest" one to figure out the problem is rewarded in some way. So, many times girls begin to think, "I can't learn it. It's too difficult!" And a resulting conclusion seems to be drawn that girls are not very good in math.

What the research has shown is: Girls, who are more relational, tend to learn math better if they can talk about it, sit at tables where they can "process it" with other students, and help each other. They tend not to learn math as well in a competitive environment. Boys learn it a little bit better when they do it by themselves -- more independently or "compete" in some way. Girls can be just as good in math. They just learn it differently.

Nowhere in the Bible does it tell us that girls learn math better in a relational style and boys learn better in an individualistic style, but this is very helpful to know if you are in the teaching profession, especially if you are teaching math.

Example 3

The Premack principle is another helpful piece of information that is useful for Christians, yet not found in the Bible. The Premack principle, developed by David Premack, states that a commonly occurring action (one more desirable for the actor) can be used effectively to reinforce a less commonly occurring one (that is, one less desirable for the actor). A common example used to illustrate this principle is a parent requiring a child to clean his or her room before he or she can watch TV.

We practiced this in our own home when our children were growing up. At the dinner table, we would allow dessert only if they ate at least one spoonful of peas or other food they found less desirable. In this case, an activity that probably does not require reinforcement, is used as a reinforcer for cleaning the room or eating vegetables, which in the context of this example the child would not normally choose to do without reinforcement. Again, that is not found in the Bible directly, yet it is a useful psychological tool.

Example 4

What about Fundamentalist Christians? Are they all the same? The intention of the study conducted in 1988 was to show that all fundamentalists are not alike (Edgington, 1988). Researchers in the past have lumped fundamentalists into a single category showing them to be rather simplistic, "black-and-white" thinkers. The attempt was to demonstrate that all fundamentalists are not alike. Some are very complex in their thinking while others are more simplistic. The findings supported the notion that among fundamentalists (those that adhere to certain conservative values), there exists a continuum of fundamentalism with rigidity, defensiveness, and close-mindedness at one end and with more tolerance, less defensiveness, and greater open-mindedness at the other end. All fundamentalists are not alike, as some might want to conclude. The Bible does not teach that directly, nor does it directly deal with the topic of cognitive complexity.

Example 5

A fifth example is of a study conducted by a Christian psychologist -- Dr. Donald Joy. His study looked at the effects of value-oriented instruction in both the church and the home (Joy, 1969).

Dr. Joy was looking at church class instruction (Sunday School class) vs. parental home instruction to see the effects of both and how they compared to each other. In the midst of his research, he discovered a "serendipitous finding." He found that boys tended to learn better in a nontraditional setting (i.e., a non-classroom setting -- which would be different from Sunday School, which tended to be more of a classroom setting) whereas, girls seemed to do better in the traditional setting.

Some have believed that boys do not learn as well as girls. But it could be that boys would learn as much as girls if they were are allowed to participate in a non-classroom instructional experience. This is helpful for Sunday School and church leaders because if we want boys to learn the basic stories in the Bible, theology, and certain biblical principles, it may be better to do it in a non-classroom situation. (Take them out in the woods and/or do things that are active that involve the intended biblical content to be taught.) You will not find that in Scripture. In fact, Sunday School is not in the Bible!

Though Dr. Joy, as a Christian, did approach his study with a "regenerate" mind; he still found truth that was not written in God's Word. We would not have become aware of his findings by just looking at the Bible, but it is very helpful research that complements the Bible.

Other Examples

Is "intermittent reinforcement" as effective as "continuous reinforcement"? B.F. Skinner conducted a study on this topic which produced helpful information.

What about Freud's "defense mechanisms"? Though those will be dealt with later, it can be stated here that there is much to be learned that can be helpful to the Christian when studying Freud's writings about defense mechanisms.

Other topics studied and written about are birth order and forms of discipline. There are a number of very informative books on those subjects that have been helpful to Christians in raising their children. Books regarding the family dynamics and the parenting dynamics that affect the development of children's personalities are all "nuggets" of information that are "out there" to be "reclaimed" by the believer and used to glorify God. In other words, numerous ideas and discoveries have been made that are helpful "nuggets" that cannot be found in Scripture.

THE COMMON GRACE OF GOD

Dr. David Plaster (2003) wrote that there are gifts that are bestowed upon non-Christians by the "common grace of God." He defined that common grace as: "The innumerable blessings, not a part of salvation that God, in His grace, gives to all people, even those that deserve death and will not be saved." Or, said more simply, "God allows non-Christians to stumble upon truth." God allows those with unregenerate minds to discover truth in His universe.

So how do we know this to be true -- that God allows non-Christians to discover truth? First of all, we see it to be true. Non-Christians have discovered countless things in our world. But what many do not realize is that there is Scriptural support for that assertion as well.

SCRIPTURAL INDICATIONS OF GOD'S BESTOWAL OF TRUTH TO NON-CHRISTIANS

Proverbs 22:2 says, "Rich and poor have this in common: The Lord is the maker of them all."

(Source: Shafer "Tuscan Sunset" from Wallpapers 2010)

Prov. 29:13 – The poor man and the oppressor have this in common:
    The Lord gives sight to the eyes of both.
Matt. 5:45 – He causes his sun to rise on the evil and the good, and
    sends rain on the righteous and the unrighteous.

And if we broaden those ideas beyond sight and rain, is it probable that God permits some unrighteous people to be smart and allows some righteous people to be "not-so-smart." It has nothing to do with who is going to heaven or who isn't. He just allows intelligence to come to a variety of different people.

Of course, the best intelligence can only come when you know God -- if you are talking about the kind of intelligence that also includes wisdom. And certainly biblical wisdom can only come from knowing God. The Bible states that the wise man says, "There is a God," while the fool says that there is no God (Ps. 14:1). So we know that biblical wisdom, certainly, comes only from following God and understanding what He has to say. But the non-Christian can also be brilliant and produce amazing contributions for our world.

The next scriptural passage provides several issues to consider. 1 Corinthians 15:33 says, "Do not be misled: 'Bad company corrupts good character.'" If you associate with bad people, sometimes you end up doing bad things. And notice that it is a quote. Paul is quoting someone when he spoke those words of warning.

The very compelling fact to consider, as it relates to our discussion of whether non-Christians can contribute to the Christian's world, is that this quotation is from a Greek comedy. "The Greek comedy, 'Thais,' was written by the Greek poet/philosopher, Menander, whose writings, the Corinthians would know" (NIV Study Bible, 1985, p. 1757). Paul used a principle that was propagated by a Greek comedy and from a Greek poet/philosopher, and said, "This is true." In fact, the accepted principle that was observed and proclaimed by Menander became biblical. It is now part of Scripture!

(Source: Public Domain)

Could Paul have used ideas from Freud, or Skinner, or Rogers? He could have, if those psychologists had been around and made true observations such as that of Menander. Bad company DOES corrupt good character. Paul knew that to be true and used the information to make his point, to teach the Corinthians and us, and in the end, to glorify God.

What about the statement in Titus 1:12, 13 which says, "Even one of their own prophets has said, 'Cretans are always liars, evil brutes, lazy gluttons,' This testimony is true"? Paul is again quoting someone. He says it is "true." Who is he quoting? Paul is quoting Epimenides (a sixth-century B.C. native of Knossos, Crete), who was held in high esteem by the Cretans" (NIV Study Bible, 1985, p. 1851). He, Epimenides, said that the Cretans were "always liars, evil brutes, and lazy gluttons." (He was definitely not politically correct by today's standards!) Paul is using a secular figure and pointing out the validity of Epimenides's "findings," his "observations." So, when considers the above evidences, it seems clear that even in Scripture there is an acceptance of the fact that truth can be learned from unbelievers.

(Source: Public Domain)

Those with regenerate minds do not always have whole truth, however. Though certainly with regenerate minds we have the capability of one understanding God, we are not always correct in all of our thinking. We continue to grow and learn throughout life. And sometimes we are wrong.

So the idea that "if you have a regenerate mind, then you can know truth, but people with unregenerate minds cannot discover any truth" is not supported by Scripture. In reality, some Christian people have some "wacky" ideas and some non-Christian people have ideas that make a lot of sense.

It is true that with regenerate minds we can go further in finding truth because we can have wisdom. We can know God and know what He is trying to tell us. Even though this is true, be careful of embracing an extreme position that says that if you have a regenerate mind, it must mean you have a nearly perfect mind.

And conversely, we need to avoid espousing the belief that having an unregenerate mind means that the non-Christian has nothing to contribute. An unregenerate person can stumble upon truth and be accurate in many of his perceptions. He can produce much that can be of value to the Christian. Discernment is the key to knowing what to accept when one considers what the non-Christian has to offer.

DISCERNMENT

Before concluding this chapter, the idea of "discernment" needs to be addressed. Hebrews 5:14 says, "But solid food is for those who are mature and who by constant use have *trained* themselves to *distinguish good from evil.*"

Our job as Christian counselors is to study the Bible and to study secular psychology/counseling -- making the distinction between good and evil. Ask yourself, "Am I able to filter out the bad?" Can you make your "grid" tight enough? To have a tight grid means that you have to have a strong understanding of the Word of God so that when you study materials other than the Bible, you can bring those materials through your grid and allow only the good and truthful things to come through. Hopefully, as you bring theories through, you can weed out the things that are contradictory to Scripture and keep the things that are complementary.

The analogy of a screen door seems fitting here. If it has huge holes in it, lots of bugs get in. When it is "tight," then it keeps the bugs out. When we know Scripture well, it helps keep the screen tight and keep the "bugs" out.

Philippians 1:9-10 says, "And this is my prayer: that your love may abound more and more in knowledge and depth of insight, so you may be *able to discern what is best* and may be pure and blameless until the day of Christ."

That is the real key to the question of integration -- the discernment of good from evil. We want to accept what is true, but we need to have a *practiced* "truth-finder," so that we can be discerning and accurate as we make the distinctions between good and evil. We want to be able to differentiate between what to keep and what to discard. The more mature the believer and the more practiced he is in knowing God's Word and applying it to his world, the easier it will be to make those determinations and the clearer it will be as to what to keep and what to discard.

CONCLUSION -- IS THE BIBLE SUFFICIENT?

There is one further question – one that this author has often been asked: "Is the Bible sufficient?" Do we who study psychology assume that the Bible is not sufficient? If we are Christians, obviously not!

Of course the Bible is sufficient. 2 Peter 1:3 says, "His divine power has given us everything we need for life and godliness through our knowledge of Him." God's divine power has given us *everything* we need to know for life, through His Word. And godliness comes through our knowledge of Him.

So here is the answer: Sufficient? Absolutely! The Bible answers all foundational and important questions about life. It tells how to find God, know God, and serve God. It is sufficient.

But is it exhaustive? (That is what many Christians are really wanting to know when they ask if the Bible is sufficient.) Does it tell us everything we could possibly know in the realm of psychology? No! The Bible is *not* exhaustive on any topic -- including psychology. It was not intended to be. So where it is not exhaustive, it is important that we study the subject -- being careful what we bring through our biblical "grid."

Some believe that we should only read the Bible. But the Bible itself says, "Subdue your world and have dominion over it" (Gen. 1:28). We need to understand it well in order to subdue and rule over it well, as God's representatives.

When it comes to the medical community, most Christians agree whole-heartedly that it is important to study and understand. But it is true in every other facet of life, including psychology.

So build a solid biblical foundation and then feel free to study the world. Be open to what God will demonstrate of Himself through that study. If we stay close to Him and compare all that we learn with His Word (keeping only what complements that Word), we can build a structure that is very helpful for counseling.

CHAPTER 3

IMAGE OF GOD

Image and Likeness

What does it mean to be in the image and likeness of God? There are six passages found in Scripture that tell that we are created in His image and likeness.

1) Genesis 1:26 says, "Let us make man in Our image, according to Our likeness; and let them rule over the fish of the sea and over the birds of the sky and over the cattle and over all the earth, and over every creeping thing that creeps on the earth."

2) Genesis 1:27 goes on to say, "And God Created Man in His own image, in the image of God, He created him; male and female He created them."

3) Genesis 5:1 says, "He made him in the likeness of God."

4) Genesis 9:6 -- ". . . For in the image of God, He made man."

5) I Corinthians 11:7 -- "For a man ought not to have his head covered, since he is in the image and glory of God. . . ."

6) James 3:9 -- ". . . men, who have been made in the likeness of God."

DIFFERENTIATION OF THE TERMS "IMAGE" AND "LIKENESS"

In the Hebrew language, the word that is translated *image* in our Bibles is the word "tselem," which refers to an "image, likeness, or something cut out" -- from the root "to carve." (Brown, Driver, & Briggs, 1968, p. 852-854). The root word of "tselem is "tsel," which means "shadow" (property or likeness) (Brown, Driver, & Briggs, 1968, p. 853).

The word that is translated *likeness* is "demuth" in Hebrew. It refers to "likeness, resemblance, and similitude." "Demah" (the root of "Demuth") means "to be like or to resemble" (Brown, driver, & briggs, 1968, pp. 197-198). The word "demuth" is more abstract than the word "tselem."

Scripture does not really give us a definition of this concept. These two words together seem to say that we are like God in some way, but more in an abstract rather than literal (physical) way. There are three views of what this concept means.

THREE VIEWS OF THE IMAGE OF GOD

The first view of the image of God is the Substantive view. Basically this view says that we have a "substance" that is like God's, but not in a physical sense. It is something resident within man's nature. We know that God is a spirit (John 4:24) and therefore He created us to be like Him in a spiritual sense. Most often people see this as a "psychological or spiritual quality in human nature" (Erikson, 1995, p. 499). In other words, we have certain spiritual qualities that resemble God's. Most would put reason or thinking as one of the predominant qualities that make us like God. Other capacities or capabilities will be discussed later in this book.

The second view is the Relational view. "Many modern theologians do not conceive of the image of God as something resident within man's nature. Indeed they do not ordinarily ask what man is or what sort of nature he may have. Rather, they think of the image of God as the experiencing of a relationship" (Erikson, 1995, p. 502). In other words, that relationship IS the image and likeness of God as opposed to something intrinsic in man. Because of this, we can have a relationship with God in a way that animals cannot.

The last view is the Functional view. It is not something that is resident within man's nature and it is not a relationship. "Rather, the image consists in something that man does. It is a function that man performs, the most frequently mentioned being the exercise of dominion over the creation" (Erikson, 1995, p. 508). Man can represent God here on earth. The idea of subduing the earth and ruling as God representative (Gen. 1: 26-28) would be synonymous with the idea of image and likeness. In other words, image and likeness means representation.

In order to get a more complete view of image and likeness (at least in this author's opinion) it would be good to combine the three views into a more comprehensive view. I would say that the essence of the image and likeness is the substantive view. In other words, we have certain capabilities or capacities that are like God's. One of those, in my mind, is the social capacity. Rather than making it a separate view, I would incorporate it into the substantive view. We have the capacity to have a relationship with God that is very unique from the animal kingdom. We have other capacities that will be discussed later. In my mind, the function of image and likeness has to do with the functional view. We have the mandate to represent God and He has given us the divine prerequisites to do so. The fact that we have certain capacities that are like His (essence of the image) allows us to carry out our God-appointed function which is to represent God (function of the image).

We will now discuss the other capacities that allow us to carry out our God-appointed function. These capacities are the social capacity, the existential capacity, the rational capacity, the teleological capacity, the volitional capacity, the behavioral capacity, and the emotional capacity. The first two give us a theory of motivation; therefore longings and strategies will be discussed after these two capacities are discussed.

CHAPTER 4

THE SOCIAL CAPACITY

Introduction

We have the capacity of relating with God and others. Where does this come from? It comes from God, who is relational and created us to be like Him in this way. That is why we can have a meaningful relationship with Him and with others like Him (other humans). How do we know God is relational?

RELATIONSHIP IN REGARD TO THE TRINITY

God sets an example of what a perfect relationship looks like through the Trinity. It is remarkable to note that God, Himself, is RELATIONAL -- intrinsically. All by Himself, He is relational.

Human beings cannot say that. We cannot say, "By myself, I do relationship." Each human is one person. We cannot do relationship with ourselves since relationship involves interaction with another. But God, intrinsically because of the Trinity, is relational. (That pure and dependable relationship is what we long for as humans.)

So, when you think about relationship in regard to God, you realize that it is "built in" to God -- that by Himself He relates to one another. It is not simply that He wants relationship, He IS relational. It is built into His very essence.

(Sources: Clipart.christiansunite.com/God, 2011; Bida, "Jesus by Sea," 2011, Dove -Public Domain)

When examining this mystery Loraine Boettner (1974) wrote, "The terms Father, Son, and Spirit . . . are the proper names of different subjects who are distinct from one another as one person is distinct from another (pp. 90-91)." Yet he notes that those three distinct persons share a relationship -- as indicated by the personal pronouns they use when speaking of or to each other (Matt. 17:5, John 17:1, 16:28, 16:13) and as demonstrated by the ways they relate to each other (Boettner, 1974, pp. 90-91).

Take a look at all of the different ways they share relationship: The Father loves the Son and the Son loves the Father (John 3:35, 15:10). The Father "entrusts" the Son -- placing everything in his hands (John 3:35). The Son goes to the Father (John 16:10). The Spirit glorifies the Son (John 16:14). The Son prays to the Father (John 14:16, 17:5). They have shared "glory" together (John 17:5). The Father sends the Son (John 8:16, 17:3, 17:18; Matt. 10:40). The Father and the Son work together (John 8:16). The Father "anoints" the Son with the Holy Spirit (Acts 10:38). God was with the Son (Acts 10:38). The Father and Son send the Holy Spirit, who acts as their Agent (John 14:16; 14:26, 16:7). This is ONE God doing this!

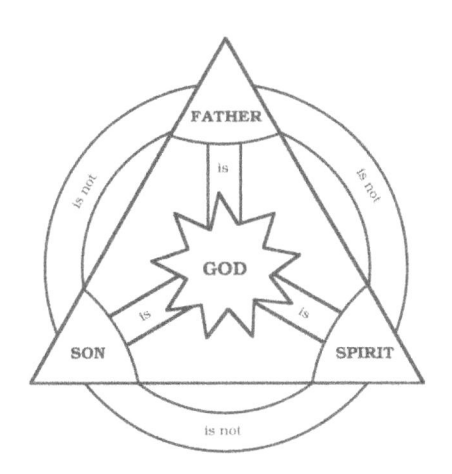

D. Broughton Knox (1982) commented on the necessity of relationship to demonstrate God's attributes. He noted, "The doctrine of the Trinity fits our experience of personality. God is the highest being that we can conceive, and personality is the highest mode of being known to, or conceivable by us. We believe that God is personal, but personality cannot exist in a monad, that is, in complete singularity of being. Personality requires relationship. The attributes of God are personal attributes. Justice is a mode of relationship. It is impossible to be just and righteous and fair in absolute isolation" (p. 63).

God's attributes are personal. They are relational. Can God be a "just" God without relationship? Think about that. Can God be a person of grace without relationship? Can God be a God of mercy or comfort without relationship? Can He be a person of love without relationship? His *most important* personal attributes DEMAND relationship. Even wisdom does not make sense without relationship. Knox (1982) says, "So, too, wisdom has no meaning or content if there is no relationship" (p. 65). Being relational is imperative for Him. And as image-bearers, we cannot demonstrate God-like characteristics without relationship.

God is a God of love and that love has to go somewhere. We see that in the Trinity. The Father loves the Son. The Son loves the Spirit. The Spirit loves the Father. It is "built in."

"This is particularly true of love," Knox (1982) declares.

"Only persons love; only persons are able to be loved. Indeed, we may define a person as one capable of loving and being loved. We must affirm the doctrine of the Trinity -- that God is eternally relational, that there are eternal persons within the unity of God who are related righteously and lovingly. Indeed the doctrine is required to give a basis to our understanding of values. Love, self-sacrifice, goodness, fairness, faithfulness are pre-eminent in our scale of values. They are personal and relational values, but if they do not exist in ultimate reality they cannot themselves be ultimate" (p. 63).

The part that is central to all of this is that in the Trinity, relationship is others-centered. You do not have jealousy, bickering, or fighting for power and position. Here you have perfect, others-centered relationships. Knox (1982) points this out.

"The doctrine also sheds light on our understanding of human life. From it we realize that personal relationship is of the essence of reality and we must learn something of the quality of that relationship. It is a relationship of other-person-centeredness. The Father loves the Son and gives Him everything. The Son always does that which pleases the Father. The Spirit takes of the things of the Son and shows them to us. We learn from the Trinity that relationship is of the essence of reality and therefore of the essence of our own existence, and we also learn that the way this relationship should be expressed is by concern for others.... Within the Trinity itself there is a concern by the Persons of the Trinity one for another" (p. 63).

So give this some thought. If we are image-bearers, shouldn't our relationships be others-centered? And yet so much of what we do has to do with ourselves. "I don't think about you because I'm more important," or "I'm jealous of you," or "I'm going to be upset that you're getting more than I'm getting." You do not see that in the Trinity.

We all long for relationship and God desires relationship too -- even in His very being. What we truly long for is for another being to be totally committed to us with no reservations. The perfect result of that would be for us to be totally committed as well and totally responsive. That is what we truly want. That is what God provides. That is what God shows us in a graphic way through the Trinity.

RELATIONSHIP IN REGARD TO CREATION

What do we observe when we view God's act of creation -- especially as it pertains to man? Why did He create man? Could it be that God created us in order to have relationship with Him? God's desire for relationship with humans is demonstrated in the very fact that He created us.

God created us so that He could pour those attributes of justice, grace, wisdom, etc., out on us. He created us in order to bestow on us His unwavering love (John 3:16; Rom. 5:8, 8:39; Eph 5:2, etc) and all that goes with that.

Now this is important when we talk about self-esteem in Chapter 10 because self-love is not enough. A few years ago, one technique that was sometimes practiced by therapists was to direct their clients to give themselves a hug and say to themselves, "I just love me." Counselors had the idea that that technique would be enough to fill the void and longings of their clients and allow them to function effectively, with contentment, in their world. They thought that if their clients could really love themselves, if they could look at themselves in the mirror and say, "I love me," it would be enough. It wasn't!

(Source: iclipart, 2011)

What many discovered was that "self-love" was not enough! It did not meet the deep needs of the clients or resolve the problems for which they were seeking help -- not that there isn't a legitimate component of self-care and self-contentment (as will be discussed in Chapter 10); but trying to love oneself in isolation, they found, was not enough. Love requires an outside source. We want to be loved by someone else! And when we have that, then we feel complete. If we do not have that, we cannot give ourselves what we need.

Many theologians believe that relationship is a key element in creation. Oehler (1883) said, "We are designed for communion with God" (pp. 211-212). Knox (1982) wrote that "God created us for relationship, for He is relational" (p. 66). "We are capable of communion with our maker" (p. 97), was a presumption that Hodge made. And Theissen (1949) talks about a "social likeness" when he states that "God made man for Himself, and man found supreme satisfaction in communion with the Lord" (his maker).

Take a look at Genesis 3:8. What does it say that God used to do in the garden? It says, "In the cool of the day, He walked with man." Davis (1975) believes that before the fall of man, God came down on several occasions, and just "walked" with Adam and Eve. He states, "The Lord had evidently visited the garden and communed with Adam and Eve on many occasions prior to their fall" (p. 92).

Why? Was He giving them instructions? Did He have to do that? Did He have to come down and walk with them? No. Why would He come down from heaven to be with them? It sounds like He wanted relationship with Adam and Eve, so He came down -- out of heaven -- and said, "I'm going to spend time with you. That's why I created you. I want relationship with you."

Is that true today? Is it true that God just wants to spend time with us? Do we want to spend as much time with God? That can be very convicting. It is very easy sometimes to see God as far off or very theological and forget that He truly wants to spend time with us. And He wants to do that for eternity.

(Source: clipart.ochristian.com, 2011)

Ryrie (1978) said that after sin, man's "intimate relationship with God was broken" (p. 11). What Adam and Eve had had before the fall was somehow very intimate.

In addition, Jay Adams (1978) said, "When Adam and Eve fell, communication with God and with one another was broken. Man, a communicating social being who needs others, began to experience the agony of being severed from relationships in life that really count. Because his social relationships were ruined, man began to suffer the misery of alienation and also began to show it" (p. 212).

Adams pointed out the needs of man (specifically the relational needs) when he stated that man is "a communicating, social being who needs others" (p. 212). That is how God made us. We are needy and one of those needs involves a need for relationship with others.

Though Adams has sometimes been known to speak against "need theology," he acknowledged a proper form of neediness that God created in us. It is clear that the Bible teaches a "neediness" that we all possess, and that neediness is for God and for His representatives whom He has placed on this earth. We need relationships. God created us for relationship with Himself. That is an important part of our existence.

RELATIONSHIP IN REGARD TO SALVATION

We have noted God's desire for relationship when He created man, but why did He desire that relationship? Was God longing for a different or deeper kind of relationship than He already had?

When you think about it, why would God have had a desire to create man? He had the angels. He had the Trinity. Why did He want man? Was there something more that He desired that was going to be part of man's existence? Did it have anything to do with man's free will? Why did God give man a free will, knowing full well that man would reject Him and He would need to provide a means of bridging the gap of sin?

What does salvation say about God's desire for relationship with man? God provides a means for our reconciliation with Him (justification). He adopts us as His sons. And He provides a place to go when we die -- heaven. We will be eternally with Him -- in relationship with Him.

God did not have to provide the cross for us. He did not have to provide heaven for us. And yet He says, "I want you to be eternal creatures who will eternally relate to Me."

When we look at justification, we realize that as Christians, God has "declared" us righteous -- even though we are not. We are still sinners, yet through the blood of Christ we are viewed as perfect in God's sight. That allows us to be reconciled with God.

What does "reconciliation" mean? When we talk about reconciliation in a marriage, what do we want? We want to bring something back together that has been separated. We want people to be reunited. "To be friends again," is the literal definition. We want "to restore to friendship or harmony" (Webster, 1983, p. 984). We want the two sides to no longer be at variance.

A number of verses express this idea of reconciliation, including 2 Corinthians 5:19, Romans 5:10, and Colossians 1:21-22. But what is the most important part of this discussion? What is the bottom line to salvation? What is it that God really wants? Is it justification or reconciliation?

Both are important doctrines. Neither doctrine is more important than the other. But, what is the bottom line? The goal of God's payment of Christ on the cross is "reconciliation" because God wants relationship with us.

Justification is a means to reconciliation. (Source: clipart-history.com, 2011)

God is saying, "I have to deal with your sin problem so that we can be friends again. I am a holy God who cannot be in relationship with someone who is sinful. I took care of your sin problem through the cross. You are now justified. You are declared righteous. Now we can have relationship."

So the bottom line to salvation, the end point, is that God intends that we are going to relate to Him. We are going to be friends again. We are going to have what God originally wanted to have with us at creation, but what was lost because of sin. Sin was a block that needed to be removed; but once it was, God was able to have what He had always longed for -- what He had with Adam and Eve when they walked in the garden.

And consider what salvation provides for us. It provides "sonship." Believers have the privilege of becoming "sons of God." We have the doctrine of adoption. The Bible teaches that we are children of God. We are part of God's family. That sounds very relational!

We sing songs . . . "I'm part of the family of God." "I'm a child of the king." Sometimes we do not realize what we are singing. We are children in His family! That is a very intimate, relational concept.

We know this because of verses such as Ephesians 1:5 which says, "He predestined us to be adopted as his sons through Jesus Christ, in accordance with his pleasure and will."

God is saying, "I wanted to adopt you. I didn't have to! You're not really part of my family because of sin. But I'm going to adopt you and make you part of my family."

Why were the "Cabbage Patch" dolls so popular? It was not because they were pretty. They were some of the ugliest dolls that have been sold. But what made them a hit?

They came with adoption certificates!

(Source: Author's doll, 2011)

A person could adopt a doll as his/her very own. Without the adoption papers, the dolls probably would not have been as appealing. But there was something about being able to personally adopt the doll and to say, "This is mine; you're part of my family now; you have my name," that attracted many people.

That is what God did with us. He said, "You don't deserve to be in my family because you are pretty ugly as a result of sin. But you know what? I'm adopting you. You're mine." And because of that, we are all beautiful. He sees us through the blood of Christ.

1 John 3:1 says, "How great is the love the Father has lavished on us, that we should be called children of God!"

Relationship is a big deal to God. Heaven, sonship, adoption, salvation, reconciliation, creation -- all of those features devised by God, point to relationship.

The "Westminster Confession," expresses this unfathomable honor of being adopted as God's sons. It says,

> *All those that are justified, God vouchsafeth* (meaning He "bestows the privilege), *in and for His only Son Jesus Christ, to make partakers of the grace of adoption, by which they are taken into the number, and enjoy the liberties and privileges of the children of God, have His name put upon them, receive the Spirit of adoption, have access to the throne of grace with boldness, are enabled to cry, Abba, Father, are pitied, protected, provided for, and chastened by Him, as by a father: yet never cast off, but sealed to the day of redemption; and inherit the promises, as heirs of everlasting salvation* (Article 12).

God says, "I am giving you these privileges and you will even have my name put upon you. You are part of my family. I am going to give you the Holy Spirit as a down payment. This means you are part of the family AND the Spirit is going to make sure you get to heaven. Also, anytime you want to come talk to Me, I am here."

A story is told that during the Civil War, President Abraham Lincoln's son, Tad, could pass all of the guards on duty and be granted immediate admission to his dad's quarters (Randall, 1955, abrahamlincolnsclassroom.org,

(Source: by Berger, Public Domain)

par 6, 2009). Yet, no one else could get that kind of access to the president!

Imagine today, going to Washington, D.C. and asking to speak with the president. All of the security personnel would say, "I don't think so." But, if you were the president's son, they would permit you to enter.

We have that access to the throne of grace, "with BOLDNESS!" We can talk to Him ANY time. When the Westminster Confession says, "We are able to cry, Abba, Father." What does that mean?

"Abba" means "Daddy." We are allowed to call God, Daddy! The most intimate kind of father you can think of is what God is for us. And He will protect us, provide for us, and "spank" us, because we are His children. Yet, though He loves us enough to discipline us, He will not cast us off, but "seals" us, and no one can break that seal! That is what God promises! We get all of the privileges, and as sons, we inherit the kingdom. It is all ours -- including everlasting salvation!

That is pretty amazing. That is what it means to be a child of God! Relationship is important to God – and it is important to us as well.

CHAPTER 5

EXISTENTIAL CAPACITY

We all have an Existential Capacity -- a part of us that wants purpose in our lives and seeks meaningful impact. God is a God of meaning and purpose and one who makes meaningful impact. He created us to be like Him in this way. The Greek language in Scripture points to this capacity.

In the Greek language the term *prothesis* has to do with "purpose, plan, resolve, or design" (Bauer, Arndt, & Gingrich, 1979, p. 713). When this Greek word is used in Scripture, it is used in reference to God (Romans 8:28, 9:11; Eph. 1:11; 2 Tim. 1:9) and it is also used in reference to man (2 Tim. 3:10; Acts 11:23). God is purposive and we are purposive.

Boulama is another Greek word that is pertinent to this discussion. Knox talks about "will" or volition -- the common translation of the word *boulama*. It often refers to the "will" of God (Knox, 1982, p. 166). *Boulama* is used to show a directing of action toward purpose (1 Peter 4:3, Acts 27:43, Romans 9:19). Here we see how "will" and "purpose" come together. We *choose* to do things with a *purposeful* intent.

Definitions of *boulama* include "the will as plan, project, purpose, goal, intention, or tendency. The question of purpose or intention is predominant" (Kittel, 1964, p. 636). In derivatives of the root, *boul*, "one can almost always find the common factor in the element of purpose" (Bauer, Arndt, & Gingrich, 1979, p. 636). *Boulama* can refer to "purpose will" (Bauer, Arndt, & Gingrich, 1979, p. 636) showing a connection between volition and purpose. In reference to the word "boulama," Knox says, "will (volition) is able to direct actions toward purpose (p. 66).

McClain and Whitcomb (1981) are even more specific, referring to "purpose" as being a part of God's personality (p. 22). Having a free will that is purposive is part of what makes us like God. We are persons with "personalities" that are "purposive."

Purpose as it Relates to a Unique Job and Tasks to Accomplish

Boettner (1974) shows how the idea of purpose begins with God. Each member of the Trinity "has a particular work to perform (pp. 90-91)." So, again, when you think of the Father, Son, and Holy Spirit remember that they each have their own purpose -- a unique function to perform. God is a God of purpose.

Man emulates that purposeful part of God, intentionally seeking to accomplish something of value while on this earth. Just as each member of the Trinity has His own purpose, each of us who are created in God's image has a specific purpose. All people search and want to know that they are special and have a unique reason for being. God can satisfy that drive for meaningful existence because He has created each of us as unique individuals with a specific job to do.

Purpose as it Relates to our Ultimate Reason for Existence

Yet, what about the question of man's existence in general? Looking beyond what we can accomplish, why do we even exist?

In order to answer that question, we first need to look at the one that we represent. What is God's purpose for existing?

Think back to the time before God created us. Did He have a purpose? What was or is His purpose? It is very simple: His purpose is to bring glory to Himself.

So, what is our purpose? Our purpose is to bring glory to Him (1 Cor. 10:31). The overall goal that we are trying to accomplish as we do our "jobs" on this earth -- our most important goal -- our responsibility -- is to glorify God. The most meaningful impact is made when it is made for God. All of our impact is "great" and "big" and "important" when it is made for God.

God's Purpose for Existence

But, return to God's purpose for a minute. Just think about that. God's purpose is to glorify Himself. Does that sound kind of selfish?

Why isn't it selfish? Why is God allowed to spend His whole existence glorifying Himself?

The answer: because He is God. God is God and He can do whatever He wants. He makes the rules. And yet, in glorifying Himself, He has demonstrated that He is a just, sacrificial, loving, "person" that is worthy of glory.

So, it is hard for us as finite humans to understand how God's purpose can be to glorify Himself, because we are not God. We are dependent creatures. He is the self-sufficient, sovereign, almighty God, who, in His perfection can say, "I'm here to bring glory to Myself."

And yet, amazingly, God brings glory to Himself by what He does for others. His love, grace, and mercy bring glory to Himself. In sending His Son for our sins, giving us the abundant life here on earth and eternal life in heaven, He glorifies Himself. He does incredible things for us, and yet, it is all about Him.

Man's Three-Fold Purpose

So what is man's purpose for existence? It is three-fold: 1) We are here to have a relationship with God (Gen. 3:8; 2 Cor. 5:19). 2) We are here to represent God (2 Cor. 5:20, Matt. 5:16). 3) We are here to bring glory to Him (Isaiah 43:7). "Whatever you eat or drink or whatever you do, do all to the glory of God." (1 Cor. 10:31) That is why we are here.

Remember that you are always going to represent God in some way -- as a friend, as a parent, as an advice-giver, as you work, as you "play," etc. You are going to represent Him. You may not do a very good job of it, but you cannot get away from it!

Even non-Christians represent aspects of God, but as Christians we can show how our God-like capacities were meant to be used. We can attempt to love and give and relate in the way that God intended for us. And hopefully people can view our lives and say, "They cared," "They were kind," "They listened," "They were fair." We have represented God. That is what part of the outworking of our purpose as Christians involves. And if we represent God well, we glorify Him.

It is important that we attempt to represent God well and not be the kind of Christian of whom others say, "If that's what it means to be a Christian, if they are representative of what Christianity is; I don't want any part of it."

When Phillip Yancey would fly to various engagements he made a habit of asking the people he was seated next to in the plane, "What do you think of when I say, 'evangelical Christian' . . . or 'fundamentalist Christian?'" A majority of the time, he received a negative response.

That is sad. Hopefully, we will try to reverse that to where others will think or say, "I was with an evangelical Christian and it was a positive experience. They represented God well. They knew how to love."

What does the Bible say that distinguishes a Christian from others of this world? Does it say, "They will know you are Christians by your 'good theology'"? Does it say, "They will know you are Christians by your 'denominational stance'" or by your "constitution"? Is that it? What is it?

They will know you are Christians by how you LOVE each other. And that is often forgotten. They ARE going to know by how we treat one another, by the way we interact, by the kind of people we are. We need to remember we are representing God, and people will know us by how we act.

So purpose/meaning is found in a relationship with God that involves both love and service -- which is why it is a secondary longing. Purpose and meaning are found in relationship, which is why it ranks second.

Meaning and Purpose for the Unsaved World

The existentialist will say that purpose and meaning are found in whatever a person can find purpose and meaning. That is the problem. They talk about "groundlessness" in existentialism. There is NO real purpose and meaning. Each person has to create his own. So, each person is to go out and find his own purpose and meaning. When he finds it, then he will find the security he is looking for.

But, in what? You create your own meaning and in that you then feel secure? And then you die?

The existentialist will say, "'Grab on' to that because that's all there is. And if you can face that and find meaning in that, then you've found all there is."

Yalom, Frankl, and many other existentialists are brilliant people who have good things to say, but they leave the common person wanting more. Most do not want to create their own meaning and purpose, live in that, and say, "Okay, now I'm secure," or "I'm not secure, but that's okay. I'll just do the best I can until I die." We want more!

Some existentialists might say, "Well, of course you do. That's part of the human condition. You have to face the fact that there is no more. And if you can face that with boldness and dignity and strength, then you have done everything a human can do." But we still want more!

And it is this author's opinion that the "more" is: "I want to know that there is someone that loves me and gives me meaning and purpose." If people start without God though, what else are they going to come up with? Existentialism make sense if you start without God.

The Specific Designations of Man's Purposeful Work (Existential)

DOMINION AND RULING

As soon as God created man -- Adam -- the Bible says that God had a purpose for him. Notice He didn't create Adam and say, "Okay, figure it out!" or "All right, see what you can come up with." As soon as God created Adam and Eve, He said, "I want you to rule over the world, as My representatives. This is what I want you to do. I want you to rule over and subdue the earth." Genesis 1:26 says "rule over." Genesis 2:15 says, "Subdue." So, having dominion or ruling as God's representative immediately gave man his purpose. That is why we are here.

In fact, in Genesis 2:15 even the preposition that is used denotes purpose. The Bible says that God put Adam in the garden "in order to . . . ." When one examines the Hebrew language used in this passage, it is discovered that the clause is "purposive," meaning God put Adam in the garden *with the purpose to* cultivate it and keep it (Williams, 1976, pp. 36, 50).

God was saying, "As soon as I put you in the garden, Adam, here is what I want you to do. I want you to work. Your purpose is to rule and subdue." So that says something -- that He made us purposive and the minute He made us, He told us what that purpose was.

Theologians Oehler and Calvin wrote of this idea. Oehler (1883) said, "Man is set over nature as a free personality, since he is *designed* for communion with God and is *appointed to exercise divine authority* in the affairs of the earth" (pp. 211-212). Notice "communion" (relationship) and "authority" over earth (impact).

In regard to Genesis 1:28, Calvin (1979) said, "Men were created to employ themselves in some work and not to lie down in inactivity and idleness" (p. 125).

The "Protestant Work Ethic" (a term coined by Max Weber) evolved as a result of the statement by Calvin that we were *made* for work. Basically, Protestants who were breaking away from Catholicism (just as Calvin and Luther did) believed that the Bible was saying that God put man here on this earth for work. Therefore we should work hard! And they thought if people would do that, God would bless them (Hill, 2005).

From that idea there came a sense of believing that somehow, if a person worked hard enough, he would receive God's blessings. And statements like that are heard by Christians even today: "God honored our hard work this year and has blessed us financially." Now, anything we enjoy is a blessing or "gift" from God – finances included. And there is some truth that if I work hard, there is greater potential for prosperity. But we also know that some people have worked very hard and have not prospered. – Maybe a storm or disaster ruined a farmer's crops or a fisherman's vessels. Did God not bless them? Other people have not worked hard and still received a lot of money due to inheritance or other favorable circumstances. Did God bless them even though they did not work hard? -- Maybe or maybe not. So, *if* I work hard, I am more likely to prosper; but one does not necessarily result in the other and whether we receive money or not does not indicate whether we are blessed or not. God wants us to work hard and He will look favorably upon us when we do. But whether we receive tangible physical "rewards" for hard work is not necessarily guaranteed.

Though devotion to one's labor does not necessarily result in prosperity (Job is a good example), God does want us to work hard. That is why God put us here. Idleness and inactivity are not endorsed by God.

WE ARE PEOPLE OF PURPOSE

When we think of the purposes of man, two major components are inherent: a *Latent Component* and an *Active Component*.

The Latent Component simply says, "We are people of purpose and meaning. There is a reason for our existence." We have that built in.

The Active Component says, "I want to make meaningful impact in my world." This is crucial. Yes, God created in me a desire for meaning and purpose and I am a person of meaning and purpose; but there is a sense that I want to make meaningful impact in my world. I want to look at the end of my life and see that I have done something meaningful, something important, something that matters.

MAN'S DESIRE FOR MEANINGFUL IMPACT

Consider that idea for a minute. Do you believe that to be true? Do you believe that everyone wants to be able to look back at the end of his or her life and say, "I did something meaningful," "I did something worthwhile," "I made impact in my world"? Is that valid?

| She had no influence. | He did nothing that mattered. | Not Worth Mentioning |

(Source: Microsoft Office Word Clipart, 2010)

Or, do we want our gravestones to be devoid of any accomplishments and to be insignificant to others?

Is there anything that would suggest the idea that we want our lives to be meaningful? Is there anything that would demonstrate that,

105

where one could say, "Here is evidence as to why I think that is true -- that every person wants to accomplish something in life"?

A psychologist named Erikson came up with eight stages of development. Of those stages, the last one is "Integrity vs. Ego Despair" (Harder, 2002).

"Ego Despair" happens when a person looks back at the end of his or her life and exclaims, "It was worthless! I didn't do anything!"

Those who have spent time with dying people will confess to having heard these types of statements: "What do I have to show for my life?" "What did I do?" "I wasted it!" "I did nothing!" And for those who make those statements, it can be a frightening and disheartening realization. What despair there can be when one looks at his or her life and thinks, "What have I done? Nothing! It's been worthless!" or "I made lots of bad choices!" or "Look what I did to people!"

And even if there isn't a regretful assessment, very few people want their gravestones to say, "Boy, could he party!" or "Man, did he make a lot of money!" or "Wow, did he dress impeccably!" If you think about it, those are not the things that we want on our gravestones.

What do we want our gravestones to say? We usually want something written that tells about the good we have done throughout our lives. "He loved his family," or "He knew what mattered," or "Look what she did for God." Sometimes it is advantageous for us to stop and evaluate what we are doing and ask ourselves, "Am I living my life in a way that my gravestone can reflect a positive contribution? Am I living my life in a way that reflects God?"

We all have something built-in that causes us to *want* to believe that we accomplished some purpose, that our life mattered, and that we did something meaningful. Understand, however, that as sinners, man is sometimes content with negative impact. If a person has had difficulty making positive impact, he may settle for negative impact. But we all want to make impact! Every person on this earth wants to believe that he or she matters. Every person wants to know that he can do something that provides meaning for his life -- even if it is burning down a building.

In that case he is saying, "Look what I can do!" It may be a bad choice, but it makes the statement, "I'm here. I matter. I want to be noticed."

So it is important to remember that all people have a built-in need for meaning and purpose that is represented in two ways: One is "Latent" in that it just exists as a truth. We want to feel that there is a reason why we exist. The second is "Active" in that we seek to do works that demonstrate something purposeful and accomplish something that we feel is valuable -- though it may not always be positive.

So that is where our Christian beliefs come in. Since God has created us to be people of purpose who desire to make impact in our world and since He has designated that purpose to be for relationship with Him, we are equipped with all of the information that we need to lead a meaningful life. We can focus our impact on representing and glorifying Him. We know how to direct our lives and the goals for living them out.

CHAPTER 6

LONGINGS AND STRATEGIES

What is it that drives man as he seeks to live on this earth? Does it involve money? Is it fame? Is it popularity? What are his prime motivators?

Think about the things that motivate you. Think about your friendships. Think about how you spend your time. Think about what occupies your mind. What are those things and what is behind those thoughts and actions?

Longing for Relationship (Social)

The most primary motivator for man is his longing for relationship. All of our needs, desires, and actions are built on our goal to seek meaningful relationships -- the most meaningful one being our relationship with God. Though many do not realize that is what they are seeking, they still behave and think in ways that seek out a relationship that will satisfy their souls. All of our relationships demonstrate our desire to meet our relational needs as we spend time with those who we hope will satisfy our deep longings within. Relationship is a prime motivator and drives much of what we do as humans.

The Bible suggests that desire for relationship is present in both God and Man in three different ways. The first is demonstrated in the very nature of God, in His existence as the Trinity. The second was exhibited when God created us -- intending for a relationship with man. And the third way that God highlighted our need for relationship was in providing salvation to bridge the gap between God and man.

Longing for Purpose (Existential)

As we reflect on what else drives man, think about the behaviors that you observe in others. What else do they seem to be crying out for? What do they seem to want and seek? Why do they desire to do something great . . . something that is written in the history books or that makes a lot of money? Why is there a need to make a "mark" that is big and bold?

People seem to want to make an impact in their world. They want to feel like there is some meaning to their life and that their life serves some purpose. Think about nearly every goal that you or others pursue. If those goals do not involve relationship, how many of them involve a desire to feel like your life is meaningful or a desire to make an impact in your world?

Dependency

INTRODUCTION

God is a relational creature and made us to be relational like Him. God is a being of meaning and purpose and made us like Him in this way as well. But He is not needy because He is sovereign. We on the other hand are needy. Why? Because we are dependent. He is independent of us. We are dependent on Him. This dependency is what motivates us.

When we look at what motivates man, we are zeroing in on some of the capacities that God has endowed in us. This textbook will divide man's nature into seven capacities -- all of which are inborn in every person. The first capacity, for relationship, was labeled the "Social" Capacity, and the capacity for meaning and purpose -- the second capacity -- was labeled the "Existential" Capacity. Dependency causes our capacities to "move" in certain directions. The capacities, which are active, will either move toward God or move away from God.

All of the capacities that are part of our being, whether they are the capacities for relationship or meaning and purpose, or whether they are capacities for emotions or behavior or thought, etc., must do something. They cannot be static. They are dynamic.

Dependency is the reason that our capacities for meaning and purpose and for relationship become longings. We long.

People long for relationship. People long for meaning and purpose. People are needy.

All of us are needy. Though some people demonstrate their "neediness" in more profound ways than others, we are all needy. God, however, provides the answer to our neediness, and as Christians we can feel content in the fact that all of our needs are met through Christ. Dependency causes us to be needy and to "long" for those needs to be met, and God provides the answer.

What about God. Is He needy? Does God long for relationship? Does God long for meaning and purpose? Or is that not the best word to use -- "long"? We know He is not needy, and yet, He does long. He longs for "something" with us.

Here is the key: He does not NEED it. God "longs" for us, but He does not need us.

When we, as human beings, use the word "longing," we are talking about our neediness. We have to have God. When He longs for us, He doesn't have to have us; but He still wants us. Or one could say, God "desires" us. There is something there that He must have wanted with Adam and Eve when He walked with them in the garden. He wants something with us in prayer. God's longing for relationship with man is substantiated throughout Scripture with all of His contact with man and through the sending of His son. He wants us.

And yet, here is the key: He is not dependent. He is independent. He is totally self-sufficient. So, He does not need us; however, God DOES long/desire for relationship with us.

God does not long for meaning and purpose. He IS meaning and purpose. He is the sovereign God.

We DO long for meaning and purpose because we are not God. Because we are dependent on God, we need Him to give us meaning and purpose to our lives.

Our capacities involve our motivations, and those motivations cause the capacities to move. They can't just lie there. The first two capacities that we are examining at this point are 1) the Capacity for Relationship (Social) and 2) the Capacity for Meaning and Purpose (Existential). They move. They are not static. They have to go somewhere.

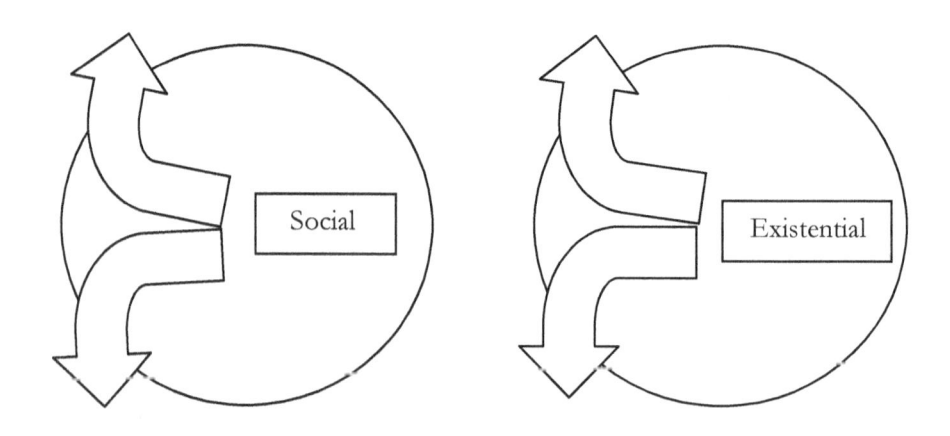

So, they are either going to move toward God, or they are going to move away from God.

What does that mean? It means that as people long for relationship, they are either going to long in a way that looks to God for satisfaction, or they are going to say, "No. I don't need God. I know I need something, but it isn't God." My longings are going to bend in one of two directions -- either toward or away from God. They are going to go somewhere.

(Source: NPS Photo, Public domain, 2003)

Even the guy who is the hermit and lives in a cabin in Montana all by himself has longings. Maybe he has been so hurt that he doesn't want to be around people anymore. He might have tried to kill those longings, to squelch them, and deny them, but they are still in there. He still longs for relationship.

Or he may have reacted to that same hurt by deciding to have lots of animals around rather than people. That is why some people have 14 cats -- which become their "family." There is nothing wrong with having cats, but if someone has animals around because he or she is avoiding people for some reason, then that person has substituted pets for people. Yet, their longings are still going somewhere. They have to. Why? Because we are dependent creatures. We are going to be dependent on something.

(Source: Moniphoto, dreamstime.com, 2011)

Romans talks about those who act self-sufficient. Chapter 1, verse 18 says, "The wrath of God is being revealed from heaven against all the godlessness and wickedness of men who suppress the truth by their wickedness." Yet, even though someone may say, "I don't need God, I don't need anybody, nobody's going to tell me how to live my life," that person is still dependent. In fact, the irony is that the very person that shakes his fist at God and says, "I hate you, I don't need you, You don't exist," could not even utter those words if God were not giving him what he needed. He would not have a breath. He would not have the words to say. All God would have to do would be to "zap" him and he would be gone. Without Him, people cannot act independently. Therefore, they are not independent!

It is not that there is not a good kind of independence. There is something good about learning to do things on one's own -- not having to depend on others for everything. There is something good about being able to function and accomplish tasks. But when that functioning person excludes the reality that he is also dependent, he is claiming something that is not possible.

So there is a good kind of independence. But when we talk about an independence that does not acknowledge any form of dependence and believes, "I am self-sufficient, I don't need anything, I don't need anyone," then we are in error.

What evidences do we have that there are longings in this world -- that we are all dependent, either moving toward or away from God? What do you see in your world that confirms that man "longs" and is dependent on having those longings met?

All you have to do is listen to the love songs on the radio. What are they saying? "I need you. I want you. I HAVE TO have you." "I can't live without you." "If you go away, I've got nothing." When you listen to those songs, what are they saying? I absolutely NEED you to make my life work.

What they are saying is that there is something deep in their souls that says, "I know I've got to have something. I believe that you're it. And if I don't have you, I don't know if I can keep going. And if I don't have you, then I'll have to go and find somebody else."

The songs are saying it! And that is: "I need something." And in some of the songs, you will also hear the need for meaning and purpose as well -- that "You give me meaning," "You're my reason for living," "You're my everything."

There is something that we like about those love songs that can be very romantic, because there is a legitimate "specialness" that we seek that seems to be fulfilled or can be fulfilled on some level. But they are also saying something about what is in the core of us -- what is deep down. We all long for relationship and we all long for meaning. And though God is the ultimate fulfillment of those longings, we also find a level of fulfillment in relationships on this earth from those who represent God to us.

THE TWO PRIMARY MOTIVATORS

All of the motivations of our lives come down to those two themes: 1) I want to know I am loved -- that I am involved in a relationship with someone who cares about me. 2) I want to know that I matter and that my life is worthwhile -- that I am here for some reason.

As Christians, those needs are met for us. And for the unsaved world, we have the answers for them when they seek relationship and purpose. We can say, "You are loved and I can tell you what your purpose is." We have the answers for people who are looking and asking these questions. We can say, "I can give you the love you are looking for. I will try to represent it the best I can, but I am going to point you to the one who loves you unconditionally. He loves you and will continue to love you forever. Also, I can tell you why you are here: You are here to represent Him and bring glory to Him."

GENDER DIFFERENCES WITH RELATIONSHIP AND IMPACT

Assuming we agree that everyone wants to be loved and have a purpose, another area to consider is the question: Does everyone seek the satisfaction of those needs with the same emphasis? Does gender play any kind of role in the way we long to have those needs met? If so, what are the implications of gender on how the desire for relationship and impact is perceived and sought?

To state it simply: Men and women attempt to meet their needs differently. Men tend to use the secondary to get the primary. Women tend to go to the primary more directly.

Men tend to make impact, saying, "Look what I can do!" as a way of getting others to love them. Men say, in a sense, "I want to do something important. I want to do something significant. Look at the impact that I can make in my world. Now you can love me." So, men start with impact in order to move to relationship.

Women tend to be more directly relational. And if their relationships are good, they tend to have a sense of meaning and purpose in their lives. Generally, women start with relationship and, with that as a basis, they build their areas of impact. Maybe there is something God-given in that He decided, "I'm going to make women more *directly primary* -- relational. And once that relationship is established, they will get the *secondary*."

It seems that God is saying to men, "I am going to make your focus more on the *secondary*. But you will still desire relationship."

Men and women still want the same thing. Both want people to love them. They want others to give them what they need. They just go about it differently.

What are ways that women seek relationship? How about beauty? Beauty is a big deal for women. Many women like to take time to do their makeup, their nails, and their hair in order to feel better about themselves and, sometimes, in hopes that it will attract others to them for relationship. Women like to feel beautiful.

It is interesting how beauty is viewed in Scripture. The Bible tells women that they are not *just* to be beautiful on the outside by *only* taking time to braid their hair or wear nice clothes and jewelry, but to take time to grow and be beautiful on the inside too (1 Peter 3:3). The Bible also does not discount the importance of beauty in attraction when it tells of the life of Esther, when it describes Tamar, and when it describes God's blessing to Job as giving him beautiful daughters that, as it puts it, "Nowhere in all the land were there found women as beautiful as Job's daughters" (Job 42:15).

(Source: Veer.com, 2011)

So there is something about beauty that God gives to women as a means of attraction for relationship. And that means of attraction is outward, but it is also inward -- the inward beauty being the most important and the most valuable to God. And though men's handsomeness is also a factor in drawing relationship, men tend to value their impact more. And women tend to view men's impact as a higher priority, whereas men tend to view women's beauty and the way they present themselves higher than women view the same thing in them. Or more simply: when choosing someone of the opposite sex, men put more focus on beauty than women do and women put more focus on impact than men do, though both sexes use both means of assessment.

Many guys like to do things like lift weights. They may discuss among themselves how much weight they can lift -- usually hoping that someone will go, "Wow! I'm impressed," and also hoping that others will be thinking, "Therefore, I like you."

Or men may feel it is important to be very successful at their jobs -- working hard for accolades, promotions, and pay raises.

(Source: freeclipartnow.com, 2004)

Men tend to use impact and involve themselves in some type of impressive activity to gain respect and love, whereas women tend to group themselves with others relationally or use a means of attraction that is not active -- such as beauty. Though women may still want to be successful at their jobs and men may want to look attractive, the sexes go about accomplishing those goals and meeting their needs in different ways.

This appears to be God-given -- intrinsic. And so when the world says, "Gender differences exist because of socialization; it is how you have been trained; there really aren't intrinsic differences," that doesn't seem to be supported theologically. There seems to be something inside men that says, "I want to use impact to get relationship." But men are still going to value relationship just as much as women do. And though men may end up bragging or fighting, they still want the same things that women want.

Sometimes women can be vain. They can take beauty too far. But there is something legitimate in that they are saying, "I want you to be attracted to me because this is how God made me." No matter whether they are "good-looking" or not, they still want to wear things and do things that improve their appearance and they still may "carry" themselves in a way that is attractive to others. They think, "I want relationship. I want to feel that I am important to you and that I matter." And hopefully they have got something inside that is even more beautiful.

So men and women both long for relationship, and they both long for impact. They just seek those goals in different ways.

VIKTOR FRANKL'S CONCLUSION REGARDING MEANING AND PURPOSE

In his book, *Man's Search for Meaning*, Victor Frankl (1959) writes a gripping account of his experience in a concentration camp during World War II. The realization that he came to in the concentration camp was that people were searching for meaning. If they found it, they did not take their own lives. But the people who couldn't find it ended up running and grabbing the electric fence and killing themselves.

Sometimes the Nazis would do things to purposely create "non-meaning." The Nazi guards would say, "I want you to move this pile of trash over to that side of the camp." So the prisoners would spend the entire day moving the whole pile. The next day the Nazi guards would say, "Now I want you to move that pile of trash back to the other side of the camp." And then the prisoners would move the trash back to the same place that it was the day before. The guards would do that every day, just to create the sense of "non-purpose." They were trying to convince the prisoners that "You have no purpose. You are doing things that are absolutely meaningless!" Then the guards would see how the prisoners would react.

Frankl explained that those people in the camp that could find a sense of meaning somewhere were able to continue doing this day in and day out. But the ones that didn't would eventually tend to go insane and many times end up taking their own lives.

Existentialists will talk about creating meaning: "You are god (small 'g'). You create meaning, and therefore it is up to you to find that meaning. When you find that, you have found all that there is, because ultimately you are going to die. That meaning will die with you. So you can create and recreate meaning."

Victor Frankl or Irvin Yalom would say, "Meaning/purpose is what it's all about. It is the primary motivator." Christians would counter that argument with, "No. Relationship is the primary motivator."

What is the difference? We are starting with God. And if we start with God, the most important thing would be relationship with God. If we do not start with God, it makes sense to say, "Meaning/purpose is the most important thing. Find it wherever you can."

So the assumption is this: Longing for relationship is a primary motivator. Longing for meaning and purpose is a secondary motivator. But both are powerful. Man needs both.

Three Categories of Motivation

When it comes to man's dependent longings, there are three categories of those motivating factors. **Sinless Dependent Longings** are good. This is what we ought to have.

A second category to look at is **Sinful "Independent" Needs**. This is often what secular writers are referring to when they talk about man's "needs." The term "sinful" is used because these needs are being satisfied AWAY from God. (It is not sinful in a "nasty" way, necessarily, but it is moving away from God. Anything away from God, the Bible says, is sin. So it seeks fulfillment in a way that bypasses God.) The label "independent" is used because the person is saying, "I don't need God." It is not really independence, because there is nothing that is truly, totally independent of God.

The last category is: **Cravings**. The Bible uses the word "lust." "They follow after their lusts" (1 John 2:16). This category is a little more intense form of the last one. Someone who says, "I don't really have any needs, I am self-sufficient," would fit this category.

So the middle group is saying, "I'm willing to talk about my needs. I'm not willing to talk about God." The last group is saying, "I'm not needy. I need nothing." And some people even say, "I am God," -- which gets a little scary. We will look at that.

SINLESS DEPENDENT LONGINGS

Now, back to the first category of motivations called, "Sinless Dependent Longings." This is longing for relationship with God and for His meaning and purpose to life. Once a person knows Christ as his savior, once he knows God, he has eternal relationship and he has eternal meaning and purpose. As Christians, that is what we already have. For the unsaved, that is what they are seeking -- though they may not know it or be willing to consider it.

When a Christian says, "I just feel that nobody loves me and I don't know why I'm here," it is because they have forgotten -- or maybe never fully understood -- what they have. Now, they could be saying, "I'm very lonely for people." That is legitimate. But if they say, "God really isn't there anymore, He doesn't really love me" (and sometimes what they mean is, "I don't feel it,"), if they really believe He is not there, that is where it becomes problematic. If the BELIEF is "I have no purpose," it is a problem.

Psalms 42 and 63 talk about man's longings. Psalm 42:1 says, "As a deer pants for water, so my soul pants for you, O God." And Psalm 63 conveys the same idea.

The words "hunger" and "thirst" are used in Scripture as metaphors for these longings. When the Bible talks about hunger and thirst, it legitimizes them. It says, "It's okay. You're allowed to be hungry." It doesn't say, "Are you hungry? Well, stop it! You're sinning!" or "Are you thirsty? Quit thinking about yourself!"

It says, "Are you hungry? Here's the answer: I'm the bread of life." "Are you thirsty? Here's the answer: I'm a spring of 'living water'" (John 4:10-13; 7:37, 38).

So, this idea of hunger and thirst is very legitimate. "Longings" are legitimate. And yet some would say, "Longings are anthropocentric – man-centered, selfish . . . We should not have them."

Yet, it is not possible to eliminate one's longings. You might say you do not have any longings, but you still do. Are they sinless? It might be hard to see that after sin entered our world, but Adam and Eve had longings before the Fall. They most likely longed for God. They wanted relationship.

So, in terms of what Adam and Eve had and what Christ desired, is it clear that they "longed." It says in John 13 that Christ longed for His Father. There is a good kind of longing that has nothing to do with sin.

So Christ legitimized longings. Adam and Eve had longings. After salvation, we have the same thing. We still long. We have a longing that is legitimate and is sinless and dependent on God. We long for God right now. We long for heaven. Those are good longings. Those do not come out of our sinfulness. That is why these longings are called "sinless."

THREE TYPES OF SINLESS DEPENDENT LONGINGS

Glasser, Maslow, and Rogers all tried to categorize man's "needs"; however, their ideas fell short because they did not start with God. A Christian psychologist, Larry Crabb (1987), categorized legitimate longings into three types: "Crucial Longings," "Critical Longings," and "Casual Longings." This categorization seems to make more sense for the Christian.

Crucial Longings
We Need God

Man's most CRUCIAL longing is for God. That longing is exhibited in both man's need for relationship and meaning/purpose. (These "crucial" needs have already been discussed, but will now be explored more thoroughly.)

Psalm 42:1-2 acknowledges this longing when it says, "As a deer pants for streams of water, so my soul pants for you, my God. My soul thirsts for God, for the living God. When can I go and meet with God?"

In this verse is heard that longing for relationship with God. This is "Sinless Dependence." Man wants this. Man needs this.

Psalm 63 -- "O God, you are my God. Earnestly, I seek you. My soul thirsts for you. My body longs for you, in a dry and weary land where there is no water."

So Scripture makes it very clear: We NEED God.

Blaise Pascal was the first philosopher to really talk about that. Pascal was a philosopher, physicist, and mathematician. He said, "There is a 'God-shaped' vacuum (Lamount, 1997) in the heart of each man, which cannot be satisfied by any created thing, but only by God, the Creator, made known through Jesus Christ."

That is it -- Crucial Longings! Every person that we come in contact with in this world, has a "God-shaped vacuum" that can only be filled by God -- a God-shaped hole -- a God-shaped "blank." And man will jump from thing to thing in life -- hobby to hobby, woman to woman, house to car, etc. – looking for something to fill that "hole." Yet that "jumping" and "filling" will produce the same result every time -- emptiness.

(Source: WPClipart, Public Domain)

Christians Don't Always 'Feel' Full

Every person has that vacuum. Every person is going to be looking for something to fill that emptiness. Christians have it already filled, though they sometimes forget or do not fully understand how complete God's filling of that void is.

The Bible talks about living the way you already are. "Be what you already are." What it seems to be saying is, "Remember what you already have" (Eph 4:1-32; 1 Cor. 4:2, etc.).

As a Christian, you have what you are looking for. It just doesn't always feel like it. And this is an important point. Sometimes when Christians talk about God being in their hearts and God meeting their crucial longings, they think somehow that that means it is going to feel like it. It is not always going to feel like it.

There are plenty of times when Christians are going to feel lonely, yet we know that God is still there. It is because we still walk by faith. So we have all we need, but we still do not have everything we will eventually get. Heaven is going to give us something that is even better than what we have down here on earth. Then, we will always "feel" that sense of fullness. As sinners on this earth, we will not always be able to maintain that reality in our thinking, but the reality still exists.

We have all we need -- in the absolute sense. God says, "You have got enough to make it in this life. You have got enough love and meaning and purpose. However, you were built for heaven and one day you are going to have it all. So you are going to feel an emptiness here, yet you still have enough.

We live with that tension. Though we may have times where we feel "fullness" -- whether it be in worship or whether it be, many times, in pain, there is something in each of us that still says, "I want more. I still want more." Of course we want more! We were built for heaven (Ecc. 3:11).

There is nothing in this life that is going to satisfy completely. Though God is going to give us morsels every now and then that will be enough for that moment, we still want the full meal. And that is heaven.

C. S. Lewis (1952) said, "If I find in myself a desire, which no experience in this world can satisfy, the most probable explanation is that I was made for another world" (p. 120).

We were built for another world. Therefore, even though God is enough, we are never fully satisfied. We were built for heaven.

Critical Longings
We Were Built for Relationship with Each Other

We were built not only for relationship with God, but for relationship with each other. God could have put Adam on the Earth and said, "Okay, here is your job and you need to do it alone."

But He said, in Genesis 2:18, "It is not good for the man to be alone." And yet, remember, this was before the Fall. This was before sin.

Adam was in Paradise. And yet, his life was still "not good" without a companion.

Could Adam have been thinking, "What do you mean 'It's not good'?" If he was thinking that, God could have answered, "Because it's not what I built you for. Not only did I build you for relationship with Me, but I built you for relationship with others like you."

Crabb (1987) says that these longings are "legitimate hopes for deep human relationships and for visible impact on our worlds" (p. 119).

There you have it again: 1) Relationship. 2) Meaning and Impact. But with Critical Longings, the relationship and impact involve other people on this earth also.

Everyone wants to know that he or she has meaningful relationships. Everyone wants to know that there are people that love him or her and that care for him or her. Everyone wants to know the he or she is not alone.

Even Christ did not want to be alone before his crucifixion. Remember He took Peter, James, and John with Him when He was "deeply distressed and troubled"? (Matt. 26:36ff).

Hebrews 10:25 says, "Let us not forsake the habit of meeting together." In fact, it says, "Let us encourage one another." And God asks us to "bear" each other's burdens (Gal. 6:2 NASB).

The Bible is saying, That we need to get together. That is what church is all about. Gathering to attend a church service is not necessarily important to do in order to hear a sermon. And Scripture seems to indicate that it is not even critical for singing and a certain kind of worship, although it involves that and certainly worship is a significant part of it. But a major aspect of church is that we are supposed to get together because it is good for us. And when we get together we are supposed to encourage one another -- build each other up -- and carry one another's burdens. That is really the essence of church -- "Let's get together, share our concerns, bear each other's burdens, and encourage each other." And we can say, "Hey. You can make it another week!" and/or "I'm praying for you," or "I'm with you." We need that.

Now, do we need that in a "Crucial" sense? No. But, we need it in a critical sense. So Crabb categorizes that need as "critical." The idea is: "This is a need. But it is not a need in the absolute sense like, 'We NEED God.'" We COULD live on a deserted island by ourselves.

In the movie, *Cast Away*, where Tom Hanks lives on an island by himself for years, the movie shows that it CAN be done. However, it is NOT what God intended. And even in that movie, Tom Hanks develops a "relationship" with "Wilson" (a volleyball!).

God wants us to be in relationship with each other. He wants us to be involved with each other. All of the "one another" passages demonstrate that: "Build up one another." "Encourage one another." "Love one another." "Bear with one another." "Bear one another's burdens."

Gene Getz (2002) wrote a book entitled, *Building Up One Another*. In that book, he discussed what all of the "one another" passages mean -- what it means to be in community. We need others.

Christians Don't Always "Feel" Content in Their Relationships

But, again, just because God meets our Crucial Longings, it does not mean we will not feel an ache in our Critical Longings. A person can have everything that he needs from God, in an absolute sense, and still feel lonely in his marriage or still feel lonely in his friendships. He can still want something that he does not have -- legitimately. Maybe he has a wife who does not know how to love him. Maybe she has friends who are not always the best kind of friends in the world. And, even if one's friends are the best people in the world, they still are not going to be perfect. So even Christians cannot always be loved the way they want to be loved. They are going to feel that ache from time to time. That is legitimate -- even for Christians. And it is true that God will give everyone the strength to deal with that loneliness or that disillusionment with friends or family, but it does not mean they will not feel lonely anymore or that they will always be satisfied in their relationships.

There is nothing wrong with wanting to have good relationships, unless those relationships become god and the thinking is, "YOU have to make life work for me." Plenty of people get married with the idea that "You are now going to always fulfill me." People do not tend to do that consciously. They just sort of do it unconsciously.

"You're going to really make me happy" is the initial thinking, and little by little the new mate sort of becomes "god." And when that newly attained husband or wife does not end up being perfectly god-like, then they get very upset. Because when perfection is demanded, there is a terrible tension.

God put perfection in our heads -- Ecclesiastes 3:11: "He has put eternity in the hearts of people." Everyone has an understanding of what perfection looks like. We KNOW instinctively what a perfect marriage looks like, and so we want one! We KNOW what a perfect friend is, and we want that! Yet, it can never happen this side of heaven. We may get morsels of it, tastes of it, times of it -- yes. But, we will never have absolute perfection this side of heaven. So we will always want perfection. And the tension between that perfection and the reality of life on this earth is going to be built in.

Casual Longings

The last one, "Casual Longings" has to do with comfort. We want comfort. Is that a bad thing? Matt. 11:28-30 says, "Come to me, all you who are weary and burdened and I will give you rest . . . my yoke is easy, my burden is light." Why did Christ appeal to our desire for rest and for a lightening of a heavy load? Was it because He knew that we all could relate to what it was like to desire comfort? He legitimized our desire for comfort when He compared that physical example with the spiritual example. We all long for comfort.

What is the first thing we do when we enter a room? We look for a comfortable chair or a comfortable area to locate ourselves. If we choose to sit in a recliner, we may decide to prop up our feet or angle the chair back. If we enter a classroom or meeting room such as a church, we may choose the same place every week because we are used to it and are more comfortable in that part of the room, on the end of the row, or with those people that we will be sitting beside.

We get "comfortable." We all find ways of getting comfortable. In and of itself, that is not a bad thing. We want a bed that we can sleep on. (The Bible says Christ slept on a "cushion" -- Mark 4:38. Why didn't He choose "discomfort" and lay his head down on the wooden floor?) We want a chair that does not hurt us when we sit on it. We want a nice house. We want a car to get us around. We want our bills paid. And we want a world that is predictable. We want a world that is comfortable. In and of itself, there is nothing wrong with that.

The problem comes when comfort becomes our god. If our being comfortable is the most important thing in the world, then that is when it becomes a problem.

We try to avoid pain. There is nothing wrong with that. God created us to naturally avoid pain. We are supposed to avoid pain as a survival mechanism. So if there is a car coming at you, you try to get out of the way. If you know that putting your finger in the fire is going to hurt, you avoid doing that. If you are climbing a tall ladder, you will step carefully and hold on tightly, in order to avoid a painful fall. If your body needs nourishment, you get hungry and crave the pleasure of eating a good meal. That is a good thing. It is a God-given mechanism for survival.

Yet God allows pain in our lives. Why? If we never experience pain, we will not know what it feels like to be "pain-free." We will not understand what it means to be "comfortable."

So where is it illegitimate to avoid pain? What about when we are doing rehabilitation after surgery? Will our muscles get stronger if we do not work through the pain? How about when we need to apologize and we know our apology may be rejected? Are there times that we try to avoid pain when we shouldn't? And are there times when we are told that we should "stay in the pain"?

Now some may take the embracing of pain too far. Martin Luther expressed disagreement with the monks who beat themselves in order to feel closer to God. Some avoid pain medication while dying because they think that is more spiritual. Does embracing pain make us more spiritual? How about taking a pain reliever? Should I say, "Maybe God wants me to have this headache right now so I can be closer to Him, so I won't take any medicine"? And what about physical disabilities and other trials? Should we always embrace weakness and hardship and never try to get out of them?

These are important questions. Where is that line between avoiding pain because it helps us survive and embracing pain because that will help our rehabilitation (or help us survive) or demonstrate love? And can embracing pain also promote maturity and spiritual growth? Or does it depend on the circumstances?

What if we have been rejected when we have made efforts to love others? God wants us to risk loving again and going through pain.

Although comfort is legitimate, sometimes God is more interested in our character growth, than our immediate comfort. In the long term, God wants to provide all of us with comfort. That is why He has prepared heaven for us. And even on this Earth, as a loving father, He longs for us to have comfort. But in order to get to that ultimate comfort, God knows that we must experience "uncomfortable" situations that will help us learn and grow and then understand and experience the ultimate comfort that He gives. Our ultimate comfort comes through godly character.

The Bible says, "He who spares the rod hates his son, but he who loves him is careful to discipline him" (Prov. 13:24). When a loving parent spanks his child, he is willing to put pain into the child's life because he ultimately wants his child's comfort. If a child runs out in the road, the loving parent would rather provide a "little" pain now, than for the child to have to deal with the "big" pain of getting hit by a car. And a loving parent wants his child to have the kind of character that produces a life that "works out better."

It works out better when we are responsible. Life works out better if we do not inflict unnecessary hurt on other people. Therefore, a parent may provide the hurt of a spanking[14] so that the child can experience the joy of responsibility and godliness. The parent is providing a "little" pain now, so that the child doesn't have to deal with "big" pains later, including what could happen if, as an undisciplined adult, he ultimately rejects God. Could it be that this is what God is doing with us? Maybe God is saying, "I want you to have some pain because I am interested in developing character."

And when we have that character, we are going to feel the peace of God. We are going to feel a comfort. We are going to feel some of the things that God wants us to feel, but only when we have the character that comes sometimes through a painful process. In fact, probably, the biggest growth time for us will be in the pain.

---

[14] We are not talking about abusive paddling here, but a small "stinger" on the buttocks where God provided "padding" to absorb that type of pain without long-term bodily damage.

Nothing is wrong with avoiding pain, unless that avoidance becomes our god. The "Rich Young Ruler" in Scripture is an example of comfort becoming a god (Matt 19:16-22; Mark 10: 17-23).

What is the greatest commandment? "Love God with all your heart, soul, and mind." And the second greatest is, "Love your neighbor as yourself" (Matt. 22:37-39; Mark 12:30-31).

On this earth, you cannot love well without pain. Somewhere, you are going to get hurt. At some time, the other person is not going to respond. Or what you do is not going to be enough. Or they are going to reject you. Or they are going to think wrong kinds of thoughts -- EVEN when you do it well!

How do we know that is true? What is the perfect example? "For God so loved the world that He gave His only son . . ." (John 3:16).

Christ loved the world PERFECTLY, and yet, they rejected Him, spit on Him, crucified Him, hated Him, called Him names, put Him down, laughed at Him. And we expect better -- we, who are sinful and messed up? We think that somehow we are going to figure it out so that it goes better -- that we will have a life with no pain? Christ promised His disciples, "If you follow me, it is going to be painful. It is not going to be easy" (Matt. 10:17, 22, etc.).

Christ understood that desire to escape pain. Before the crucifixion He asked the Father, that "this cup pass from me" (Matt. 26:39; Mark 14:36; Luke 22:42). And He demonstrated His need for comfort when He sought a place away from the crowds (Matt 14:23, etc.), when He reclined and ate with his disciples, friends, and others (Mark 14:17, etc.), when He took his disciples with Him to pray (Matt. 26:37), when He slept because of tiredness (Luke 8:2), and when he laid his head on a cushion (Mark 4:38).

But, God is more interested in us being good lovers, than avoiders of pain. So, "love" is the most important thing. And yet, it is going to hurt. Are you willing to enter into that? Are you willing to say, "God, do what you are going to do. And I pray that I will learn."

As we do that then, we can still ask (as Christ's example demonstrated), "Could you bring some relief?" That is legitimate.

So, to summarize this topic, the ultimate point is this: We all long for comfort. Having that comfort is not crucial to our existence or to our eternal state. Having that comfort does not always mean that my critical need for relationships is met. But having comfort provides a measure of enjoyment. We can enjoy the world that God made and because of that, enjoy God. And comfort gives us something to thank God for. We realize His provision and the reality that our comfort is only present because He gives it to us. Comfort is a real desire in all of us.

SURVIVAL NEEDS?

When looking at Crabb's ideas regarding the most important needs of man, you may be wondering, "What about survival needs?" What about the need for food, water, and air?"

This is the argument that is often made by Christians: People need God. They need each other. They want life to go well. But if you do not feed them and you have the capacity to feed them -- if you do not give them what they need physically, how will they be able to focus on the message? If you simply share the gospel with them and do not take care of their physical hunger, is not some of their ability diminished to relax and give their full attention to the message you are giving? Shouldn't we be giving people what they need physically, if we have the where-with-all to do that, BEFORE we share the gospel? But if going to heaven and finding God IS the most important thing, then, is that at the base and is that even more important than food? Is that more important than bread and water? What is at the base?

When Psalm 63:3 says, "Your love is better than life," does that mean that we should share Christ's love before we give those people physical necessities that will enhance their physical lives? It appears that Crucial Longings/Needs should be at the base. Crucial Longings would be a primary need.

Christ fed the crowds, but it is interesting to note that they stayed and listened to Him, even though they were getting hungry. They didn't know he was going to provide food for them, yet they gathered and listened (Matt 14:15-22, Matt 15:36; Mark 8:1-8).

So helping with eliminating physical needs is godly, but physical needs may not be primary needs. Yet, if someone is on the brink of starvation and going to die, obviously, if we have the where-with-all to feed him, we want to help meet that need.

(Source: thebiblerevival.com, Public Domain)

The biblical examples seem to indicate that when Christ was with people for an extended period of a day and knew that they would be without food, He fed them. Yet why didn't Christ give food everywhere He went? He had the means to give food to everybody. Why didn't He deal with the hunger problem in Israel? And the people that Christ did feed, eventually got hungry again. Why didn't He take care of their physical hunger in a more permanent way?

And there was a poverty problem. There was a slavery problem. There was an abundance of social problems in Israel. Why didn't He address those? Why didn't He form groups to picket certain issues? Could it be that it was because He saw spiritual things as the most important? And yet, where He could address those things, He did.

Does that mean that as Christians, we should not get involved in social movements -- that they all ought to be spiritual movements? Those passages probably are not teaching that. But it does seem to show us that man's desire and need to know God surpasses every other need.

So if you have to pick between giving food or giving the gospel -- knowing that the next moment the person would either be in Heaven or just have had his stomach filled up, but be in Hell, obviously as a Christian, you are going to say that the spiritual needs are at the base. But that does not mean that feeding the hungry cannot be a means of showing kindness -- paving the way to sharing the gospel. We can do both.

MASLOW'S CHART OF HIERARCHY

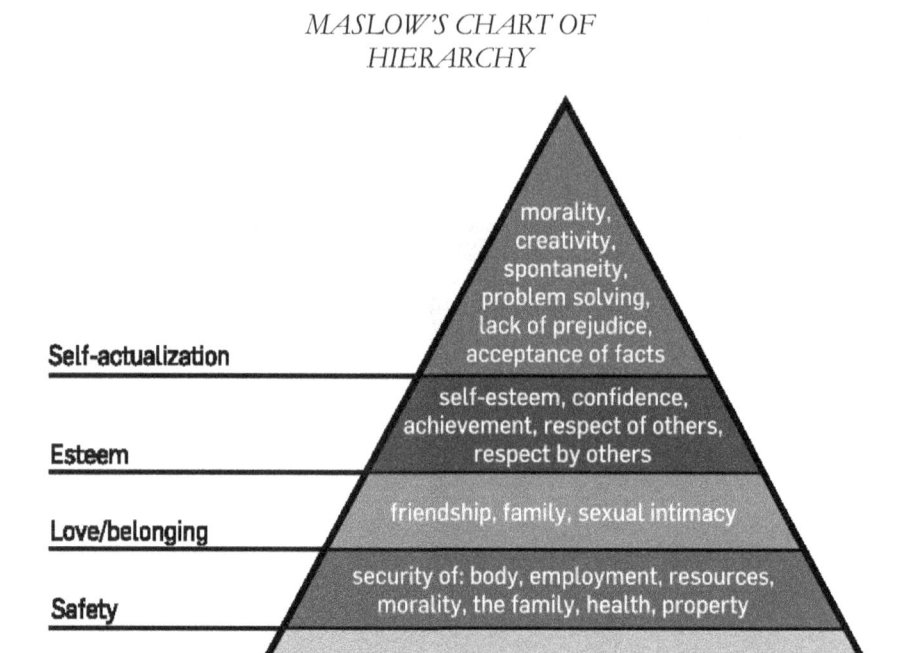

Self-actualization	morality, creativity, spontaneity, problem solving, lack of prejudice, acceptance of facts
Esteem	self-esteem, confidence, achievement, respect of others, respect by others
Love/belonging	friendship, family, sexual intimacy
Safety	security of: body, employment, resources, morality, the family, health, property
Physiological	breathing, food, water, sex, sleep, homeostasis, excretion

(Source: Wikimedia.org, Factoryjoe, 2009)

What does Abraham Maslow have to say about all the needs of man and which are most primary? Maslow would say that "physiological" needs are at the base.

But, if you start without God, you miss the importance of our spiritual needs. He started without God. There is nothing spiritual there. Yet, he is right in that, if we can feed the hungry and give them what they need, we ought to be doing that.

GLASSER'S FIVE NEEDS

Next, take a look at William Glasser's five needs. He also talks about the "survival need" -- our one physiological need. (The rest are psychological.) He suggests the need for "belonging (love)." It is his assumption that that need is built into us as social beings. His ideas correspond very closely with the relationship needs that we believe are God-given and were discussed earlier.

Glasser's 5 Basic Needs

- Belonging
- Power
- SURVIVAL
- Freedom
- Fun

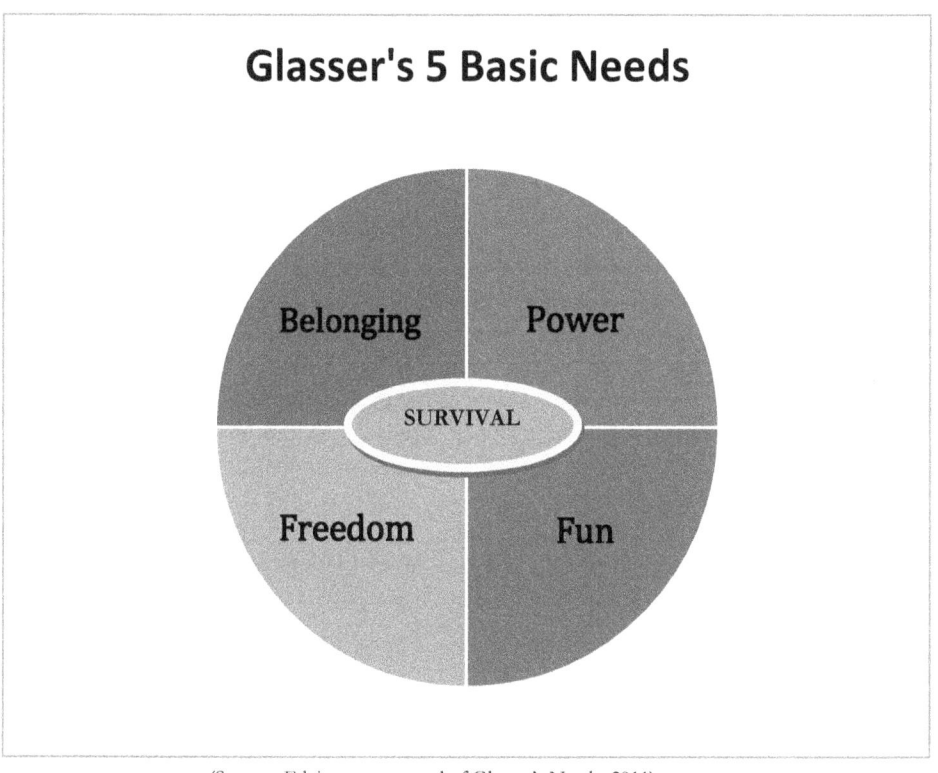

(Source: Edgington portrayal of Glasser's Needs, 2011)

"Power" is another need he gives. Could he be talking about the need to make meaningful impact in our world? This author believes that could be the case. Glasser (1998) says that we feel powerful (at least at a minimum) when we are respected and listened to. Could that need for respect correspond with our discussions on impact? So far, Glasser seems to be enlightened in seeing some of the same psychological needs in man as were discussed at the beginning of this chapter. He is an example of "The Lord gives light to the eyes of both" (Prov. 29:13).

The last two needs that Glasser proposes -- that usually are not included in psychologists' listings of man's basic needs -- are: Freedom and Fun. Do you think we have a need for freedom? Do we have a need for fun? Are they needs? Glasser thinks so. A discussion of how God created us with a capacity for freedom of choice can be found in later chapters.

Every society has a sport. Could that point to a need for fun? Do those needs have the same kind of intensity compared to others we have discussed?

You can see that he has his own ideas about what man's basic needs are, yet he still sees some of the most primary needs being a form or relationship and impact. Though secular psychologists do not see God in that picture, it is amazing how many of them still see the needs that God created for relationship and impact.

BACK TO CRUCIAL, CRITICAL, AND CASUAL LONGINGS

Now we return to the ideas on crucial longings and draw some conclusions. Though survival needs may "feel" more compelling, they are probably NOT the most basic. If you are out of food or if you are out of water, you want those needs met NOW and that can feel very overwhelming; however, that does not mean that they are the most basic. This author believes that our spiritual needs are at the base. Our Crucial Longings -- our longings for relationship with God -- are the true foundational longings.

So here is the next question: "If our survival needs are being met, how do Crucial, Critical, and Casual all fit together?" Probably the best way of explaining that is with a cup.

The "Cup" Analogy

Imagine that you are looking, from the top, into the bottom of a Styrofoam cup. You are looking from up above, down into the cup. Casual is at the top. Critical is in the middle. Crucial is at the bottom.

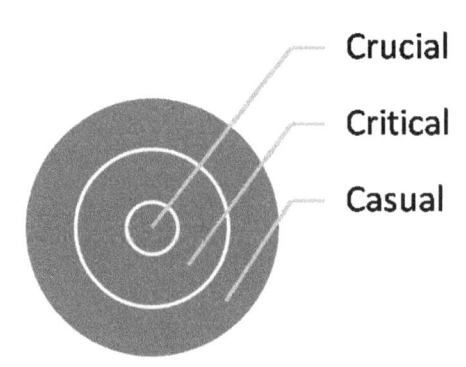

Crucial

Critical

Casual

If you don't have a <u>bottom</u> to your cup, if you haven't found God and those crucial needs are not being met, you will be like this cup, pouring in things to satisfy critical and casual longings, and never being able to do so. That is why people often feel "empty" -- because they have "tried relationships," or "material things," or "being addicted to something," and they are still empty. What they need is a bottom to their cup.

Now, that is not to say that if someone has a bottom to his cup, that he always feels full -- that he is always feeling happy and thinks that everything is great. Sometimes a person can have that bottom to his cup and still have that ache that his critical longings are not being met, or his life is not comfortable or it isn't going as well as he would like.

But here is the key: When we have the bottom to our cup, we have hope! We have enough! We can go on. We can put one foot in front of the other. We have enough, even though we may not have everything we want and we may still feel that ache.

If we do not have a bottom to our cup, we can have all kinds of relationships, we can have all sorts of material "comforts," and still always feel empty. We still always feel like we do not have enough. We are looking for the bottom of the cup.

That does not mean that when we get that "bottom" that we will always feel "full." But FULLNESS is now a potential. When we don't have a bottom to our cup, fullness is NEVER a potential.

And if we do have a bottom to our cup, what happens is usually that our relationships are now more enjoyable -- because we are not needy and demanding of them. We can just enjoy them. We can enjoy the things we DO have, rather than believing, "I need another car," or "I need another job," etc.

Now we can just enjoy what we have -- those casual longings are not grasped in an attempt to promote fullness. The "casual" longings truly feel "casual" because we have got a bottom to our cup.

When we do not have that bottom to our cup, we go to our relationships with more of an intensity and demand saying, "Come on! You've got to be God, for me!" We go to life and say, "Come on!" to material things (or whatever we're addicted to) -- "Do it for me!"

So, though it can happen for Christians too, people without the bottom of the cup often have a subtle demand that somehow life ultimately should satisfy. They believe, "I've got to find it here!" And they get more and more demanding. They get more and more intense and, sometimes, more and more empty.

CHRIST LEGITIMIZED LONGINGS

So what did Christ think about man's "neediness"? Did He think it was legitimate to long? Did He judge man as selfish for being needy?

We talked about the hunger and thirst metaphors used in the Bible. John 6:35 says, "I am the bread of life. He who comes to me will never go hungry.

John 7:37 -- "If anyone is thirsty, let him come to me to drink.

These usages of the terms "hungry" and "thirsty" are analogous to physical hunger and thirst. Never would we say to somebody, "Oh, you're physically hungry? You're selfish!!"

Or, "If you eat food at that party, you're selfish!!

We would not say that satisfying those needs is selfish. We would not say, "You should not have any food and just go hungry, because that's more spiritual." Right? We don't say that!

God created us to enjoy the fulfillment of eating and drinking and satisfying those physical cravings. God says in Ecclesiastes 2:24-25, "There's nothing better than to eat and drink and find satisfaction in his work." Why? God made it! He says, "Go eat, drink, and enjoy." Why? "I made it! Go have a good steak!" Now, if we are gluttonous -- if life is all about good steaks, then we have got a problem. But, when we go the opposite way and say, "We cannot have anything enjoyable, and we cannot eat or drink because that would be selfish, that is contrary to what God desires for us!

"SELF-CARE" – A GOOD KIND OF "SELF"-ISHNESS"

There is a GOOD kind of "self-ishness." The "good" kind of "selfishness" we are going to call "Self-Care" (which can include enjoyment of the world that God created for us and worship and praise for His gifts). That good kind of selfishness includes taking care of ourselves. If we do not eat and we do not drink, we do not live.

And you say, "Yeah, but if you die, you died for Jesus!" Well, you could say that! And that sounds more spiritual, but I do not believe it is really more spiritual. If you die for Jesus because you did not partake of what He has provided for you, then you are no longer here to represent God to others on this earth.

And what about working hard without rest? The story of Jethro and Moses (Exodus 18) was highlighted in Chapter 2. If you "'burn out' for Jesus!" as some have encouraged, if you just keep putting your head down and pushing forward and eventually "burn out," some would say, "That's okay! You did it for God!" But what has happened to your ability to serve God? How useful are you to God if you are totally incapacitated?

God wants us to be "full" of what we need to function for the Lord. As Psalm 1:3 says, "He is like a tree planted by streams of water, which yields its fruit in season and whose leaf does not wither." In my publication, *Healing Helps*, I say, "We are to look after our own interests with the end goal being to then look after the interests of others. Once we are 'filled,' as a tree planted by the streams of water, we can then bless others with the 'fruit' and 'shade'" (Edgington, 1995, p. 90).

God has given us physical and intellectual/spiritual capacities so that He can use them. We have a body and a mind that God wants to use. We have a digestive system that God created to use nutrients that help keep us healthy and functioning. We have a body that gets tired, but God gave the ability to revive it through rest. We have a mind that functions best under certain time and stress limitations.

Maybe "burning out" for Jesus is not such a good idea. Maybe I am supposed to take care of myself so that I can serve Him even longer. An adage that has been communicated to seminary students illustrates this principle: "God gave you a horse and a message. If you kill the horse, you won't be able to deliver the message" (Edgington, 1995, p. 91).

Self-care is a biblical thing. Remember Jethro with Moses (Exodus 18:13-27)? Jethro was saying to Moses, "Moses, what you are doing is not good! You are going to 'burn out!'"

In *Healing Helps from the Bible*, it says, "His (Jethro's) suggestion was that Moses could select capable men to help him with the smaller matters, and he would handle only the most difficult ones. In this way, Moses would not 'burn out' and would remain able to fulfill God's purposes" (Edgington, 1995, p. 87). And Moses followed Jetho's advice.

Moses could have said, "Wait a minute! I'm doing God's work here. What are you talking about? I'm the spiritual one. Jethro, take a back seat!"

But he listened to his father-in-law and God blessed him. Self-care is biblical if ultimately our goal is to care for others. It is legitimate to think about ourselves. Sometimes we NEED to think about ourselves.

Christ took care of Himself by resting/sleeping, withdrawing from crowds/getting alone, and praying numerous times (Mark 1:35, 4:38, 6:30, 6:45, 14:32, Luke 4:28-30; 4:42; 6:12; 8:22,23; 21:3; John 11:53,54). He even picked a "quiet" time and place to get by himself. Mark 1:35 says, "Very early in the morning while it was still dark, Jesus got up, left the house, and went off to a solitary place where he prayed." Luke 21:37 says, "Each day he was teaching at the temple, each evening he went out to spend the night on the hill called the Mount of Olives...." Christ took care of Himself. He ate, drank, slept, avoided crowds when he needed a break, got alone, sought peace and quiet, and prayed, so that He was able to care for others. He even sought his friends' accompaniment at Gethsemane, asking them to "keep watch with me."

The monks took care of themselves in a "twisted" way. The monks tried to be "selfless," and yet, weren't they really still being "self"-ish? Even though the monks were trying to deny themselves, they were still "taking care of themselves" when they chose to self-inflict pain and suffering. They were wanting to be more godly -- and in essence be more loved and accepted by God. They were still trying to get that legitimate love and purpose that all of mankind strives for. The Bible says to LOVE each other as we (already) LOVE ourselves. (We naturally seek care, respect, love, comfort, purpose and constantly look for ways to satisfy those needs.) Though they "took care" of themselves in a different way, the monks were still being "self"-ish in that they were trying to obtain a "higher stature" for themselves before God. They wanted a deep love and respect. Nowhere in the Bible does it say that God wants us to "flog" ourselves, but He does want us to take care of our physical and spiritual needs. It is legitimate to long for God, for love, for value, for relationship, for comfort, for security, for direction, and purpose.

What the monks were longing for was legitimate. They were longing for love from God, acceptance from God, relationship with God, and purpose. God programmed us to need those things -- love and purpose -- and to "self"-ishly seek them.

In fact, why do we get saved? Did you accept Christ because you just wanted to love other people? Many people get saved because they do not want to go to Hell. They want to go to heaven and be with God. Isn't that selfish?

When teaching a three-hour class, a college professor will usually provide the students (and himself) breaks at different points during the lecture. What is the students' normal reaction when afforded that break? Do the students say, "Oh, please don't stop! Please tell us more"? No. They are anxious for some time to relax before having to direct their focus again, to learning the material given.

But would it be more "godly" if we didn't take breaks? The monks thought that the more suffering they endured, the more godly they were. Taking a break would mean giving some comfort and minimizing the tediousness of learning material in a lecture. The monks beat themselves, hurt themselves, and put themselves in difficult situations in order to be more godly. They would probably claim that it would be more godly NOT to take breaks in a three-hour class. Is that what God expects of us? They were doing something that seemed logical to them. -- If in pain I find God, then I should inflict myself with more pain, and as a result, find more godliness. So, is it more godly to avoid breaks?

I mean, aren't we selfish? Absolutely! That's how God draws us. "If you're hungry and thirsty, come to me. I'm the bread of life." He didn't say, "Stop it!" "Quit being selfish! You're wrong!" He said, "Come to me, and I'll satisfy" (John 7:37). Can we make bread and water our God? Yes. Though we have often gone too far to take care of our own needs or to "deny ourselves," we all still have legitimate sinless dependent longings.

SINFUL INDEPENDENT NEEDS

The second category of Motivation is labeled "Sinful Independent Needs." Those who fall under this category acknowledge that they have needs, but not that those needs can be met by God. Though in reality, they are still dependent on God, they -- as the Bible says is Romans 1:18 -- "suppress the truth by their wickedness." They are still dependent on God, but they act like, or talk like, He is not there and that they are dependent on something else.

The thinking goes something like this. "As a nonbeliever, I would rather talk about my needs than talk about my need for God." And even non-believing psychologists are willing to talk about man's needs. They say, "We all have needs. We need love. We need purpose. We need affirmation. We need freedom. We need . . . ." But the minute you ask, "What about God?" they deny that He is the source and fulfillment of those needs.

They say, "No, I need those things, but I find fulfillment wherever I can find it. I do not look to God to find that fulfillment. (Though some secular psychologists acknowledge that "God may 'work'" for some people, they say He is not the answer for most. And the secular psychologist does not believe that God is the answer for himself.)

These theorists are still dependent on God, but they do not want to believe in that dependency on God. They do not want to talk like they are dependent on God. They want to talk about needs in a way that bypasses God.

So when secularists say, "We have psychological needs," what are some of the needs that they would give? They would say that we need love and acceptance. They would acknowledge those types of needs.

William Glasser's ideas about man's needs were mentioned earlier. They included needs that corresponded to love and purpose, but also added freedom and fun.

Do we have a need for fun? Every culture has a sport. Every culture has some sort of fun. They all seem to have a form of dancing, singing, and games. So do we have a need for fun? Maybe we do. It certainly seems to relieve stress at times and active "fun" often seems to also increase clarity of thought along with other positive outcomes.

Remember Maslow's Chart of man's five needs? What are Maslow's five needs? He talks about "Belongingness." That would include the idea of relationships. When you look at Maslow's hierarchy of needs, "Self-Actualization" is at the top. Next down would be "Esteem Needs," then "Belongingness." Then there is "Safety." We need to know that we are safe.

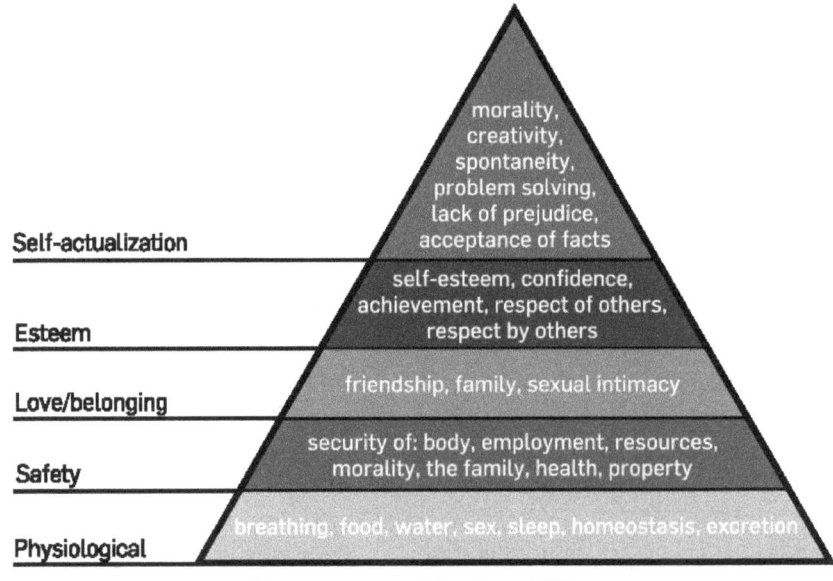

Self-actualization: morality, creativity, spontaneity, problem solving, lack of prejudice, acceptance of facts

Esteem: self-esteem, confidence, achievement, respect of others, respect by others

Love/belonging: friendship, family, sexual intimacy

Safety: security of: body, employment, resources, morality, the family, health, property

Physiological: breathing, food, water, sex, sleep, homeostasis, excretion

(Source: commons.wikimedia.org, 2009)

(Some would say that is still kind of a physiological need.) And on the bottom of his "Hierarchy of Needs" chart are basic needs -- the "Physiological (Survival) Needs."

Notice what Glasser and Maslow are talking about. They are saying, "Here are our needs." Yet, nowhere do they say, ". . . and God." So, Maslow and Glasser are two psychologists, along with numerous others, who talk about psychological needs that bypass God.

That is what is meant by "Sinful Independent Needs." Yet, people whose beliefs fall into the category of "Sinful Independent Needs" are still dependent on God. So something in them acknowledges that they have needs; but they are going to act like their dependency is not on God. And they talk about their neediness in a way that says, "I don't need Him."

These thinkers are willing to acknowledge that they are needy. But are they getting at man's real needs? Sometimes the unsaved man is willing to talk about his neediness, but without admitting a need for God. This is a form of idolatry.

The Bible talks about this kind of idolatry in Jeremiah 2:13 and Proverbs 27:20. Jeremiah 2:13 says, "They have forsaken me, the spring of living water, and have dug their own cisterns, broken cisterns that cannot hold water." Proverbs 27:20 says, "Death and Destruction (Hebrew words "Sheol" and Abaddon") are never satisfied, and neither are the eyes of man."

Those who fit this category try to find things to "fill" that void of neediness that are apart from God. (In truth, all people -- even Christians, being still sinful and vulnerable to temptation -- try to meet their needs in illegitimate ways. So everyone would fall into this category at times. But those who truly fit this category have no intention of ever acknowledging that God is the only true fulfillment of their needs.) Whatever is chosen to fulfill their needs becomes a god. It could be a wife or husband or kids, a job, prestige, beauty and/or their physique, a career, fame, money, cars, houses, sex, pornography, etc. All of those things are sought as a way of fulfilling needs. There is a belief that "I need this in order to be happy." "I need this to have self-worth." "I need this to be fulfilled." "I need this for meaning and purpose in my life."

Albert Ellis, the founder of Rational-Emotive Therapy, would say, "Do you? Do you need the money? There are people out there without it. They are going on." And he would have a way of cutting through that thinking and challenging those beliefs. And the client would say, "You're right! I really don't need the money." Things would be said like: "I need this man in my life" or "I need this woman in my life. I cannot go on." Ellis would have a way of countering, "Oh, if you didn't have this person, there's no way you could live!? There's no way you could survive? You couldn't take another step?"

Then the counselee would say, "No, I know what you're saying. I don't really need that person."

So secularists like Ellis have a way of cutting through that, challenging that belief. They employ techniques that promote the client to realize that he is not as needy as he thinks.

However, do I need God? Absolutely. You cannot say "Well, I don't need that. That's not that important. I can go on without it." You cannot go on without God!

Again, if you do not start with God, you will end up in a different place than if you start with Him. But, the fact of the matter is: People are saying, "I still long for something." As Christians we can say, "I can help you find what you are looking for."

These are needs that secularists talk about in their theories. Carl Rogers says that we are needy; we need unconditional, positive regard.

What does that mean? Love. We need to know that weare unconditionally loved. He says we all need it. So most secularists are willing to talk about these needs, but not our need for God.

CRAVINGS

The third and last category of motivations is "Cravings." We talked about the word *lust* which is the Greek word *epithumia*, in Scripture. It is found in 1 John 2:15-17. This category involves those who are totally self-consumed and self-absorbed. It is anthropocentric -- man-centered. Those in this category are thinking, "It's all about me. I'm God. I have no needs."

If you are familiar with the criminal, Charles Manson, you will remember that he preached to his followers that he was Jesus. Here was a man who did not believe he had any needs, yet in truth, he was very needy. People who come across as the most self-sufficient, professing: "I need absolutely nothing in this world," tend to be the most needy people.

(Source: wclipart.com Public Domain)

The narcissist who says, "I am the greatest of all time" is the one who thinks very little about himself. Down deep inside (if you get down in there), there is a little boy who is saying, "I'm not very good with life. And I'm not very good with relationships. I'm going to overcompensate by being incredibly narcissistic. I need to endorse myself in a LARGE way in order to fill the massive emptiness and neediness inside."

But there is still an image-bearer in there that says, "I long for God and I long for His meaning and purpose to life."

People in this category see themselves as "God" and life becomes merely the pursuit to glorify themselves and make themselves happy through greed, sex, power, and pleasure. Indeed, they are still dependent, but they make no acknowledgment of that dependency.

SIN'S EFFECT ON OUR LONGINGS

So, where does sin come in? Basically, sin comes in when we do not believe that God meets our crucial longings. Now, as Christians, we all believe internally that He does. But even Christians are sometimes swayed externally into thinking on some level that "This isn't enough! I could get more!"

We know that God is enough, yet sometimes we live our lives as if it is not true -- as if we do not have what we really need. Eve's big sin was in thinking, "God, you have given me all I need, but I want a little bit more."

Sin slowly creeps into our hearts, where we think, "I could do better than this." It is at that point that Critical Longings (and often, eventually, Casual Longings) become *viewed* as Crucial Longings.

When stories are told of those who have been in captivity or war, one theme that often comes to light is that during that captivity or battle, they did not worry about the "little" things anymore. They did not worry about what outfit they were going to wear or whether their clothes were in style or how much money they made or whether they were popular. Those things are not crucial. In fact, there is a saying, "There are no atheists in foxholes." People in captivity or war are often faced with what is crucial to them. At that point, the only thing that seems to be important is living, dying, and where they will spend eternity.

God has given us <u>everything</u> we really need, even though we can find ourselves thinking that we need more. To really grasp that would alleviate much stress and tension.

So, if you do not believe that God meets your Crucial Longings, then your Critical Longings feel like Crucial Longings. When that is true, you start living life as if others are going to meet your needs -- your friends, your mate, your kids. You rely on your Critical Longings to satisfy you. And if that does not work, you eventually move to Casual Longings, thinking, "Maybe material things (or something you become addicted to) will make life work!"

The person in this situation thinks, "God, you are just not doing it for me, so I have got to get this relationship -- this person -- to do it for me, to be 'God' for me," or "I have got to get this thing, or this job, or money, or whatever I choose to depend on, to be my 'god.'" In other words, that person is going to go to people or things to get his needs met. Now, this is not always a conscious decision, but the individual's actions demonstrate the belief.

Many get married with the thinking, "Just be God for me. You made me feel really good at the beginning. Now, just make me feel good the rest of my life! That's all I'm asking." And the spouse often thinks, "Well, I was kind of hoping for that too!"

But there comes a point where they do not always give of themselves the way they did when they were first dating. Because no one can! No one can keep that up.

So at some point people say, "I demand you. I'm really going to try to 'push' you and try to make you be my god." Maybe they "push" their spouse. Maybe it is their friends. The "god" could be family. But no matter who it is, Critical Longings are now viewed as Crucial.

As sinners, we all try to control other people. We try to get others to give us what we want. Most marital problems occur for that very reason. One side is thinking, "You are not doing what I want, and I have got to get you to give me what I want," while the other person responds, "Well, you are not giving me everything I want, and I have got to get you to be different too!" That is when problems arise.

Relational problems arise when Critical Longings are substituted for Crucial Longings -- when there is no bottom to the cup (p. 229). But if one goes to his Critical Longings for satisfaction and then gets hurt or rejected or ignored, he often moves to his Casual Longings -- living his life making "things" his gods.

Billy Joel wrote a song in 1973 called, "The Piano Man." In the opening verse, he sings of an old man "makin' love to his tonic and gin." When Critical Longings fail to satisfy, they are traded for addictions. An addiction becomes the new "relationship" -- that alcohol, those drugs, that sex, that pornography, etc. This new "relationship" is always there whenever called upon. It brings a level of temporary satisfaction. It brings a sense of "comfort" as it is sought to replace those failed relationships.

The irony is, as comfort becomes the god, there is less and less "comfort" experienced. So begins the pursuit of more comfort -- more drugs, more pornography (then "harder" drugs or hard-core pornography), etc. And the new system for getting needs met eventually implodes. Eventually there is more discomfort, because comfort became the god. It is Satan's great lie. "This will do it for you." "You don't need God. This will satisfy you."

At this point, a proper dependency is replaced by desperation. We are dependent. We will always be dependent. But in this case, we have come to believe, "I have GOT TO have this thing!" "You have GOT TO come through for me!" "You cannot leave me!" "I cannot lose this job!" "I cannot lose my money!" A desperation comes in life because there is no realization that all of man's needs are met, in a crucial sense. When we do not believe we have all we need, we get desperate.

Some relationships actually grow out of desperation. When that has happened, strategies are developed based on how needs were met. (Strategies will be the focus of pages that follow. People tend not to employ strategies unless previous relationships did not "work" or satisfy. But if the previous relationships did not "work" -- if they did not meet needs -- and a new strategy seems to meet those needs, or "works" on some level, then the tendency is to try to make it "work" in that same way again and again. Crabb (1987) writes about relational strategies in his book, *Understanding People* (p. 147).

But relationships cannot be perfect and cannot give us everything we want. So when we go to our spouse or our friends, or our family or whoever, demanding that "Somebody's going to be God for me," we fall into the trap of trying to control things that are uncontrollable.

The topic of controlling others to get needs met and the strategies developed to control them will be dealt with in upcoming pages; but let it suffice to say at this time that strategies are methods developed to try to get another to give us what we want. The bottom line is, sin has caused us to grasp at the unquenchable, the "broken cisterns," desperately "digging" them (Jeremiah 2:13) -- trying to control through strategies rather than seeking the perfect one, the one who gives us the bottom of our cup, filling it from a spring of living water.

LONGINGS AND STRATEGIES –
WHERE WE ARE MOVING

So, here is where we are moving. We have been talking about "longings." Longings are legitimate. We will move to the discussion of "strategies." Strategies are illegitimate.

It is legitimate when people have a longing -- a desire: "I want my life to be better." "I want my friendships to be better." "I want my marriage to be better." "I want my relationship with God to be better." Those are legitimate longings.

"I'm now going to find a way to MAKE life give me what I want." "I'm going to find a way to get people to give me what I want." Those intentions are illegitimate. As sinners, we all develop strategies to try to make life work apart from God -- EVEN as Christians. We all try to find ways to make life work WITHOUT God or ways that bypass God. Strategies are the methods we devise in our attempt to manipulate others to meet our "needs."

Think about the events that come along in your life. Is your first thought, "What can I do to make this better?" or is it, "I need to pray about this first"?

How many times is the first thought, "What can I do to control this, to get it my way?" We go to strategies SO quickly! And part of the reason is because strategies have worked in the past. We do not follow certain strategies if they have not worked. We give them up. We follow the ones that have worked.

happens in time is that we develop a list of certain ... be ten, maybe one hundred, or there could be thousands ... have different strategies (based upon our background and ... to work in our situations) that bypass God. Everyone ... and everyone (because each of us is a sinner) also has ... gies to try to meet those longings -- to make life work. Unfortunately, many of those strategies are going to lead to more misery and more heartache. Even though in the past the strategy may have achieved the desired result, ultimately strategies are going to lead to destruction.

THE IMPORTANCE OF LONGINGS

So why look at longings? Longings are important aspects of relationship. To whom are we going to go with our longings?
And how will we protect ourselves from longings being unmet? We do not want any more pain. We do not want any more rejection in our lives. How do we try to prevent any more hurt?

There are really two things to consider when it comes to relationships: 1) How does one **get** his relational needs met? 2) How does one make sure he does not get hurt? How does he **protect** himself?

"I don't want any more hurt. I've had enough hurt." At least, that is what we think sometimes.

So to whom do we go with our longings? Do we go appropriately to God?

This is where prayer comes in. Every time we pray, we are acknowledging, "God, I need you."

With God we have been given enough to live fully, to be godly, and to put one foot in front of the other. He has given us enough to do that. We do not have everything we want or that would be nice to have, but He has given us enough.

Do we realize that? Are we going to God with our longings or are we going somewhere else with them? If we are going somewhere else, we are doing it inappropriately. If we are going to a relationship or job or kids or money or an addiction, then we are going to something that says, "You've got to do it for me. God isn't enough. I need more."

We do have enough, even though we cannot be fully satisfied on this earth. Even though "walking by faith" brings peace and contentment, we were built for heaven and this earth cannot fulfill our deepest longings for God (Ecc. 3:11). We will not feel fully complete until we have reached heaven, and yet, we can be content that God is there for us. We know that we have enough to be content, even though we still long for heaven.

But when people discount God's fulfillment of their needs, they have moved beyond that. They are saying, "God, what you have given me isn't enough. I need more. And somebody or something has to give that to me. I'm desperate."

Met longings bring pleasure. We like it when we are admired by others. We like it when they care about us. We like it when we are shown respect or attain prestige. We like when our longings are being met. That brings pleasure. And we learn something from that. We learn that we want that enjoyment to continue. We want more of it.

And we function better when we feel content. Why do we feel better when pleasure comes to us? The Bible says a "merry heart doeth good like a medicine" (Prov. 17:22 KJV). There is something good about feeling good. So can we serve God better when we are feeling good psychologically/mentally/spiritually? Probably. And does that make us feel better physically? The Bible seems to indicate that it can. But the Bible also exhorts us to seek the things that bring enduring pleasure, not the things that are fleeting -- those things that will not bring ultimate contentment.

But when longings are met, we learn what it feels like. When we experience that pleasure, we often think, "Hey! That worked! I think I will do more of it." We then look for ways of achieving that pleasure again. The problem comes in, though, when we turn that pleasure into a need, into a demand, into a "god."

Maybe the first time the gratifying experience was achieved by accident. That is usually the best way -- where sometimes God gives us what we want or relationships go well.

We think, "That felt good. I like that." But when we go beyond that and add, "Now I've got to find a way of keeping it. I've got to find a way of getting this to remain constant," that is when we start to develop strategies to "make" it happen again.

So we learn certain beliefs from those pleasurable experiences. And we begin acting on those beliefs to get more of those pleasurable experiences.

People get addicted to falling in love because it feels so good! The problem is, if you "fall in love" with that one person that you are going to marry and stay with for life, you are only going to "fall in love" with that person once. You can still be "in love," but that first romantic meeting and getting to know each other can only happen once. So for some the thinking becomes, "Well, that felt really good. I want more of that."

But if you want more of it and you believe this is the right person for you, then you have a choice. You can either get rid of that person and look for someone else to fall in love with or you can DEMAND that person give you that feeling again -- which probably is not going to work.

You may try a number of different techniques or "strategies" to get back to that feeling of "falling in love." And your implementation of those strategies can become your way of making life work.

Your choices may then cause you to find yourself in a vicious cycle that still does not satisfy. You could keep dating new people over and over again in order to keep getting that feeling, and yet, you may still want something deeper. But if you go for "the deeper," then you lose the newness of falling in love. So how can you have it all? You can't!

So ask yourself: What beliefs do I have about how to keep certain things in my life? What strategies have I developed that I think will give me what I want? Should I be developing a different approach in regard to my relationships? What am I going to believe about them?

Christians are not immune from formulating beliefs and techniques to get needs met apart from God; therefore, it is important that we challenge ourselves to discover those practices that may have become entrenched in our being. A Christian can think, "Oh sure, I believe in God. I pray and go to church," and still live his life as if it is under his control.

Ways that Our Longings Bend Away from God

When sin entered, man's God-given capacities still remained. People continue to have the desire for relationships and impact and can still think thoughts, feel emotions, etc. But now the direction is different. Instead of dependency going toward God, the sinner says, "I don't need God" or "There is no God." "The fool says in his heart, there is no God" (Ps. 14:1).

> The image was not destroyed in the fall, but was catastrophically affected. Genesis 9:6 clearly shows that the image was not destroyed after the fall. But the image was marred considerably due to sin. It is this writer's opinion that the capacities remain, but the direction of the capacities has been altered catastrophically. In other words, man now longs for relationship, longs for purpose, believes, thinks, chooses, acts, and feels in ungodly directions. Man has now become anthropocentric instead of theocentric, since he has declared his independence from God. He is still a dependent creature,

but believes he is independent and acts accordingly. The question is: What does man do with his dependency? (Edgington, 1985, pp. 33-34).

So in man's foolishness, in man's sinfulness, he says, "I don't need God," or "He's not enough" or "He's not really going to do it for me; therefore, I'm going to go somewhere else to get relationship and meaning and purpose." Man has to go somewhere with it! Because man is still needy and dependent, he has to go somewhere with that neediness. But the direction has now changed.

SELF-ENHANCEMENT

With the entrance of sin, the goal became "self-enhancement." It started back in the garden. "How can I GET what I want?" That is the thinking behind "self-enhancement."

So if you think about the first sin, it actually took place before Eve ate the fruit. Eve's first sin was her thought (Gen. 3:6). What was going on in Eve's thinking that caused her to choose against God's warning? What was she wanting? Could she have been thinking, "Hey, you know what? I don't need to do this dependency thing. I can make life work myself! I don't need to follow what God said. If I eat of this fruit, I'm going to get MORE of what I'm looking for (whatever that is). And I want more. I demand more. God is not enough."

Eve was into "self-enhancement" at that point. "I'm going to get what I want, and I don't care about God or what He has to say."

What was Adam's first sin? Adam's first sin was not his action either. It was also a thought.

Maybe he was thinking, "I don't want to lose Eve." Maybe he was not willing to trust God to take care of his needs if Eve were gone because of her sin. Or maybe he was thinking, "I want to have what she has," or "I want to be 'like God' too." What we do know is that Adam was thinking in a direction that moved away from God and he acted out his thinking by eating of the fruit as well.

Rather than going to God and saying, "Hey, wait a minute! We have a problem here! She is not doing what she is supposed to do," Adam decided to look at what he perceived were his own needs and attempted to meet those needs on his own.

Man has struggled with that ever since: "God, I know you are there, but you are not really in the picture right now, and I am not going to follow what you have to say. I am going to live life to get what I think I need." The goal has now become "ME" -- "Self-enhancement."

PRIDE -- THE CAUSE OF SELF-ENHANCEMENT

The causative element of self-enhancement is Pride. Pride is a core ingredient of sin and says, "I want to be like God. I don't want to be just an image-bearer; I want to be GOD. I want to be in control of my own little universe, in which I can be God." Pride causes us to try to "get" what we want to "enhance" ourselves and totally "control" our world.

The "world" may be our family. It might be a place of work. It might be a number of other places where one can be "God" and in control. But the insistence on those who are part of that world to meet needs is the key element.

In the TV sitcom, *The Office*, that element has been well portrayed. Michael (the first boss on the show) had his own little world where he was trying to get his needs met. Anyone who has watched the show has probably thought, "What an insecure man, trying to look big!" It seems comical because it is so obvious.

Yet, how is it any different from any other place where people are trying to get their needs met apart from God? There are people everywhere, from every culture, who think, "I want people to like me," "I want more money," "I want prestige," and they go after those goals without acknowledging that God is in the picture.

On *The Office*, Michael just happened to do it in a way that was clearly identifiable. It was not subtle on the show. Most of us do it in a more subtle way.

So what else is involved in "pride" besides the desire to be God? The next thing we want is *to be comfortable*. We want our world to be comfortable. We want our world to be predictable. We want to know what is going to happen tomorrow. And we want instant gratification. This is especially true for us Americans.

You have a headache. You don't want a headache. You want it to be gone in five minutes.

You want good things. In fact, you *deserve* good things! You are "worth it"!

And so we develop a belief of entitlement. Americans are pummeled with this everyday on TV. "YOU deserve this! You are not getting it? Why not? You deserve it!" In fact, if you talk to people who are in the advertising business, one thing that is taught to sales people is: "Create a NEED." Even if the consumer does not have the need, CREATE the need.

"Are you still driving a two-year-old car?"

"Yeah!"

"You could be driving a brand new car for the same amount of money that you are paying for that old wreck!"

Or maybe the "pitch" is for a better cell phone. "Do you still have the kind of cell phone that DOESN'T have a camera?"

"Yeah!"

"How can you endure life? How can you make it through?"

Some consumers have shared that after watching an infomercial, they actually wanted to buy the same item again -- even though they already had one.

Another common tactic is used for body-building products. "With just 15 minutes a day, you could look like this," the ad says. Then it shows a guy who is "ripped" with "six-pack abs"!

Then there are hair commercials for men and women. For each, if you use their product or their service, people will love you.

Some watch those commercials and start thinking, "That's what I want!" Two years later the purchased workout equipment is in a garage sale or they try another hair product hoping that will work.

We have this "I need that! I've got to have it!" mentality. And it stems from our thinking that somehow, *having more* will make life work.

The point is not that there isn't a time for comfort and convenience; but many have "bought into" the idea that if they do not have more, then something is wrong. As a result, they make themselves miserable because a "need" has been created where they are convinced they need something that they really don't. There is a tension that has nothing to do with one's identity. But people begin to believe they are "less" if the created "need" is not satisfied. So if they do not look like the guy using the weight machine, then they do not think they will be able to get somebody to love them. They think, "In order for me to get what I really need -- relationship and meaning and purpose – I have got to have these things!"

That is Satan's great lie! What he's saying is, "You do not have enough! You'd better get that! You need more!"

"Women, you'd better look like that person on the magazine cover. If you don't, I'm sorry. Life is not going to work for you." And you know what? We accept that rationality!

"Men, if you don't look like that, if you don't have that job, if you are not making that money, if you are not driving that car, if you do not have that woman, then life will NOT work!"

And people respond, "You are right!"

It's Satan's great lie -- Self-enhancement! It is all about me. And so I now try to manipulate my world to get me what I think I need. We are talking about the "get" part now. *I'm going to manipulate my world to* **GET** *what I need.*

MANIPULATIVE STRATEGIES -- **GET**

So how do people manipulate to "GET" their longings met? The following are some strategies that are used.

GUILT

Guilt – The "gift" that keeps on "giving." A good example of someone who tries to manipulate through guilt is the TV character Marie Barone from *Everybody Loves Raymond*. In a number of episodes of the show (that played in the 1990s through 2000s), she demonstrates techniques that continue to pervade our world. She is a master of that skill. How does she get her needs met? She "guilts" people into giving her what she wants.

She gets a pitiful look on her face, and then as she turns her head away, she says, "Yeah. That's fine! You boys go ahead and go golfing. I'll just stay here and be unappreciated! It's okay. I'm used to it." The "boys" (her adult sons) then start feeling that "tug" of *guilt*, and think, "We can't go golfing now!"

College professors are often the recipients of numerous requests by students to be excused from classes or quizzes. One such scenario has involved the author of this textbook. On the day before fall break, students have asked, "Are we having class tomorrow? When the answer has been, "Yes," sometimes a student will begin telling what their other professors are doing. The students have said things like, "Well, my other professors cancelled class, so I was wondering if you were going to cancel class."

When the initial answer has been restated, "No, we are having class," there is often still a student who will continue with, "You are the only one of my professors that is having class."

What is the student trying to do? He/She is trying to manipulate the professor -- to "guilt him" into canceling class. In fact, it appears to have "worked" with some of the other professors to the irritation of the dean, who finally one year issued a notice that professors were not to eliminate the last class in order to accommodate students desiring to leave early. But because that strategy had worked with some professors, the students were more likely to try each consecutive year.

Another example that often takes place among families over the holidays has to do with when and where to have the family gatherings. A young couple may call their parents and say, "Since we are married now, we are going to have our own traditions, and we are not going to be coming home on Christmas day like we used to do. We will come the day after."

The response is sometimes silence on the phone. What is going on?

Mom is quiet. Then she says something like this, "Why are you doing this to us?"

What do you hear beneath those words? Because the son/daughter has grown up with his/her mother and has become accustomed to her tactics, he/she probably knew this was coming before the call was even made.

Mom is communicating, "We need you here." In fact, she might say, "Christmas won't be the same without you. If all of you aren't here, it won't be the same" (which is true). "You HAVE to come on Christmas Day!"

"Well, we really want to start our own traditions, and we will be there the next day."

Now Mom says, crying, "Fine! We'll just cancel Christmas then!"

If you are the son or daughter, how do you feel now? -- just a little guilty?

And if Mom continues with, "I'll just call your brothers and sisters and tell them not to even come! And we'll have no presents either! We'll take down the tree and everything!" you may start thinking, "What's happening here?"

Mom has determined, "I'm going to get you to come Christmas day. If you're not here and I don't get what I want, then I can't be happy."

But probably the most disturbing is the accusation that often follows: Mom says, "You know what? I think you're just being SELFISH!"

Wait a minute! Who is the selfish one, really?

Some will even add the "spiritual" element to the situation. Mom says, "What about honoring your father and mother? The Bible says to honor your father and mother." These tactics can cause the young Christian couple to become very "torn" in their thinking and unsure of what choice is the right one.

A number of people misuse Christianity, the Bible, and religion in order to manipulate others. Is the mother using that passage correctly? Is she right in assuming that when the Bible talks about honoring your father and mother in Ephesians 6:2, that means married children need to come whenever the parents want them to or do whatever the parents want them to do? Is it not legitimate for a couple to start their own traditions?

The Bible says in Genesis that husbands and wives are to "leave and cleave" (Gen. 2:24). The marriage bond is to be the priority -- leaving the claim of the parents and establishing an independent unit.

Deuteronomy 24:5 specifies that couples are to refrain from customary duties their first year of marriage, bringing happiness to each other -- establishing their committed bond.

Do you see how Mom is trying to use guilt to manipulate and GET what she wants? Yet, people often allow themselves to be manipulated by guilt in a way that is not necessarily right before God -- even though Mom is trying to make her wishes seem spiritual. And sometimes the married children do what is "easiest" by not upsetting Mom and going along with her wishes rather than to do the more difficult thing of challenging Mom's authority and instituting the new marriage's boundaries. (Challenging Mom actually holds Mom accountable and does what is best for her by not reinforcing her foolishness and, in the end, helps her to learn to be more godly. That also "honors" her, if done respectfully.)

These examples are not anything new. These strategies have been used for years. And there are Christians or maybe some "so-called Christians" who use the "spiritual" strategy, like that mother, that "God's going to be disappointed in you if you don't come for Christmas." And if you are a good son or daughter, you may become confused as to what you ought to do. Some people use guilt very effectively when trying to manipulate others and to get what they want.

BRIBERY

Bribery – I will give you what you want if you give me what I want.

I will look after your interests if you vote for me. I will give you that new dress if you give me sex. Those are all examples of bribery.

Rewarding is not a bad thing, but sometimes rewarding turns into bribery. A parent may say, "If you play in the band, I'll buy you a car."

Bribery is used to manipulate. If the child chooses not to play in the band (and not get the car) and the parent is okay with that decision, then it is not bribery. It is bribery if the parent is trying to manipulate the child into doing what the parent wants and will become angry if the child does not choose what the parent wants.

COMPLIMENTS

Compliments. I used to try this strategy to get my wife to make phone calls for me. I would compliment her on how well she handled herself on the phone. The truth is she is good on the phone. But I tried to use that to my advantage.

I would say, "Honey, you have such a pleasant phone voice and you are so thoughtful in the way you word things. This phone call needs to be made and I wondered if you would make it for me."

A number of times, she responded, "Yeah, I could do that."

But after doing that for awhile, she came to a point where she said, "Uh, I don't want to make that phone call for you. I think you can make your own phone calls."

My response: "Uh-oh!" The old strategy was not working anymore. So I decided to try a new one. My new strategy? -- guilt. "Why don't you want to help me out here?" And if that did not work, then I might try anger. And if that did not work, I might pout. And if you are someone intent on getting a particular desire met through a strategy, you just keep going down the strategies until you find something that will work (Edgington, 2006).

Salespeople often use the "compliment" technique. Some of them can do it pretty well. Compliments can be a way of trying to get what one wants, and complimenting is a strategy that often works.

EMOTIONAL BLACKMAIL

Emotional Blackmail. "Emotional blackmail is a powerful form of manipulation in which people close to us threaten to punish us to get what they want" (Forward & Frazier, 1997). The intention is to cause guilt or other trauma if the intended victim does not comply. The previous example of the mother using guilt would apply to this strategy. But there are other aspects.

Emotional blackmail involves six stages (Forward & Frazier, 1997, pp. 4-6), identified by Susan Forward as: a demand, resistance, pressure, threats, compliance, and repetition.

"If you leave me, you'll never see your kids again." "If you don't support my project, I will delay your recommendation." Those statements could be classified as emotional blackmail.

Ex-wife may say to ex-husband, "If you don't take the kids this weekend, I will tell them that you don't want to be with them."

Withholding affection can be a form of emotional blackmail. "I'm not going to be relational with you. I'm not going to give you affection unless you do what I want." "Until you give me what I want, you get nothing from me."

Or it could be as extreme as, "If you don't do what I want, I'll kill myself." Someone using emotional blackmail may even indicate that he will neglect himself or become depressed if you don't do what he wants.

Child molesters sometimes use this strategy with young children. The little girl or boy is told that if he/she tells, "I will kill your parents." The children believe the perpetrator and, subsequently, fearfully withhold that information from their parents (or other authority figures).

APOLOGIZING

Apologizing. Some people apologize, yet they aren't really willing to be specific about what they did wrong. Or sometimes they know what they did was unacceptable and can be specific, but really do not feel bad about it. Also, a person can be truly sorry -- but sorry for themselves, sorry that they got caught and not for what they did. In reality, then, the apology is not a true apology. The words, "I'm sorry," are just empty words.

Why would someone do that? Why would someone say he was sorry, yet not really feel bad for the wrong that was caused to others? He is apologizing to get his needs met, yet sometimes not even believing he has sinned or damaged the other person. Maybe he apologizes because he is feeling lonely, thinking the apology will mend the rift that is promoting some of the loneliness. What he is really saying is, "I'm sorry that I don't have what I want, so I'm going to say the words that I think you want to hear so that I can get my needs met. Now let's be friends again and everything will be okay."

SAUL REJECTED AS KING
1 Sam. 15:13-23.
GOLDEN TEXT:—To obey is better than sacrifice.
1 Sam. 15:22.

(Source: thebiblerevival.com, Public Domain, 2011)

But that is not a true apology. That is a manipulative strategy. Could that be the motive behind Saul's apology in 1 Samuel 15:30? Maybe.

Sometimes it is so subtle we are not even aware that we are doing it! But we all use strategies such as this to try to get our needs met -- whether we realize it or not.

A NOTE ON SELF-ENHANCING STRATEGIES

To be noted regarding self-enhancing strategies: There is a proper sense of self-enhancement which is self-care. Taking care of oneself is a good thing – as was mentioned. It is godly to do things to promote your health. It is good to eat nutritious food and exercise. It is advantageous to get enough rest, to be around godly people, and to read and listen to uplifting things. It is good to take care of oneself and be a good steward of the body and life that God has given each of us.

But when the self-enhancing belief becomes an all-pervasive drive and all of life is about "getting my needs met," then the person is heading down the wrong path. The ultimate goal of life is not comfort and the avoidance of pain.

PROTECTION FROM LONGINGS BEING UNMET – **PROTECT**
REJECTION HURTS

The second thing we do to meet our relational longings besides attempting to GET is attempting to PROTECT. Pain in life has to do with unmet longings -- especially being rejected.

"At one point, you were meeting my longings -- ESPECIALLY the longing to be accepted. Now you don't want to be in relationship with me anymore." "You don't like me anymore." "You are confronting me." "You are hurting my feelings." "You have betrayed me." "Now you are their friend and you are not my friend." "You used me." "I did not realize that you were in relationship just so you could get what you wanted and when you were done with me, you would throw me away." Do any of those statements sound familiar?

All of us have stories of rejection. We have stories of times that we thought a person was committed to us in some way -- or we hoped he/she was, but that person turned on us or turned out to be different than we had hoped. Maybe we thought someone was going to come through for us and then he/she didn't. We know that feeling. We know what it is like.

And painful feelings of rejection run deep! What we really want is to be able to trust people and know that they are going to be there for us. So what happens when they are not there for us?

Sometimes there is a legitimate realization, as in dating, where one person recognizes that the other person is not a good "fit" for him/her. Then one says to the other, "I just don't want to date you anymore."

That is a part of dating. Though it is legitimate, it can still hurt -- especially when one person thinks the other may be "the one" or that the other feels the same way he/she does. So at times, rejection could be legitimate, but even there, the pain can run very deep.

BELIEFS AND STATEGIES TO DEFEND AGAINST THE PAIN

What beliefs, then, do we learn from pain? First of all, we learn that we do not want any more of it. No one likes pain -- especially the pain of being rejected in relationships. And we do not want the pain of being RESPONSIBLE. So how do we keep ourselves from the discomfort and sometimes debilitating effects of pain? How do we protect ourselves?

One way we deal with it is to get defensive -- "No, it's not me!" If we can convince the other party that we are not responsible, maybe we can keep them from disliking us. We find ways of saying, "No, no! I'm a good person. I wouldn't do that! I wouldn't say that." "No, it's not me."

Another method of protection would be to avoid getting into the same painful situation again. "I was hurt in a dating relationship that I was in, so I don't want to date anymore." "My speech did not go well. I want nothing to do with speaking in public." "I was hurt trying out for a sport. I don't like sports now." Whatever the specifics are that we tell ourselves, we determine how we got hurt and make a choice not to do that again.

Another way we protect ourselves from pain is to "kill" our longings. Sometimes the decision is made to "stop feeling." "I won't feel anymore; therefore, I won't hurt!"

"You can't make me feel!" "I won't be sad!" "I won't ever be happy." "If I'm happy, then I can come down from that. That can hurt. I just won't feel!"

Some people go through life somewhat stoic -- like there is no feeling there. They refuse to feel anything. It is a way of killing pain.

We can protect by killing longings. "I won't want anything in life." "I won't care about anything in life." "I won't love or be loved."

The person who "kills" his or her longings thinks, "I'll just kill my longings and, therefore, I won't be hurt. I might be cynical. I'll LAUGH at life! I just won't care about anything. You can't hurt me!"

Teenagers are sometimes known to respond that way. An authority figure may say, "Well, you're going to be grounded!" or "You're not allowed to have a friend over!"

And the teenager says, "I don't care!"

"Well, you can't have ... uh ... your video game."

"I don't care."

"Well, we won't let you have the car then!"

"Fine!"

And no matter what the authority figure does, it does not matter. What the teenager is saying is, "I'm in ultimate control because you can't hurt me! I won't let you in!"

If godliness is the goal, however, then there is a willingness to hurt -- a willingness to be rejected. There is a willingness to love and endure pain -- to get involved, and if it does not work out, to accept that.

Again, God built within us a mechanism that causes us to try to get away from pain. That is a good thing. It is a survival mechanism.

But sometimes something else is going on. Rather than being committed to godliness, the commitment is to comfort and no pain.

Remember, there is nothing wrong with comfort. Even Jesus slept on a "cushion" rather than on the hard floor in the stern of the boat (Mark 4:38).

And there is nothing wrong with saying, "I don't want pain." None of us do. Even Christ openly acknowledged that He would prefer to avoid the pain and rejection of the cross (Matt. 26:39). That is legitimate.

But when the GOAL in life is comfort, if that is what life is about, then too much importance is being placed on it. When comfort is the most important thing, then we are no longer seeking God's best for us.

God says, "Will you believe you have enough (2 Cor. 4:7-9, Rom. 8:38) and will you live your life for godliness -- even if it involves pain sometimes?" "Will you live your life to love well -- even if it is painful sometimes?"

When we say, "NO! I don't want to do that! I WANT my life to be comfortable!" then we are going in a direction that is opposed to godliness. Getting our needs met apart from God becomes our god!

There can be a fine line between taking care of oneself and making comfort one's god. You might say, "Oh, yeah, I know God is all I need. I want to go out there and love well." You can say that and believe that, and yet live a life where that is not true. You can still live your life to get others to like you and try to keep yourself from being hurt. And sometimes you do not even know you are doing it until something happens where it is pointed out to you or you get caught in the act and see it.

Every sinner's commitment is to remain comfortably in control of his/her world. In other words -- no pain! We want NO pain.

So when sin entered, a major goal became "Self-Protection." We try to protect ourselves from responsibility. We try to protect ourselves from rejection.

And again, remember that there is a proper sense of self-protection in the same way there is a proper sense of self-enhancement (self-care). The message here is not, "Let's walk into abusive situations" or "Just stay around and take abuse." Even Christ escaped the clutches of the crowd at times (Luke 4:28-30). And as a baby, Christ escaped abuse from Herod when his parents left during the night with Him and fled to Egypt (Matthew 2:13). To say one should never, ever protect oneself from pain is foolish!

There is a difference between "turning the other cheek" and being abused. When one is making a choice for the ultimate good of another -- that will teach a lesson, promote the gospel, or "heap coals of fire" on his head, then it may be legitimate to "turn the other cheek." But to allow abuse in a way that reinforces another's sinfulness in not what God intended.

Christ took abuse when He allowed Himself to be crucified, yet at other times He avoided going to a particular place because He knew some would try to kill him -- John 11:54 -- or he escaped crowds in order to get rest, or told His disciples to get rest -- Mark 6:30. In most cases it seems that God wants us to take care of our bodies and our spiritual lives and protect them from harm if we can. If He brings abuse or pain along that we have no control over, that is one thing; but to purposely put ourselves into abusive or painful situations is not typically what God asks of us.

There is a time to say, "You know what? The way you are treating me is not right and I'm not going to allow you to treat me this way anymore." And you can actually not only protect yourself by leaving, but you can be doing what is best for the abuser by not reinforcing or rewarding the foolishness of thinking that he/she can get away with being abusive. Leaving can be others-centered. It can help the abuser grow. That is legitimate.

There is a proper sense of self-care. There is a way of taking care of oneself and thinking about oneself in the correct way that comes from a proper sense of self-enhancement. But the point to be made in this section is that in his sinfulness, man has made a commitment to avoid pain at all cost and has developed strategies to avoid that pain. One's commitment to getting his needs met is the impetus for using the protective strategy of pain avoidance. Self-protection has become his "god." That is illegitimate.

FEAR -- THE CAUSE OF SELF-PROTECTION

The causative element of self-protection is fear. FEAR is another result of sin. Remember PRIDE is the causative element of self-enhancement.

Eve said, "I want to be like God. I'm in control of my world. I'm getting my needs met. It's all about me." That is pride.

With self-protection, the main element is fear. Fear is what causes us to want to protect ourselves. What was the first thing that Adam and Eve did when sin entered? They hid! (Gen. 3:8-10).

When sin entered, the thinking became, "I want to hide and protect myself." "I don't want anybody to see me." And all of a sudden, I know I'm naked.

Donald Miller commented on "nakedness" when he spoke at the Warsaw (Indiana) Community Church in 2006. He made the point that it is all relational! God made us relational creatures, and hiding is a way that we say, "I don't want anybody to see me -- because if you do, you're going to reject me."

Before sin, the reaction of Adam and Eve was, "I don't care if you see me."

Why?

"Because, I am focused on you. You are focused on me. We love each other."

In marriage, you can be naked and not ashamed. In marriage, you can be exposed and vulnerable and say, "This is nice. This is appropriate."

But it is not appropriate in a fallen world. It would not be good if all people took their clothes off right now because in a fallen world, when you do that, bad things happen to you.

Nakedness HAS TO BE in a love-trust relationship, where each knows that the other wants what is best for him/her and that one is not going to take advantage of the other. Each knows that the other is not going to hurt him/her.

Some of the worst forms of rejection are lovers who have been vulnerable physically and then one of them says to the other, "I don't want you anymore." Or one sees the other in his or her vulnerability -- whether it be emotionally or physically -- and says, "I don't want you."

Now that is what hurts deeply. That type of rejection is the focus here. To be seen in one's most vulnerable situation and to be told, "I don't want you," is what we try to protect ourselves from.

So we find "covers." We find ways of looking good, wearing nice clothes, presenting a certain image -- covering up our imperfections and presenting whatever we feel we need to, to protect ourselves.

Man is the only species of the animal kingdom that wears clothes. Think about that. Animals do not clothe themselves. Because they are not relational in the same way that man is (as image-bearers), they are not aware of their nakedness and vulnerability in the way that man is. Thus, they have no fear in that regard.

We (man) are the ones wearing clothes AND, add to that, we want them to be a certain kind of clothing. They have to be in style. They have to be new. And we want them to be the kind that help our body appear the most perfect: black -- to slim down some areas or to look "tough," gathered in some places give a fuller appearance or a lighter color to make some areas appear bigger, maybe a tank top to show muscles, nylons to cover leg imperfections, heels to make the person appear taller, or a jacket to make the person look slimmer or more "rugged" or more professional, etc. They have to be kind of WOW! Why?

We want our "covers" to look good! We want people to think, "You're impressive!"

And add to that, if someone has a little extra weight, or the muscles are not what they used to be, or there are scars or certain parts of the body that he or she does not want others to see, he/she looks for clothing that covers the imperfections and enhances the way he/she looks. This is especially a concern of many women. "Does this make me look fat?" "Does this make me look more bright or dull, short or tall?" We all want clothing that will make us look better -- maybe even a little deceiving -- making us look better than we actually are.

Now it is not always beauty that is being sought. Some might think, "Hiding is better than revealing. If you know what is really there, if I do not have clothing that does a good job of hiding things, you may not like me. You may not want me. You may not want to be in relationship with me."

So we have ways of protecting ourselves from rejection, even in our clothing! If that is true with clothing, how is that true in our personalities, in our spiritual lives, or in our emotional lives? "I want to find covers that make me look good." How often do we think, "I want to find covers that will make you impressed with me"?

So what we want to look at next is all of those different covers that we use that we hope make us look good. But before we do that, it is important to remember and understand that our deepest **LONGING** is: **To be known and to be loved**. Our deepest longing is that "you know me completely and you still love me."

But our deepest **FEAR** is: **To be known and to be rejected**. The thinking is, "I'm afraid that you're going to see me naked physically or emotionally or spiritually and not want me. You're going to see my blemishes. You're going to see my sin. You're going to see my faults. And you won't want me."

Fear is a core result of sin -- fear of exposure, fear of vulnerability, fear of being responsible, fear of feeling negative emotions, fear of failure, fear of being destroyed or undone.

That is the tension we live with: Our deepest longing -- "Please know me and love me," Our deepest fear -- "You are going to know me and reject me." What do we do with that?

Well, each of us has choices. We can take the risk to go ahead and let others get to know us, hoping that they love us. But if they don't, we will have to live with that pain OR we can make the choice NOT to let others get to know us, but allow them to fall in love with our image. We can let others fall in love with the person that they "think" we are. That will hurt less. And then, maybe in time, we can slowly throw in those little faults. "If I've already got you loving me, then maybe you can handle those little faults -- or big faults -- little by little as they come." At least, that is our thinking.

It usually does not work that way, though. Often the reaction comes out more like, "Why didn't you tell me?" or "Why did you try to hide this from me?" and the response is, "Well, I didn't think you could handle me if you knew this about me; I didn't think you would love me."

So again, remember what was mentioned earlier. This does not mean that people should all run out and be naked physically or emotionally or spiritually. That is not appropriate in a fallen world.

But do we have places where we can go with those vulnerable parts of us and be accepted? Is there a place where others can know us, where someone knows us, where we can take our clothes off emotionally and still be loved?

Just as in the physical world, if we wear clothes all the time -- in the shower, during intimate relations with a spouse – there is a problem. The same thing is true if we live our emotional, spiritual lives in such a way that we never take our clothes off, ever. Then something is wrong. Our lives are being dominated by FEAR. We are being controlled by the idea that someone might see through and reject us. Now there is a problem!

We need to ask ourselves, "Do I have those places where I'm known and I'm loved?" "Do I take the risk to be known and loved? Or do I never allow myself to take that risk?" And "Is fear of rejection driving me more than it should be?" God gives us ultimate acceptance and love, seeing all of our flaws, yet without rejection. We can move out into our world knowing we have His continual involvement and support. As ambassadors for Christ (2 Cor. 5:20), we can represent God by showing that kind of love to others, and as part of God's family, we have others who can give us "tastes" of that kind of love as God works through them. We do not need to fear, as God is always with us.

FREUD'S DEFENSE MECHANISMS

So what happens when we protect ourselves from rejection? We get defensive. And we employ various mechanisms when we do. Freud called the **defensive** tactics that we use **Defense Mechanisms.**

Freud was the first psychologist to acknowledge this phenomenon. Freud did not come up with something new. He merely categorized and labeled something that he observed happening. We employ defense mechanisms in order to avoid pain, to divert attention away from our sin, and/or so that people will like us -- without knowing the REAL us.

Crabb calls the idea of relating without really knowing, a "Layer-to-Layer" relationship. The idea is something like this: "I like your layers. You like my layers. We have that kind of relationship. But let's not ever take our layers off, because we may not like each other."

So we may go around smiling a lot. We may act spiritual. We may act happy. We may act in control or confident. We may act mean or strong-willed. Whatever method we employ, in essence what we are saying is, "You will like my layers and consequently like me."

So what are the defense mechanisms that help keep layers in place? The following are some that Freud noticed and labeled.

RATIONALIZATION

Rationalization: If one acts in an unacceptable manner, he/she finds a way of making the unacceptable behavior SOUND acceptable. When one rationalizes, the attempt is to hide the true motivations by justifying the actions. What are ways that we rationalize?

"I really didn't want to do that, but I had no other choice! I had to."

"You know, I'm typically not like this. This is not me at all!"

When the author has heard those words, the question that looms is, "Well, then who was it? Is there someone else in there?" Maybe those who used to be categorized as having "multiple personalities" may not have been that bizarre after all! Maybe we do the same thing, but just haven't labeled it with a name.

"Boy, I don't know what happened. I was really tired and . . . I had a test coming up and . . . I had to be in class from 1 to 4 . . . and so, you know, if it wasn't for all that, I wouldn't have acted the way I did."

What are we doing? Rationalizing!

"My roommate really needed someone to talk to last night, so that's why I didn't get my paper done."

"I'm a good person and I don't get angry. I'm very spiritual and better than this, so don't think badly of me"

Can you think of any biblical examples? What about Saul's conversation with Samuel in 1 Samuel 15? Though Samuel had instructed Saul to attack the Amalekites -- totally destroying "everything that belongs to them" (v. 3), Saul had disobeyed. Yet, when he met with Samuel after the battle, Saul said to him, "The Lord bless you! I have carried out the Lord's instructions" (v. 13).

So Samuel said to him, "What then is this bleating of sheep in my ears? What is this lowing of cattle that I hear?" (v. 14).

Saul answered, "The soldiers brought them from the Amalekites; they spared the best of the sheep and cattle to sacrifice to the Lord your God, but we totally destroyed the rest" (v.15).

Samuel continued, (v. 19) ". . . Why did you not obey the Lord? Why did you pounce on the plunder and do evil in the eyes of the Lord?"

"'But I did obey the Lord,' Saul said. 'I went on the mission the Lord assigned me. I completely destroyed the Amalekites and brought back Agag their king. The soldiers took sheep and cattle from the plunder, the best of what was devoted to God, in order to sacrifice them to the Lord your God at Gilgal'" (vv. 20-21).

What was Saul doing? He was trying to put what he did in a "good light." He was rationalizing.

Do we try to "spiritualize" our actions as well? "I wasn't really gossiping. I just wanted them to know about the incident so they could pray more effectively." I will find some way of making this legitimate!

"I know I was watching movies with nudity, but I really want to be informed about what the kids are watching today so I can help them. I want to know what they are putting in their minds so that I can be better prepared." That is rationalization.

This author recalls a remark made by a former pastor of his youth that illustrates this defense mechanism well. When at the wheel of his vehicle and racing to an event, the pastor realized that this author was peering at the speedometer and noticing that he was speeding (going 10-15 miles over the legal limit). The pastor excused his actions by remarking, "I'm on God's time."

PROJECTION

Projection. We find examples of this in the Bible as well. Remember how David's brother Eliab treated him? (1 Sam. 17:28). He said, in essence, "You insolent brat! I know why you're here! I know you're conceited and how wicked your heart is! I know what's going on!" He was projecting himself onto David.

"Projection" means: attributing one's own unacceptable feelings to others. People who attribute their own unacceptable feelings to others are PROJECTING those feelings onto the other person. "David YOU are wicked. YOU are conceited. YOU need to repent."

DISPLACEMENT

Displacement (or what this author likes to call, "Kick the Cat Syndrome"). You are at work and you get called in by your boss. Your boss says, "You know, this is your annual review. You didn't do a very good job this year. You'd better work harder or I'm going to fire you."

You are feeling very upset, but you cannot yell at your boss because he or she signs your paycheck. You think it is unfair, but because you cannot express it to anyone there, you walk out of the office at the end of the day, kind of miffed.

(Source: Co-Author, Edgington, 2011)

So you go home and your wife says, "We're having pizza." You respond by yelling, "Pizza again! Why do we have to have pizza again! Can't we have anything good?!"

Now she is upset, but she does not want to yell at you because you are angry and you will get more upset, so she goes and yells at the kids. "Kids, you're room is dirty and you haven't made your beds! Don't you have your homework done yet?!"

But they cannot yell at Mom because then they could be punished, so what do they do? They kick the cat!

When a person takes out his unacceptable impulses onto some innocent stimulus rather than the one producing the anger, it is displacement.

If you have watched the old movie, *It's a Wonderful Life*, you have seen another good example of displacement. After George finds out that his Uncle Billy has lost a large sum of the Building and Loan's money, George comes home, yells at the kids, scatters all of the stuff on the desk, and yells at his child's teacher.

(Source: doctormacro.com, 2011)

Displacement is where one redirects his emotions and actions from the original object to another -- usually to a "safer" or more acceptable substitute. This can happen after a romantic breakup. Sometimes one of the affected parties will quickly begin dating someone else. It has been called being "on the rebound." The Beach Boys sang about this in their '60s song, "Help Me, Rhonda."

One may caution a friend, "You don't want to 'go out' with that person because he's/she's 'on the rebound.'" What does that mean?

It means that you cannot trust the reality of his/her love because he/she may just be compensating for the loss of a relationship. He/She does not want to feel the "hurt," so he/she immediately replaces the previous person with someone new. He/she is willing to fall in love right away, as a way of not hurting. He/She "redirects his/her emotions" from the original source to a new one.

Some people are always in a "love relationship." That does not necessarily mean that is not appropriate sometimes, but many times it is a way of not hurting about the previous relationship. It may just be that they are "displacing" their love to a different stimulus rather than the one they were really in love with.

COMPENSATION

Compensation. Here is a guy who is not particularly handsome, probably was not the star athlete, probably was not the most dated guy in high school, but he found a way of making himself feel good. He found a way to be successful and even gain the respect of others. Compensation is the striving to cover up a deficiency or unmet desire in one area of life, with achievement and/or excellence in another area.

Compensation can take many forms. Sometimes the compensator is the computer "geek." Or the compensator may decide to compensate with musical ability, artistry, intelligence, a unique skill, etc., to make up for an imagined -- or real -- deficiency. He will emphasize or build on a strength in order to *cover* the deficiency. And if he got "picked on" in high school by one of you, he may enjoy the power he feels at the company where you are working for him.

Could Leah have been compensating for her lack of beauty and love from her husband by intending to make use of her fertility and bear as many children as possible for Jacob (Genesis 29, 30)? (Peninnah could have been flaunting that same "gift" to Hannah in 1 Samuel 1 to cover up the deficiency that she was loved less by her husband, Elkanah.) Could young men compensate for their youth by flaunting their strength and old men use their gray hairs to signify wisdom -- avoiding focus on their degenerating bodies (Prov. 20:29)? Compensation takes various forms and can be seen in many situations.

(Source: Fotosearch, 2011)

UNDOING

Undoing. Undoing is where we attempt to "undo" the harm that we did. We try to take back our improper thoughts or behavior.

You may have had times when you have talked about someone, really "ripping" on him or her, and the person you are conversing with agrees. Then it gets quiet and you both start feeling a little guilty for gossiping about him. So what do you do next?

You say, "Well, he is a brother, isn't he?"
"Yes, he is. He's somebody we should pray for."
"That's right."
Or sometimes someone adds, "But bless his heart."
Or you might say, "But I really do like her new hair cut."

We have a way of "making it okay." Instead of saying, "You know what? We should not have gossiped, We should not have talked about him or her like that, It was wrong," we try to *undo* the harm that we really wanted to do.

Proverbs 26:18-19 says, "Like a madman shooting firebrands or deadly arrows is a man who deceives his neighbor and says, 'I was only joking!' Could pretending to be joking be a way of attempting to "undo" the wrong that has been done -- at least in the eye of the offended? Maybe for some it can.

REACTION FORMATION

Reaction Formation: "Actively expressing the opposite impulse of what you really want to do" -- that is *Reaction Formation*. "A common pattern in Reaction Formation is where the person uses 'excessive behavior,' for example using exaggerated friendliness when the person is actually feeling unfriendly" ("Reaction Formation," par 2). Maybe you fear that you will be criticized for something, so you very visibly act in a way that shows you are personally a long way from the feared position. You probably know stories of preachers who have "harped" about sin, especially sexual sin, and sometimes homosexuality: yet sometime later they have an affair with their secretary or another man. And you wonder, "How did that happen?" The evangelist, Jimmy Swaggart, and pastor, Ted Haggard, fit this category.

When preachers demonstrate reaction formation, they seem to be saying, "The more I preach about it, the more, maybe, it will go away in me. The more I can preach about it to YOU and get YOU to stop doing it, maybe it will stop happening in me. That is how I will deal with it in ME." Instead of just saying, "You know what? I have it in me, I am a sexual being, I lust, I have problems, but here is what God is doing to help me deal with that," they would rather allude to the idea that "I don't have it in me." They make it sound like "You have got it in you! And I am going to call you to repent!" That is how they try to deal with what is in them.

Someone using reaction formation thinks, "The harder I push in the opposite direction, the more I hope it will go away." Some people will take up a cause as their way of compensating -- "If I really put all of my energy into this cause, then I do not have to deal with this stuff inside me." Reaction formation means expressing the opposite of what you feel inside.

DENIAL

Denial. In denial, one simply denies a reality that exists – one that is too uncomfortable for him to accept. He denies that he has certain feelings -- that certain things are in him. He denies an event has occurred or that the consequences of an event or situation will occur.

Sometimes it seems to be God's way of helping people deal with a situation. Some have called it, "the shock absorber of the soul." If someone comes to him and says, "Your loved one just died in a car wreck," the first thing he may say is, "No! It can't be!" The first thing people often do is deny.

"No! I just talked to her a half hour ago!" Why do people say things like that? Do we really think someone cannot die in a half hour? Of course not. But in our minds, it just does not seem like it can happen. "That can't be! If I talked to her a half hour ago, she can't be dead!" We know that's not true rationally, but emotionally, that is how it feels, so we say, "No! I can't believe that!" "The initial denial protects that person from the emotional shock and intense grief that often accompanies news of death" (Friedrich, 2007).

But for some people, the denial of death can last a long time. Some women have been known to do things like continuing to set out a place setting at mealtime for a husband who died twenty years previously. It is a way of saying, "No! He's not gone!" Some do not sell his clothes or move anything that was his. Everything stays in its place, the same as when he lived there. The thinking is, "I cannot deal with the fact that he is gone. Therefore, I will not accept it."

When people are diagnosed with a chronic or terminal illness, you often see denial. The receivers of such news may think, "It's not so bad," or "I'll get over it," or "I'm going to beat this." Often they make no changes in their lifestyle and act as if there is no truth to the diagnosis.

But denial can involve things other than death. Sometimes people use lies -- even to themselves -- to prevent facing a variety of unpleasant realities.

Denial can happen in response to any painful event, thought, or feeling that we don't want to acknowledge is real. ". . . For instance, some children are taught that anger is wrong in any situation. As adults, if these individuals experience feelings of anger, they are likely to deny their feelings to others. Cultural standards and expectations can encourage denial of subjective experience. Men who belong to cultures with extreme notions of masculinity may view fear as a sign of weakness and deny internal feelings of fear. . ." (Friedrich, 2007).

Certain personality disorders tend to be characterized by denial more than others. For example, those with "narcissistic personality disorder" deny information that suggests they are not perfect. Antisocial behavior is characterized by denial of the harm done to others (such as with sexual offenders or substance abusers).

"Denial can also be exhibited on a large scale — among groups, cultures, or even nations. . . . The large-scale denial . . . by some that the World War II Holocaust ever occurred is a good example" (Friedrich, 2007). We certainly see denial at work in addictive disorders. People deny that they have a problem or that there are any negative consequences, even though life is caving in around them.

Do we have biblical examples of denial? What about Sarah when she heard that she was going to have a child in her old age? What did she do? Genesis 18:12 says that she laughed! She thought to herself, "After I have become old, shall I have pleasure, my lord being old also?" (NASB). She was given information directly from the Lord, yet she protected herself from the pain of being disappointed if that pleasure never came to her and therefore she chose not to believe it.

OTHER EXAMPLES OF BEHAVIORS AND TRAITS THAT CAN BE SELF-ENHANCING AND SELF-PROTECTIVE STRATEGIES

As we continue to look at the ways that our longings "bend" away from God, we now focus more at length at the topics of self-enhancing and self-protective strategies. It is good to remember throughout this discussion that not all self-protective and self-enhancing behaviors are wrong. There is a time to take care of ourselves and make ourselves better people. There is a good kind of pride we can have in our work. There is a time to protect ourselves. We shouldn't disclose everything in a fallen world where people could hurt us. Those would be good self-enhancing/self-protective behaviors.

The word "strategies" will be used to talk about methods employed to self-enhance and/or self-protect that are *not* what God desires. As each of the following strategies is introduced, try to determine how it could be used illegitimately/sinfully to get needs met or protect from pain. How are the strategies used in ways that are not pleasing to God?

(Souce: Hironaka, dreamstime.com, 2011)

"Sweet and Nice." How could that be used as a strategy to get needs met? There is nothing wrong with being sweet and nice, in and of itself; but it can be a self-enhancing, self-protecting strategy. What could "sweet and nice" **get** you?

It could get people to like you. It could get people to say nice things about you: "She is so sweet! She is always smiling. I have never seen her angry!" And the observer thinks, "I like that person."

What could it **protect** you from? Think about a sweet old grandmother who never gets angry -- she bakes you pies and seems like one of the nicest people you know. Maybe no one will ever know she has problems.

Maybe no one will ever get angry at her or confront her. Who is going to say, "This might be a self-enhancing, self-protecting strategy"?

If someone dared, it would be very likely that another would turn on the confronter with a question such as, "How could you talk to my grandmother that way?" followed with, "You mean, nasty person!!"

And you know what? "Sweet and Nice" could be a way of making life work without God. Even though it is "sweet and nice," it could still be sinful! (Of course, that does not mean that it IS sinful -- just that it COULD BE.)

Make an attempt to get in your mind that some of the behaviors that you may have thought were good, might not always be. What you are seeing may be a self-enhancing or self-protective strategy.

Now it does not mean that every time you encounter a "sweet and nice" person that you need to think, "I know what you are doing; you are sinning right now." Just keep your mind open to the fact that sometimes it is a protective strategy. Challenge yourself with, "I wonder what might be happening in this person's soul as I see this possible layer." Maybe it is not a layer! Maybe he/she really IS sweet. But if it is a layer, what happens when "sweet" does not "work"?

We talked about "faces" in chapter three. The two reasons why we wear illegitimate "faces" are to enhance ourselves or to protect ourselves. That is all it is. So when we are not feeling happy and we feel the need to look happy, that is when our "happy face" -- our "sweet and niceness" -- becomes a strategy. That is when the "face" or a "persona" is intentionally "donned" with the intention of accomplishing a self-centered purpose.

Caretaking. "He's always thinking of other people." (We call it "co-dependency" in the counseling world.) People in this category are always caretaking – nurturing others, taking people in. If you were a "caretaker," how could you benefit from that?

Maybe you are going to **get** the kind of love and admiration that you never received growing up. Nobody ever took care of you that way. Maybe you hope to get the kind of love you always wanted.

Maybe people would appreciate you and make comments like, "He/She is SO giving!" "He never thinks about himself. He is always thinking about other people!" Maybe people would like you more if you were "there" for others. People may depend on you or need you if you were giving. So you may "latch on." You may depend on their dependency on you. Co-dependents tend to latch on to people who are needy because when the co-dependent is needed, he feels wanted and loved.

It is kind of a crazy system because after awhile people take advantage of the caretaker, and then the strategy does not meet his/her needs anymore. He/she does not want to be taken advantage of, but because co-dependent/caretaking people tend to gravitate toward people who are needy, there are those who want to avoid effort and allow the co-dependent to do their "grunt" work or perform tasks for them that they really could do themselves.

(Source: Dreamstime.com, Deal, 2011)

What does caretaking **protect** you from? (This is a little more subtle.) If you are always taking care of others, concerned about others, and focusing on others' needs, you don't have to look at yourself. It protects you from others looking at you or, even, from you looking at yourself.

You do not WANT to focus on yourself because then you might have to be responsible or face pain you would rather not face. You would rather keep the focus on the people that you are taking care of. It is a POWERFUL protective strategy!

Controlling. When one is being controlling, what does it get him? Well, ... whatever he wants! One controls to **get** what he wants.

Marie Barone, the mother of Raymond in the 1990s TV show, *Everybody Loves Raymond*, is also a good example of a controlling person. She gets what she wants.

What does controlling **protect** a person from? When we control our world, it may protect us from surprise. Life is always predictable because we are in control.

What else does it protect us from? Rejection? Nobody is going to reject us because we are in control. (At least that is what is thought. And it can work for awhile.)

And how many times have you heard, "Just go along with what they want because it's a lot worse if you don't!"

What are we doing if we "just go along"? We are giving in to their control, so they can get what they want and do not have to feel pain. And we do not have to go through the pain of dealing with them being in pain or being upset with us.

If you have the mother demanding that her children come home for Christmas, sometimes the father gets involved too. While the mother is still crying and after she has been told that one of her children is not coming on Christmas day, then the father gets on the phone.

"What are you doing to your mother? Why are you doing this to her?" Why do you think he is saying this now?

Now the father is trying to control! Why? He is thinking, "Do you know what I have to deal with now? I am going to have to live with her like this! I don't want to deal with that discomfort, that pain. No! You guys ARE coming for Christmas!"

What is her fear? She is afraid of their not coming and her being hurt. If she can "control" them, then she protects herself from that pain. And he is protecting himself from the discomfort and pain of his wife being disappointed.

Busy-ness. What does Busy-ness **get** us? If someone is always busy, always on the go, seemingly always able to add "one more thing" and do it well, what does that get for that person? Satisfaction? Acceptance? People tend to like busy people. People tend to give them awards and accolades and say, "Look at all you're doing!"

What does busy-ness **protect** us from? It might protect (Source: Dreamstime.com, Georghiou, 2011) us from having to think about whatever pain we are dealing with. And busy-ness can protect us from having to get involved with others. We do not have time for messy and threatening relationships.

What else does it protect me from? Purposelessness? If I am not busy, I do not feel like my life has any point. I do not feel valuable. "Busy-ness can cover over a lot of insecurities and pain.

And what about silence? There are those that keep their lives busy and noisy -- because if their lives are silent, they may have to think about what is inside. They may actually have to think about feelings and pain, so they stay busy and keep it noisy.

Withdrawal. If I keep things hidden from others, if I am quiet and reserved, what does that **get** me? How about control? I can control what you know about me and my feelings and what is inside.

What does that **protect** me from? Criticism? (If they do not notice me, they cannot criticize me or make fun of me and they cannot hurt me. If they do not have any information about me, then they cannot use anything against me.) Withdrawal can protect me from being "wrong." It can also keep people from getting too close.

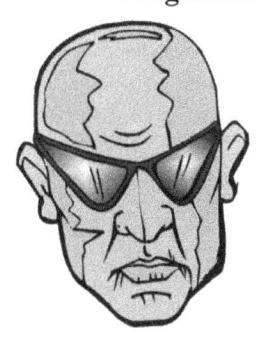

Toughness. How about the **"tough" face**? Do some people seem to want to portray a "tough" demeanor? How would a person go about looking "tough"? He might choose to do things that would intimidate others. He could portray that Clint Eastwood, "Nothing gets through" mentality -- that "bullets bounce off of me," Superman image!

Why would anyone want to look or appear tough? What does it **get**? -- A feeling of power! This is the kind of guy that gets what he wants!

The actor previously mentioned and (Source: Clipart, 16183624, 2011) known for "toughness" in earlier movie days was

171

Clint Eastwood. (A more current example might be Bruce Willis.) In many of the old western movies he walks into town and declares, "I'm going to get what I want and NO ONE is going to mess with me!" When some men have watched those movies they have started thinking, "YEAH!! That's what I want to be like!"

Many times men think that is the definition of a man -- he gets what he wants. He intimidates. He puts fear into people's hearts. He threatens and they melt! He gets a level of respect.

Then there will be women who will admire that and say, "Oh! I want him!" Why? Because he's tough!

How can "toughness" be **self-protecting**? No one ever gets too close. If you are "tough," you never get close to others and they never get close to you. Can you imagine Clint Eastwood going up to a guy in the movie and saying, "Can we talk about *feelings* today? I'm feeling just a little hurt and disappointed." No! He's not going to do that! Why not? Because he is tough! He never gets too close to anyone. No one ever has a chance to look very deeply inside.

But there are women that want to appear tough too. Why would a woman want to appear tough? -- Maybe for some of the same reasons as men. Maybe she does not want others to get close. Maybe she wants to divert attention away from her so that others do not see the pain inside.

When this author has taught prisoners, one thing they have expressed is that "toughness" helps keep a distance from others. If people are "tough," they can protect themselves from others getting too close and hurting them emotionally or physically. It is certainly unlikely that you are going to confront the tough person and tell him he has got problems. Billy Crystal, in *Analyze This*, said, "I don't want to tell him that he's got problems . . . He could kill me!" (Warner Brothers, 1999).[15]

Intelligence. Sometimes people put on an intelligent "persona." They try to appear intelligent or put on an intelligent "face."

Do you know of people who wear the "intelligent face"? Could you put on a "face" that might cause others to believe that you are smart? How would you go about doing that?

One way would be to use big words. Or you could discuss your accomplishments. You could spend time reading or appear to be reading impressive books and literature. You could be quick to give advice -- even when you are not asked for it.

What would that **get** for you? Respect. Admiration. What might that **protect** you from? How about being belittled and the rejected

---

15

feeling that goes along with that? Portraying intelligence *can be used as a strategy to meet needs*.

Humor. What about humor? How could "cracking" jokes or being the "clown" be a strategy? Maybe it **gets** people to "like" us. Maybe it **gets** us to be noticed.

What could it **protect** us from? It could keep others from getting to know the pain that is hiding inside. One song talks about the "tears of a clown, when there's no one around." Or maybe it diverts attention from reality and things not wanting to be faced. The "clown" is not always as jovial as he or she may seem. Though many "clowns" really just want to have fun, to get everyone involved, or to cheer people up, at times joking and "clowning around" can be used as a self-enhancing and/or self-protective strategy.

Leadership.

"He's always a leader." "He manages so well!" "Wow! She can really take charge! She is so comfortable in front." What does leadership get us? -- Again, lots of accolades. It gets us attention. People notice us and admire us.

(Source, Dreamstime.com, Lindie, "King Penguins on Ice Bay," 2011)

And when you are the leader, you can be in control. You can make things happen. You call the shots. You have power.

What does always being a leader **protect** us from? It protects us from feeling worthless or from people thinking that we're not important. It can protect us from being "confronted" or from having to trust or depend on someone else's decisions. It can protect us from vulnerability. If one is a leader, he does not have to ever let someone else take over or help him -- guide him -- because then he could get hurt.

Perfectionism. What is the definition of a perfectionist? Some say it is "someone who takes great pains and gives them to others." There is a lot of truth to that -- that we not only make our own lives painful, but we make others' lives painful as well because WE HAVE to have things a certain way.

What does perfectionism **get** us? It can give us a sense of control. We also gain respect and the reliance of others on our performance. We gain admiration when our work is evaluated. People go, "Wow! You always get the best score," "You are always the top person," or "I can trust you to provide a nice product when I assign you a task." We gain the trust of others.

What does it **protect** us from? Failure. If you are perfect, you never have to fail. (We may think it earns us favor with God -- though we know Scripture teaches the contrary.) You are never below the standard because if you are ever below the standard, bad things can happen to you. It can protect you from the disappointment of things being done wrong. It can protect you from feeling out of control.

Self-contempt. Why do some people "beat themselves up" all the time? What does that **get** them? (Yes, it REALLY CAN get them something.) -- Maybe attention. People feel sorry for them. Maybe it will get them care and concern. -- Maybe involvement and support. If they are "beating themselves up," others may go, "No! No! You're a good person! Don't think that about yourself!"

It can be a way of getting relationship. Maybe people will see them as humble and they will like them better.

Maybe it gives them a sense of control. If they berate themselves, others will not join in. We tend to not want to "whack" someone who is "whacking" himself.

What does it **protect** us from? As was just stated, it may protect us from others berating us. It protects us from expectations. Nobody is going to expect anything out of us because we are so deficient!

Maybe it protects us from being confronted. (This goes along with protection from being berated.) Who is going to criticize somebody who's already beating himself up! You are not going to confront him. If you did confront him, he may reply, "I am worse than what I thought! Now I feel even more terrible and you made me feel this way!" Chances are that no one is going to confront him!

And it protects us from taking specific responsibility. If one thinks he is such a horrible, defective person at everything, then he feels he does not have to take responsibility for anything specifically. This is a bit like protection from expectations. "It wasn't that I didn't study for the test. I am just stupid and I will never get it, and I don't know why I am even in school!"

That is different from, "You know, I probably could have studied another hour last night and that would have helped. It is really my fault. That could have helped my grade."

But the "self-contempt" strategy is used so that the user can believe, "I would rather have this 'global' responsibility -- that I am a problem in every way and just stupid, so I don't have to take on specific responsibility." It protects him from being responsible for specific tasks and events.

Super-spirituality. If someone is "super-spiritual," what might you think about him or her? You may think, "Wow! She always shows so much emotion when she prays!" "He knows so much Scripture and Bible doctrine! Isn't he wonderful?" "She's always humming praise songs. She's so close to God!" "He's always got his Bible with him!" "He's always claiming God's promises." "She's always quoting Scripture." And the "super-spiritual" person on a Christian campus can draw a lot of praise. The "super-spiritual" person might **get** admiration and positive treatment along with leadership opportunities. He can make his mark and feel valuable.

What does it **protect** him from? Who is going to challenge the super-spiritual person? Who is going to say, "Maybe this is a self-enhancing, self-protective strategy!?" -- Probably no one! It feels as if you are confronting God! It does not tend to happen.

So if you find yourself thinking, "I could never say something like that to that person because she is sooo godly!" you may be witnessing a self-enhancing and self-protective strategy.

Counseling. Remember Dr. Leo Marvin on the movie, *What about Bob*? He was doing counseling and wrote a book in order to feel important. He used that to **get** his needs met.

What does counseling and advising others sometimes **protect** us from? If you are a counselor who is getting your needs met apart from God by making yourself look like a renowned, famous counselor (like Dr. Leo Marvin), and someone confronts you, you might turn the responsibility back to them. You might say, "What is going on in your life right now that would cause you to feel the need to confront me?" If you confront his arrogance, he may "interpret" that as *your* arrogance being projected on him.

The counselor could keep up his arrogance and façade along with the self-imposed authoritativeness that he draws from his professional title, with a reply like, "I noticed that. I notice that you don't like to talk about yourself, do you? You really like to talk about other people, and I notice that you like to point out their faults, don't you?" As a counselor, you could also give this person a diagnosis of narcissistic personality disorder or something similar. Again, there is a sense of power that comes with being an advisor or counselor.

What would the counselor be doing? He would be turning things around. Counseling can become a great way of self-protecting. Being in the authority position, the counselor has the means to insure that problem is never him. It is always the other person.

And even if the other person turns out to be obviously right, you may now react with, "Huh! So you think you're right, don't you? You like to think you're right? That's really important to you."

Counseling can protect a person from looking at himself or from others looking at him -- seeing his shortcomings. And that could keep circling around and around with the counselor continuing to keep the negative focus on the client and protecting himself from any pain or admission of wrong-doing.

CONCLUSION OF SELF-EHHANCING AND SELF-PROTECTIVE EXAMPLES

We should all have some of the previously mentioned traits. (Ecc. 3 -- There is a time for every purpose under heaven.") There is an appropriate time to be "sweet and nice." There is a time to take control of things. There is a time for humor. ("A merry heart doeth good like a medicine" -- Prov. 17:22 KJV. Happiness and humor are good for our person, our soul). It is good to "help" others as a counselor or as a leader. If you are going into surgery, you hope that your doctor is a perfectionist. Humility is appropriate -- as opposed to self-contempt where one does not value what God has given him (like Moses degrading his ability to speak -- therefore degrading that with which God had equipped him -- Ex. 4:10). Intelligence, toughness, withdrawal, busy-ness, caretaking -- all can be used for godly purposes. But when those traits become the only way one relates to his world, then it is possible that he is using them as strategies to get personal needs met and/or protect himself from pain.

Take some time to think about your own life and ask yourself, "What are my self-enhancing, self-protective strategies? What may be my ways of making life work apart from God -- that I might not have been aware of until now?"

Christians Do Not Have to Employ Strategies

CHRISTIANS WILL NOT BE DESTROYED

We will begin to stop using strategies when we deeply believe that we will not be destroyed if we are exposed and rejected. As Christians we can be hurt, but we will not be destroyed. Nothing can destroy the believer (2 Cor. 4:7-9).

If we believe that other people or things can destroy us, then we are going to have anxiety problems or other kinds of psychological difficulties. That is when we look for ways to protect ourselves. We think, "I've got to watch out. I've got to make sure I don't put myself in certain situations -- never speak in public, never relax, never smile, etc. I've got to make sure people don't see me in a certain way, because if they find out what I'm really like, they can destroy me."

God says, "No, they can't. ONLY I can do that, and I won't. I WON'T do that."

We know that from Scripture. 2 Corinthians 4:7-9: "But we have this treasure in jars of clay to show that this all-surpassing power is from God and not us. We are hard-pressed on every side, but not crushed; perplexed, but not in despair; persecuted, but not abandoned; struck down, but not destroyed."

We have something better. We have God. We have Christ in us, in jars of clay. The passage is talking about typical, common jars -- like our peanut butter jars, mayonnaise jars, or mason jars that we have cleaned out -- just common old jars that we keep things in. God is saying, "I am putting my most precious treasure in your average jar. And because you have got my diamonds in your old peanut butter jar, that jar is now priceless."

(Source: clipart.com, pbJar, 2011)

That is what Paul is trying to tell us. You have so much in your common jar that you are going to be "hard-pressed on every side, but not crushed." Nothing can crush you. You are perplexed, but not in despair. You are persecuted, but you will never be abandoned. You will be "struck down" – they will hurt you -- but you will never be destroyed.

Nothing can destroy the believer -- Romans 8:38. It does not matter what it is; nothing can separate you from the love of God -- height, depth, powers, principalities, Satan himself, tragedy, trauma, turmoil . . . NOTHING! That jar will always have what it needs. We have all we need to make it -- to be godly and to live fully. God says, "I'm on your side. I'm with you." and if He is with us, who can be against us?

QUESTIONS TO PONDER

Do I really believe that, as a Christian, I have nothing to hide? -- Not that I'm going to share everything about myself with everyone I meet, but do I have the freedom to share when I feel like it is beneficial for me or for others?

The risk is that others may take the information I share and hurt me with it. But do I have the freedom to share, knowing that they really cannot destroy me? Do I have the freedom to love, knowing that they could hurt me, but that will not destroy me? Or do I say, "Hiding is all important, I have to make sure no one knows this about me"? Do I really believe that nothing can devastate the Christian? Or do I think some things can? Those are good questions to ask myself.

THE FREEDOM OF NOT HIDING AND REPENTANCE

What does NOT hiding look like? Ask yourself, "What are the ways I hide, so that no one knows what is inside?" and "What would it mean for me NOT to hide?"

Again, it is not that we are going to go out and share all of our "dirty laundry" with people. But are there times when we might need to talk, or others might need to hear our story? What are the ways that we hide? And what does not hiding look like for each of us?

Repentance means that we are choosing to go in a different direction. We are going the other way. As we consider self-enhancement and self-protection, what does going the other way look like? What are our present strategies and what would it look like if we changed them?

First of all, we need to make sure that we are going to God first rather than attempting to manipulate other people, or going to things, or addictions, or whatever, to try to get needs met. Jeremiah 2:13 says, "My people have committed two sins; they have forsaken me, the spring of living water, and they have dug their own cisterns, broken cisterns, that cannot hold water." It is important to acknowledge the places we go to (to get our "water") that do not work, that will not fill the bottomless cup.

1 John 4:19 -- "We love because He first loved us." The only reason we can love others is because we have what we need. Therefore, we can always love. We always have enough. He loves us. For that reason, we can give love away to others.

It is like the analogy of a feast. We have a feast set in front of us. We cannot eat all of the food, so we go out and invite all of our friends and acquaintances to our feast and say, "Hey, dig in! There's enough for everybody." That is the love of God.

That is what we have when Christ is in our lives. We have fullness. We have what we need. Now we can give it away.

If we are hungry, we are not going to give our food away. Many people out there are loving others, but they are hungry. And eventually, they get tired of loving, because they do not get filled up. So they say, "I've given and given and given. I'm tired of giving! I don't feel like giving anymore. I'm done!" And they become very angry people -- even though they had been loving.

What happened? They were giving out of emptiness. God says to love out of fullness. You have a feast! Now, as you feel that fullness, give it away. (John 4:13: . . . "Whoever drinks the water I give him will never thirst. Indeed, the water I give him will become in him a spring of water welling up to eternal life.") We love because He first loved us (1 John 4:19). As with the feast, we are full and bubbling over --running over, as in Psalm 23:5 -- "My cup overflows." We cannot help but let it spill onto others.

So how do we begin trying to change our sinful strategies? First of all, we have to be willing to enter pain, to minister as an aspect of godliness. Are we willing to "move in" to pain, if it means loving well? Are we willing to "move in" to pain, if we believe God is calling us to something? If we are, then what we are saying is, "Godliness is more important than no pain." Are we willing to love, even when it is painful?

If you say, "No! I'm not willing to do that," even if you know it is the right thing to do, if you are still saying, "I'm not going to do it," then you are saying that avoiding pain is more important than godliness. You are saying that avoiding temporary pain is more important than long-lasting contentment. Being willing to enter into pain is an aspect of godliness. Will I love, even if it hurts? Do I believe that nothing can devastate the Christian?

1 John 4:18 -- "Perfect love casts out all fear." When we understand the love of God, we do not have to be afraid.

What can others do to us? Psalm 118:6 says, "The Lord is with me; I will not be afraid. *What can man do to me*?" Others can hurt us a little bit. But we have God. Therefore, what others can do to us is very little. Others can laugh at us, ridicule us, even kill us; but they cannot get to our souls. Do we really believe that?

Further Thoughts

The most important motivators for man are his longings. We all long for relationship and we all long for purpose. We want to be loved unconditionally and we want to feel valued and that our life is worthwhile.

Our longings help develop a thirst for God. When we realize what we long for, such as, "I long for this from my father," then we can also learn that we have a heavenly father who wants to give us those things (Matt. 7:11). When we realize what motivates us, those longings can help develop a thirst for God.

Sin is more than just ungodly behavior. We need to be aware that there are often deep-seated, practiced (and often unconscious) strategies in a person's soul. It is more than simply, "Oh, I am doing the wrong thing." Often, we are not even aware that the way we are "doing life" -- our "sweet and niceness," or our "super-spirituality," etc., could be sinful!

This could be our way of making life work that bypasses God. Sin runs deep in our souls in the form of strategies! There can be that "good guy" that is hard not to like. And yet, he is a sinful guy. Be careful about equating a "good guy" with meaning a "godly guy." Sometimes someone can be a "good guy" or a "good girl" and be very sinful!

And beliefs are learned from both pleasure and pain. That will be part of the discussion in the next chapter on the rational capacity.

Man is motivated in life through his longings. Those longings can cause us to choose to move toward good or evil.

There is a danger when we acknowledge our longings. We should not make longings our god. Longings can be another form of self-centeredness. Once we realize that we have been victims in some ways and long for some things that we may never receive, we must move to the place of taking responsibility for our present lives and for any sinful strategies we may have. Sometimes we land so hard on longings and victimization that we never move to a sense of responsibility. Some people's psychological teachings reinforce that belief -- that we are ONLY victims, not responsible for anything, and that getting longings met is the most important thing in life.

We are not responsible for being victimized or how we were victimized, but we ARE responsible for how we react to our victimization. It is important to realize this important truth. Sometimes when we have been victimized and hurt and abused, we then choose to self-enhance and self-protect -- inappropriately-- as a way of making sure that that never happens again. We need to take responsibility for our inappropriate strategies -- for what we are doing now.

So do not make longings your god. If you have been victimized, then that is a legitimate area for you to acknowledge, but you are also responsible for how you live your life today.

It is important to remember that we have all been perpetrators, in some form, as well. On one side of the coin, we have all been victims, yet on the other side, we have all done damage to people too. We have all hurt others. So we need to focus on both our longings and our responsibility.

It is very easy sometimes to think, "God is really here for me" as opposed to, "I am here for Him." Though God will never leave me and will always love me unconditionally, I am not here to get all that I want. I am here to serve and glorify God, knowing that I have all that I truly need. Sometimes it is easy to think that God is nothing but a cosmic Santa Claus -- that if we pray right or if we pray enough, He will give us what we want. That is dangerous. God is not Santa Clause, but His existence DOES guarantee that our true needs are met (though not every whim and worldly desire -- even though He still wants us to bring our heartfelt requests to Him – Phil 4:6).

We have enough; but we do not have all that we long for (in an absolute sense), because we were created for heaven (Ecclesiastes 3:11). We were created for eternity. And here is the big question to ask yourself: "Is enough, enough?" What God has given me, in a life that I have to live by faith, is that enough for me to go on?

Answer: Yes.

Does it always feel like it? No.

We want more! We were created for more! But we have to find a way of believing that what we have is enough. If we don't, we will be miserable and we will cause others around us to be miserable too.

Knowledge of our longings being met is helpful, but living by faith when we intensely long for sight, still makes living in a fallen world difficult. Do not think that knowledge is somehow going to make it all feel good. There will still be times when we will feel pain and hurt and rejection.

Even though you may think, "But I KNOW He is there" and "I KNOW He loves me," do not assume that somehow that knowledge is going to make life become everything that you want. It does not work that way. What you have IS enough though. It is just not always going to feel like it.

Conclusion

So what is the grand conclusion? We all long for relationship and unconditional love. We all long for purpose. We develop strategies to "get" those longings met and to "protect" us from the pain of those longings being unmet. But God ultimately fulfills those longings. We have enough. Believing we have enough -- even though we want more and even though we were built for more -- frees us up to be others-centered. We can focus on loving God and others. When we come to understand that reality, we can quit worrying about ourselves so much and instead of being desperate to **get** filled up, we can move into our world -- knowing that we have enough. Of course we want more, but we have enough. Now we can ask, "What can I do for you?"

CHAPTER 7

THE RATIONAL CAPACITY

Do animals have a conscience? When our dog, Sandy, was living, I would sometimes go downstairs to our basement and observe the rocking chair rocking, but no one was on it and no one else was in the room. It was obvious that Sandy had quickly bounded off the chair when she heard my footsteps and in time to avoid being caught on the "forbidden" chair. Even before I said anything, however, she would shrug her shoulders and cock her head to one side -- cowering, as she peered up at me. "Oozing" out of her "sheepish" stare was the epitome of a guilty look. Even if I had not seen the evidence of the chair continuing to rock, I would still have known that she was guilty because of the way she was looking at me.

Now is that behavior modification -- that she learned through punishment to be that way? Or is that a conscience -- she KNOWS right from wrong and is aware she has committed an offense? The answer could be argued. But it is more likely that her actions were a result of behavior modification rather than of an internal conscience.

People, however, have an internal conscience. We can think. We can process things. We can decide whether we believe something is right or wrong. We are aware of ourselves.

Dogs are probably not asking themselves, "Huh! I wonder why I just had that thought." They are probably not considering, "That was an interesting idea. Let me ponder that." There is probably no introspection and they probably don't think, "Why did I say that? I'm not quite sure."

People ask existential questions. Dogs do not contemplate why they are here or what "dogness" is all about?" A person may gaze at the stars some night and think, "What does all this mean?" "How did it happen?" "What am I here for?"

People have a capacity to think in a deep way -- to reason. We are cognitive creatures. "The Bible seems to make clear that the image of God is what distinguishes man from the rest of the creatures. (While man is described as created 'in the image of God,' the other creatures are described as being brought forth 'after their kind.')"(Erikson, 1995, p. 72). We have something that is higher than the animals. Our capacity for rational thought is another way that we are like God.

Consider the following verses:
Psalm 94:11 -- "The Lord knows the thoughts of man; He knows they are futile." (NIV)

Ephesians 4:23 -- ". . . to be made new in the attitude of your minds." (NIV)

Proverbs 23:7 (from the NASB -- the more literal rendition of the Hebrew here) -- "For as he thinks within himself, so he is." The KJV says, "As he thinketh in this heart, so he is."

All of those verses acknowledge that ability of man to do something with his brain -- his mind -- that is a deeper form of thinking than that of animals. The previous verses also lead us to the realization that those thoughts are the basis of our being. Have you heard the expression, "You are what you eat"? Not true. You are what you think. Proverbs 23:7 is a great verse for Cognitive Therapy. Cognitive Therapy says that the way you think determines if you have problems, if you get depressed, if you get anxious, or if you are doing well. The way you think truly determines how you are going to be. That is biblical!

Thinking is a part of the image and likeness of God -- the Rational Capacity. We think in the same way that God thinks -- not always in the right direction, but we are thinking beings in the same way that He is.

The statue of *The Thinker* (Rodin, [Sculptor] 1901, weltum.de – Public Domain) is a great portrait of the essence of man. We think. We reason. We wonder. If we have a brain that is working correctly, we "think." That "thinking" capacity, that self-awareness, that ability to reason, to evaluate, and to form beliefs is one way that makes us like God. It separates us from the animal kingdom because we are capable of a deeper kind of "thinking" than animals.

Theologians' Descriptions

Theologians use a number of different words to describe this aspect of being in God's image. Hodge (1979) describes it as a propensity for "reason and conscience" and a "rational agent" (p. 97). Davis (1975) uses the terms "self-consciousness" and "moral discernment" (p. 81). From Chafer and Walvoord (1974), it is "intellect" (p. 167). "Laidlaw (1879) describes it as "intellect or rationality" (Gen. 2:19) and "self-consciousness" (Rom. 8:16) (pp. 121-122), and

Thiessen (1949) uses the term: "mental likeness" (Col 3:10) (pp. 219-222). Erikson (1995) says, "reason" is the favorite candidate -- with the ability to "think, reflect, and deduce... It is in his cognitive, 'cerebral aspect' that man is most like God" (p. 499).

All of the previously mentioned theologians recognize that God created something in our being that has the ability to be rational -- to think, to be aware. That "Rational Capacity" is an important way in which He created us like Himself. It is an aspect of our "image" and "likeness" of Him. The theologians all acknowledge this mental likeness -- this mental capacity that is "like God."

Three Greek Words Involving/Explaining thinking

But if the theologians are not convincing enough for one to accept that man has a rational capacity that makes us "like God," take a look at the Greek language.

The word, *dokeō*, essentially means: we can think. We can think thoughts (Matt. 3:9, John 5:39). Animals, on some level, can think thoughts. Their neurons fire and they can think about the rubber ball that they want to play with or the dog dish and the water that is in it. Man's neurons also fire in a way that allows thinking, and the Bible makes reference to man's ability to think those basic thoughts -- *dokeō;* but man's basic thinking also interconnects with higher levels of thinking.

The Greek word, *Ginoskō*, has to do with the fact that we can understand concepts (John 13:12; 15:18). *Ginoskō* is a level "up" from *dokeō*. It is doubtful that a dog or an ape or any other animal, can understand concepts in the same way man can. Dogs probably do not wonder if the water is safe to drink or whether they should save some of it for later. They do not know what water quality is or how to evaluate what is given to them. They cannot reason in that way. They cannot understand those concepts. They may have some form of understanding, but certainly at a far different level than man's level of understanding.

The last word, *Pisteuō* (found in I Corinthians 13:7 and I John 4:16), is where we get our word, "epistemology." *Pisteuō* has to do with having deep beliefs. We have deep convictions about life. We have *faith*. Epistemology is the study of "the nature of knowledge, in particular its foundations, scope, and validity" (World English Dictionary, n.d.) Animals do not have convictions. There is no belief or faith. They just react to the stimuli and input provided to them.

We do all of those thinking processes in the same way that God does them (John 21:17, 10:15; Luke 16:15). God thinks. God understands concepts. God has deep beliefs and convictions. Obviously, God's convictions and God's beliefs are the true convictions and the true beliefs about life.

Now why is this important? It is important because in order to understand ourselves and others, we need to realize that within each one of us are automatic thoughts. If we want to conquer a problem or help someone else conquer a problem, we need to alter the way we think about it. We need to alter our automatic thoughts.

Sometimes when trying to understand concepts like, "God really does love you," you can think about it -- *dokeō*, but you may not really be able to grasp it -- *ginoskō*. You may have been taught the idea that He loves you. You know that fact, but you may not understand it. Or sometimes you just cannot believe it -- *Pisteuō*. That complete *understanding* of certain concepts can be a difficult.

When it comes to our deep convictions or beliefs, many times we may not even be aware of what we are believing! We may not realize that we do not really believe a concept like the previously mentioned one -- that God loves us just like He loves everybody else.

Christians in counseling often say, "Oh, I KNOW that I have no reason to feel ashamed. God has taken care of all that. But given what I've done in my past, it's too hard for me to really believe that I'm forgiven. I can't believe that it's all okay." Those deeply rooted, foundational beliefs are *Pisteuō*.

The rationality of some Christians goes something like this: "I know it's true! I think it. Yes! The cross has taken away all of my sin (dokeō). I understand the concept. That makes sense to me that His work covers everything and everybody (ginoskō). But I just can't really believe that applies to me (pisteuō). Somehow I see myself as a little worse than everybody else -- that somehow His forgiveness doesn't get to me. It doesn't cover me." That is a very common theme heard over and over again in counseling sessions -- "Somehow all of this that I KNOW and that I UNDERSTAND on one level, doesn't apply to me." When a person says that, it indicates that the "pisteuō" kind of thinking (that inner belief or conviction) regarding the concept of God's love has not taken place.

Those levels of thinking distinguish man from Earth's other creatures. All are capacities of reasoning that God has. Yet, though man has a rational capacity with which he can think on a variety of levels, sometimes because of sin, that thinking and those beliefs move in directions away from what God intended.

Primary Distinction from Animal Kingdom

So returning to the original distinction being made: the primary difference that separates us from the rest of the animal kingdom is our Rational Capacity. It is the major reason why man is different from the rest of God's creation. Animals may be able to think, but they cannot think as deeply as man can.

As human beings, we can think thoughts and form beliefs, and then evaluate those thoughts and beliefs. We are self-conscious, which means that we can think about our thoughts, actions, emotions, etc. While animals can "think" on one level, they do not have the same capacities either quantitatively or qualitatively.

Animals and humans do not think on the same level. Animals do not have man's quality of thought, man's quality of beliefs, or man's quality of understanding. They are not philosophers. And they do not think the number of thoughts or concepts that man does.

Some apes have been trained to communicate in ways that resemble human communication. Kanzi the Bonobo (Pygmy Chimpanzee, *Pan paniscus*) learned to communicate with his trainers using a keyboard with lexigrams (Raffaele, 2006). He also picked up some sign language and seemed able to communicate normally ("Kanzi," Wikipedia, 2012). Some have said, "Look! He understands!" (Chaddha, pbs.org, 2008).

The problem with animals is that it is sometimes hard to distinguish how much is behavior modification and how much is true understanding. An ape can be trained through rewards to react, and no one ever knows when that eyebrow goes up a little bit or when there is some cue from the trainer that triggers a response.

In the early 1900s there was a horse named Hans whose owner proclaimed that he was able to think. He could be asked mathematical questions such as, "What is 2 plus 3?" and be able to indicate the correct answer by stomping out the number with his hooves -- in this case, five stomps. Though proclaimed by a committee of "experts" in 1904 as a genuine achievement (validating the horse's ability to calculate the answer), it was later discovered that the horse responded to miniscule movements of its trainer's head or eyebrows that conveyed the time to stop stroking his hoof. It was all behavior modification! (Dehaene, 1997).

So the idea that apes can be trained to use sign language is amazing. They can learn and can do things so that, to some, it appears that they understand. It is hard to know how much is behavior modification and how much is really the "ginōskō" and "pisteuō" kind of understanding. But even if they can be taught sign language and other communication skills, they still fall far short in the number of words they are able to use, and there is still no evidence that they can think deeply and hold convictions and beliefs.

Biblical theology seems to indicate that there is still a gap. Qualitatively and quantitatively, animals cannot get there because they are not image bearers. But can they do more than what we think they can? Possibly.

Marooned in the Canary Islands during the First World War, Wolfgang Kohler did some now famous studies with chimpanzees. He put them in a pen with a variety of objects including boxes and sticks and ran several experiments -- one with a bunch of bananas hanging from the ceiling and out of their reach. He wanted to see what they would do. And after a while, a chimp would realize that if he stacked the boxes on top of each other, he could get up and get the bananas. Or he realized that he could use the stick, stand on the boxes, and "whack" at them to get the bananas. They called that "insight" (Gould & Gould, 2004).

(Source: clipart.com, 2011)

Animals have the ability to have insight. Nobody trained those chimps to stack the boxes and climb up to get the bananas. They were not rewarded. But they discovered, on their own, how to use the boxes to get to the fruit.

It is amazing what animals can discover on their own. But to say that that equals what humans can do is a HUGE leap.

Core Beliefs and Convictions

So humans differ from the animal world in the depth of their thinking. And all of us as humans, including you as you read this book, have beliefs that we hold and carry. We may not even be aware of some of our beliefs, yet those beliefs drive us. And though we may not even know that they are there, they will "leak out." Sometimes they leak out in our shame. Sometimes they leak out in anxiety. They leak out in the way we talk about ourselves. They leak out in the way we respond to others or to crises. They leak out in our actions and our conversations. They are there. But we often do not realize they are there. Yet, if we really want to grow in our faith and godliness, we need to work on changing those deep beliefs.

Connections To Longings

So that leads us back to those two key words again (discussed in the previous chapter): GET and PROTECT. We develop beliefs about how to get our needs met and how to protect ourselves from pain. We develop beliefs about how to GET longings met and how to PROTECT ourselves from the pain of longings not being met.

Now notice what happens in regard to those Godlike capacities that we have discussed so far. Our motivations and longings drive us. Our thinking or rational capacity is formed based on our longings. Understanding how our God-like capacities interconnect is important in understanding people. In this chapter, we will be looking at our thinking (Rational Capacity) -- our *beliefs* about how to get our *longings* met (Social and Existential Capacities). In the upcoming chapters, we will discuss capacities to set goals (Teleological Capacity), make choices (Volitional Capacity), behave in certain ways (Behavioral Capacity), and express emotions (Emotional Capacity). Each is built on another, so understanding that interconnection is vital.

How do the emotions (Emotional Capacity) connect with the will? How does the Volitional Capacity (choice) connect to the Existential Capacity (longings)? How do they all work together? Understanding that is going to give a better grasp of what is going on in your life or in the lives of others.

So when we consider the Rational Capacity (beliefs), what are our beliefs formed around? They are formed around how we get and keep relationships and how we make them work. All of us have a way of making relationships work. We have beliefs about what will make them work. If you were asked right now, "What do you believe is a necessary component of making a relationship work?" you would have an idea. But some may say they have one belief or idea, yet do something that totally contradicts what they say they believe. If that is true, if what they actually do is different, then that would indicate that there is a belief that the person is not aware of.

You may say, "Oh, it is very important to be sweet and nice," but you actually go about intimidating a lot of people. And you say, "Well, I'm not *trying* to be intimidating." But maybe your deep belief is: "If I intimidate, I'll get what I want -- more than if I'm sweet and nice," even though you understand or have a surface belief that being sweet and nice will work. What you REALLY believe is that intimidation is the way to go.

How do you get relationships? How do you keep them? Look at the answers to those questions realistically and decide whether what you think you believe about getting and keeping relationships is really what you believe.

How do you avoid getting hurt? We all have beliefs about how *not* to get hurt. Sometimes those beliefs have been encouraged by parents. They may have had ways of telling us or modeling for us, "Don't tell people anything about yourself. Don't ever open up!" Our parents may have been thinking, "All that will do bring you pain! If you stay closed, life will work better."

So that becomes ingrained into the thinking and the internalized message becomes, "I never want to open up to anyone. I never want to be honest. I've learned not to do that."

Or it is learned experientially. "I opened up one time, got hurt, and I'm never going to do that again. I'm never going to expose anything personal in my life to anyone."

We also learn beliefs about how to find meaning and purpose in our lives. We find things that are meaningful. We grab onto some things and discard other things.

We learn beliefs about how to make impact in our world -- what works. All of us are trying to make impact. Some do it in good ways. Some are out there doing very noble things for others and feeling "fulfilled" in the ways they are impacting others' lives.

But others are nasty, thinking, "Look how I'm making impact!" while they hurt people -- damage people. Yet they still are saying internally, "Look what I can do."

Think about it. You can build something and say, "Look what I built. It's beautiful!" Or you can blow up something (that someone else built) and say, "Look what I did!" Both behaviors can give a sense of impact. What kind of impact do you want?

When we see people destroying and hurting others and causing damage, we want to say, "NO! That's not the right way to make impact!"

But people are still are trying to make impact that way. And they have developed beliefs about how to do it. Why? Because things have worked! If their actions "work," then they are going to do more of them. (If blowing up a building gets people's attention, if people are talking about it or if it gets in the newspaper, etc., then there can be a feeling that "impact" has been achieved -- even if it is something bad.) If their techniques and attempts do not work, if they do not get any form of attention or cause any notable damage, then they will tend to do fewer of those behaviors. So somewhere the beliefs have been formed around what "worked."

Beliefs Based on Pleasure and Pain

What do we respond to that causes us to develop our beliefs? Sometimes they are things that bring us personal pleasure, and sometimes they are things that bring us pain -- maybe intense personal pain.

As you read the following examples, try to come up with instances in your own life where you have learned beliefs and upon which you may have developed your own belief system. Think through: "Where have I learned my beliefs about how to make life work?"

When we think about which is the better teacher, it seems that it is probably "pain." Pain is probably the teacher that gets our attention most often. It is the one in which we say, "Okay, I got it!" because we do not want any more pain. Through pleasure, we learn, but pain has a way of really grabbing our attention.

Examples of Beliefs Based on Pleasure

Pleasure, however, *can* also be a great teacher. The following example was related by a friend of the authors, about an incident that happened when this friend was a young boy. We will call him Matt.
Young Matt decided that he wanted to make some money. But as is true of most of us, he did not want to work too hard to get it.

So as he was deliberating on what to do, he noticed that there were beautiful red roses growing in bushes at his next-door neighbor's house. He started to think, "I could sell them and make some money. I think I'll try that. I'll take those roses around the neighborhood and sell them to people."

So he cut off the roses in her rose garden and went from house to house, selling roses for one dollar. And many of his neighbors smiled and said, "Yeah. I'll buy one."

He returned home with a "wad" of money, but he had one rose left. So he thought, "Well, I've been to every house in the neighborhood, I'll visit the lady next door (that owned the rose bushes!) and see if she'll buy one from me." So that is what he did.

And when he asked her to buy a rose, she agreed and actually bought one of her very own roses! Then he went home and began counting his money.

As he was counting, his father walked in and asked, "Where did you get all of that money?"

Matt said he was tempted to lie, but he decided that he had better tell the truth. So he said, "I cut down the neighbor lady's roses and went around selling them and I even sold one to her."

Now if you were the father, what would you do? Would you punish him?

His father had a different response. His father patted him on the head and said, "That's my good little businessman!"

Matt said, "I never forgot that."

What did he learn from that intense pleasure and what was the pleasure? It was not merely, "I got money." That was fine. But he learned something that felt even better: Someone is proud of me! Replaying in his mind were his father's words, "That's my good little businessman!"

So how would that translate to the years of his life that followed? Matt said he internalized a message, something like this: "It's okay to lie, cheat, steal, or whatever you need to do, as long as you get what you want." And in the years of his life before he became a Christian, he sold drugs and exploited people to get what he wanted.

That is a good example of how a belief is learned and how that can lead to a way of making life work -- from just one event! Now, it is not always just one event. It is most likely his dad would have reinforced his belief other times. But sometimes we can learn things from ONE event -- one very pivotal event, either pleasurable or traumatic. One event could be that powerful!

Think about what some young men and women learn from sports when they are growing up. What do you think can be learned about life through sports? What beliefs are learned or reinforced there?

We may learn hard work and teamwork. Those are positive ones.

How about: "Try to be the best." And in order to be the best, you need to defeat them! It is very important to *beat* another person or team. You must be *better* than they are!

I remember that thrill I had as a kid. My high-school-age brother took me along to a "pick-up" game he was playing with his friends. I was probably around ten years old, and they were all high school guys. When they divided into teams, they realized they were short one person. I was shrieking excitedly, "Pick me! Pick me!" And they kept saying, "No, no." But they kept trying to figure out what they were going to do. So finally, they said, "Okay, you can play."

I was thinking, "Oh man! This is great! I'm playing with all of these high school guys."

And as they were playing, of course, they would not throw the ball to me. But it got down to the last play of the game. The score was 9 to 9 and they were playing to 10. Then the ball went squirting out and everybody was fighting for it, including me and I got it! And grabbing the ball I thought, "Here's my chance. I get to take a shot!"

And the only shot I could take was a hook shot because they were all so much bigger than I was. So I did. I did one of those 20-foot hook shots. And the ball went in!

I will never forget how they responded! They picked me up and put me on their shoulders. They were all going around praising me, and I learned something from that event. What is it that I learned? If I win, they will like me! If I make the shot, if I score a lot of points, if I am successful, people will like me.

Now all we have to do is watch it on TV and see the famous athlete that is acclaimed by the media and/or makes a lot of money. We see the movie star who is on the cover of magazines. Seeing that acclaim may entice us to begin thinking that being a star is what it's all about. And being a star will get your needs met. Right? . . . Wrong!

It will work in the short run, but it does not work in the long run. As a child, this author did not know that. All I knew was, "It's working." The harder I practiced, the more it seemed to work -- on some level -- until I hit a major block and then had to think, "Now what?"

And we all have situations like that -- things we have learned from pleasure. But sometimes the things we learn from pleasure, the very things that seem to bring us "life," are also the things that bring us pain when they do not work. Then we have to develop a new belief about what to do with things that do not work.

The unfortunate thing about sports is that you learn that you have to be BETTER than someone else. That means that someone has to feel bad about not being better than his opponent. Rather than affirming our growth and improvement, we base our "value" on whether we are better when compared to someone else. And we cannot maintain that. We cannot guarantee that we are always going to be better than our challenger.

Intense pleasure and intense pain develop beliefs. The previous example was one belief that the author learned through pleasure -- that if I win, if I am successful, then everyone will like me.

What happens if you are the oldest child in your family? You are given a lot of responsibility to help raise the younger ones. And what do people say to you when you are the oldest? They may compliment you on the way you take on responsibility.

Sometimes parents will talk positively about one sibling and negatively about another -- comparing their differences. What kind of beliefs develop in those siblings? Sometimes when a child hears his parent dismayed over one sibling's behavior, he determines to do the opposite, hoping the parents will think positively about him. And often that is exactly what happens.

What do you think we learn from that -- when we do it and do it well and people notice? What do you think happens inside that man or that woman when he or she realizes that, "When I do things well, or when I'm responsible, or when I am the opposite of my sibling, people will like me." Do you see how that person may begin thinking, "The more I do it well, and the better I do it, the more I can get my needs met." Do you see how that could develop into perfectionism or other personality traits?

Going back to the basketball example, do you remember the belief that began to take shape? -- "If you are successful, if you do it well, they will like you. If you do it perfectly, they will all like you." Now did anybody say, "Let me teach that to you. Let me tell you how life works." No, not directly. But that is the way those incidents cause thinking which leads to the formation of beliefs. Even though, in actuality, those learned "beliefs" are not necessarily valid and life does not exactly work that way, rationally, it seems to make sense in our minds. And if it worked once, we often keep trying to get it to work again and again -- to get back to that pleasurable feeling.

And people go on living their lives. They are responsible. They are successful. They do all of those things that they think work. And those things DO work, for awhile. But, eventually, the perfectionism starts to implode. They try to be the best and get 100% on every test and be the best on the team and/or at their jobs, and it becomes impossible as finite human beings to keep up that level of performance. Then they have to start dealing with things like disappointment, sadness, depression, guilt; and the very things that brought life to them are now bringing problems. And so, as they get depressed, what do they do?

If you were a perfectionist who was getting depressed, what would you say to yourself -- based on your deep beliefs? How about, "Try harder! The reason you're depressed is because you're not trying hard enough!" And all it takes is a few Christians out there or a few other people who are perfectionistic, to go, "Yeah, that's right. You're depressed? You're doing something wrong. You're not reading your Bible enough. You're not praying enough." That is why it is so hard for some of those people to understand God's grace. It does not make sense to them. The model of -- "You must be on top to gain acceptance and praise," does not fit with God's grace, that -- "As a Christian, you don't have to do anything to earn God's love and you are still loved and accepted by a perfect and almighty God." What does fit is, "You're not trying hard enough!"

So the perfectionist reacts with, "Yeah! That's what is wrong. I need to try harder. That is how life works! I've got to read more. I've got to study more. I've got to pray more. I've got to do more." And usually there is also that unconscious belief that, "I've got to earn God's favor. And only when I am satisfied with myself, will God be satisfied as well." But the perfectionist keeps getting more depressed and wonders, "What is going on? I must be doing something really wrong!"

Now he "beats himself up." He is burdened with guilt. What message is he telling himself? "You're not trying hard enough!"

Do you see the cycle? Beliefs are causing the problem. The same beliefs that once brought the person joy and happiness (They "worked!") are now the beliefs that are bringing him down. But he cannot figure all of that out.

And if a mature Christian says to that person, "You don't need to try that hard," the one with the irrational beliefs may look at that mature Christian like he/she is crazy. That is because the only reality the person understands is that trying hard is how you make life work, being the star is how you make life work, being responsible is how you make life work. Grace does not fit.

But if you are implementing that "strategy" -- that belief that you internalized long before -- why doesn't it always work? Why does it eventually implode? -- Because it is not God's design. It is not the right way to think.

Hard work is commendable, but working too hard will cause problems -- especially when it is for the wrong goal. Why might one be trying so hard? -- Often because of the learned belief that it will get people to love him (he thinks). Now, we're back to longings.

And another strange thing occurs. The beliefs can become so internalized that the need is not only for others to love him or her, but now "I must do this or I can't accept myself."

So it is important to understand what is driving us. If we are perfectionists to an extreme, that affects our functioning; so laying more guilt and more "Christian" responsibilities like Scripture memory or lengthy praying, may not always be the best advice. It may look biblical, but it may be reinforcing the wrong thing. Sometimes we need to revamp our thinking. Sometimes we need to "rest" in the Lord and learn to give out of "fullness" -- like the tree in Psalm 1. Sometimes we need to just think on the things that are good and lovely and of good report (Phil. 4:8). Sometimes other scriptural principles come into play. That is why well-meaning pastors and Christian counselors sometimes give the WRONG homework to those they counsel, even though it looks biblical! They sometimes reinforce the very thing that is causing the problem. It is important to get to the root of the thinking that is fueling the depression, or the anxiety, or other problem that affects the ability to serve God well.

Examples of Beliefs Based on Pain

The following is an example of a belief developed through a painful circumstance. When John was a boy, he was very excited one day to be asked by his dad to help him. His dad owned rental properties and needed to do some repair work.

John jumped into the truck and rode along eagerly with his dad to the property. When they arrived, John's dad gave him specific instructions, "Sit over there and I'll let you know if I need something." Then his father proceeded to work on some pipes under the main floor of the building.

The boy sat patiently until his father finally called out, "Go get me the socket wrench that I brought."

The boy was elated to finally be summoned by his dad who now needed his assistance. He jumped up and scurried to the place where his dad's tools had been placed and quickly returned with a wrench.

Unfortunately, the wrench that he brought was not a socket wrench, but a more traditional wrench -- sometimes known as a "spanner." His dad looked at the tool his son was carrying. His face quickly took on a disgusted grimace! "Can't you get anything right?" he yelled as he grabbed the wrench from his son. The father then angrily tossed the wrench to the side where it hit a wall, ricocheted, and struck the boy in the head.

His dad then angrily marched toward the location of his tools, found the correct wrench, and returned to finish his work. As he walked, he swore continuously -- shaking his head and demeaning the boy for his failure to bring the correct tool.

Now, pretend you are that boy. You are sitting there on the floor. What are you feeling? Ashamed? Worthless?

Though his head was then throbbing, that was not the worst pain. The worst pain for him was disappointing his dad. And in the midst of that pain, he developed a belief. What do you think he said to himself as a way of dealing with that pain? What might be some of the ideas or beliefs he may entertain?

He could have thought, "I don't want to help my dad anymore." He may even go so far as to think, "I don't want to help people." Why? "Because if I help people, I probably won't get it right and then I'll feel that pain again."

Or he could have developed a belief that he might as well not try. "Why try? If I try, I'll probably fail!"

He might have said, "I'll never get anything right. I am stupid. And I'm going to live out my life and live out that reality that I am stupid." So if he *does* well on a test, he'll say something to himself like, "It must have been an easy test, because I'm stupid." If he *doesn't* do well on a test he'll respond with, "That makes sense because I'm stupid." Either way it goes, he's going to hang on to the belief that he is stupid.

What other things might he begin to believe as a result of that incident? Maybe he would think, "Next time, I'll get it right! I'll never, ever be wrong again! I never, ever, want to have another wrench thrown at me or have somebody be disappointed with me."

And maybe from then on, no matter what he might do, it may never be enough. He might have a good job and a decent life, but it may never be enough. And his dad could even die, but what often happens is that the belief remains -- "I still want to make Dad proud."

Do you see how those beliefs determine behavior and feelings and lifestyle? Underlying beliefs are powerful! Many times people are not even aware that they are "still trying to make Dad proud!" or whatever their belief system is built around. But they live their lives and make choices based on those beliefs.

Imagine being a young woman who thinks, "I can never be pretty and smart like my sister. I'm big-boned. I have a big nose. I can wear all the makeup that I want, but she's got the natural beauty. And I don't do well in math; algebra and geometry just don't make sense to me." Then your parents add to that by saying, "Why can't you be more like your sister? Why don't you work more on your appearance? Why don't you study harder?"

If you were constantly compared with your sibling, what belief might you develop as a way of dealing with that pain? The basis of your needs is always the same. "I'm not being loved and accepted the way I want to be. I'm not finding the meaning and purpose for my life that I long for."

So what might the young lady do based on her perceptions and her formulated beliefs? She might think, "I'm always going to be a little heavier and a little uglier than my sister." How can I make life work?" What do you think she might do? What are the options?

Sometimes girls in this situation choose to joke about themselves. They become comedians and make others laugh as well. They use jokes about their weight and looks to incite laughter from others and ease their inner pain.

Now, in reality, it is not funny. But in social settings they can be the "life of the party." They are getting their needs met, but getting them met in a different way.

Sometimes girls will deal with that situation by becoming anorexic or having plastic surgery or withdrawing from people or getting ten tattoos or finding other "outcast" friends or a number of other options. But if you are a girl and those are your circumstances and you "feel needy," YOU WILL do something because you have got to find acceptance somehow, and you are desperate to have it.

It is all about *getting* needs met. It is all about *protecting* ourselves from more pain.

Every eating disorder makes sense. Each makes sense because people with eating disorders are trying to get their needs met -- just like all of the rest of us.

The only problem is that all of those methods of "getting" needs met will not work ultimately because what we get is not really what we want down deep. We want to be accepted unconditionally. But if that is unlikely to happen, we can still determine, at least, to lessen the pain.

The last example to examine regarding beliefs is the following. Picture a guy who is in the ninth grade, is small for his age, not athletic, and has big ears. Let's say this guy is not just short, but a good seven inches shorter than most of the guys his age.

Now what do older or taller boys tend to do to small guys like that? They like to push them around, carry them and put them places, or do other things that tend to ridicule the small one. (At the same time the older or bigger boy is trying to make himself feel bigger, stronger, and more important.)

So imagine you are the small guy and you are "picked on" every day. You are put in a trash can or forced into a locker. Or maybe they just make up elephant antics to make fun of your "elephant-like" ears. What strategies would you develop to avoid that pain and what beliefs might you form about yourself?

Maybe you would try to "win over" the boys by being a manager of an athletic team. Maybe you would laugh at their jokes and smile at them, or maybe you would try to avoid them by ducking into a room when you see them coming or by leaving school early. Maybe you would withdraw from people in general. Maybe you would put your energy into schoolwork and try to excel there. You may even let them cheat with your homework or you may give them answers on tests. Or maybe you would take on "bad" habits like smoking, in order to demonstrate your "bravery" and "toughness."

Boys deal with this situation in a number of ways. One strategy that can be chosen is to never say "no" when asked for help. As that carries into adulthood, how might that belief impact the short man? When that boy becomes an adult and the boss asks him to stay late or do extra projects, he may feel that he cannot say no (which in his mind, could lead to him being "picked on" again). That strategy could cause problems in marriage, with children, and with other commitments.

Now if he wanted to be the best father and the best worker, those two goals may conflict sometimes. Resolving that conflict can be a real challenge.

The thinking could go like this: "But I definitely have to be the best worker because that's what I know how to do! I'm not sure how to do the father thing. I know I probably need to spend more time with my kids, but I can't turn down overtime."

And besides family problems, that thinking can lead to depression and "burnout" at work and life. The man whose shortness was the impetus for his developing certain traits, could collapse under the pressure. One can see, however, how "workaholism" would make sense for a guy in this situation.

Everyone in this world has a story based on his or her needs and the strategies that he/she picks to try to meet those needs. When you understand everyone's story, his or her life choices make more sense. You may realize why he or she chose to become a comedian, or a perfectionist, or a workaholic, or a sports phenomenon, or a top salesperson, or a "bum," etc. Each one is trying to get needs met and trying to avoid pain.

In fact, we can be so "tied" to our strategies, that if the perfectionist is asked to leave the bed unmade or go out with friends rather than study one more hour or to decline an opportunity to work overtime, he can be struck with panic and be very fearful of giving up that strategy.

These are POWERFUL images that we carry -- powerful beliefs that are the key to how we function and why we do what we do. And when we begin to look deeply, things start to make sense.

So spend some time thinking about your own story. What are those incidents of intense pleasure or pain in your life? What worked for you? What was painful to the point that you said, "I never want to be in that situation again"; "I never want that to happen"? What beliefs did you learn about how to make life work?

We all have a story and we all have beliefs. We hold to beliefs that, in the long run, do not work, and often we hold to beliefs that we are not even conscious of, but they are there nonetheless.

Rationally Based Therapies

The Rational Capacity was given to us for the purpose of evaluation. Beliefs are vital places to explore. They are the roadmaps that lead us to life or death. That is why psychologists such as Aaron T. Beck, David D. Burns, and Donald Meichenbaum have found Cognitive Therapy and Cognitive-Behavioral Therapy so helpful.

Cognitive Therapy and Cognitive-Behavioral Therapy are secular methods of helping others that make sense. Both systems of treatment assume that everyone has powerful beliefs that guide them. Their beliefs are the foundation upon which is created the map by which we choose to navigate our lives. Major consequences result from whatever beliefs and paths are chosen.

Albert Ellis used what he called the "Rational Emotive" approach. Applying his "Rational Emotive Therapy" (and later "Rational Emotive Behavior Therapy"), Ellis promoted the idea that irrational beliefs cause problems. While the assumption that "irrational beliefs cause problems" is not incongruent with biblical teaching, Ellis's conclusion to solve those problems was for people to eliminate all of the "shoulds" in their lives -- "I should do this!" "I must do that." "I ought to do this." He urged his clients to replace the "shoulds" with "preferences" and to view all of the things that they felt compelled to do as preferences, not "oughts." He wanted them to grasp the idea that if they did not attain the "requirements" that they held for themselves, they would not then think of themselves as reprehensible (Ellis, 2004).

What Ellis advocated, begged the question, "Wouldn't it be better if our *oughts* were our *wants*?" -- "I WANT to do that," as opposed to "I OUGHT to do it and so I force myself to do it. And if I don't succeed in forcing myself to do it, then I need to chastise myself."

While true that living a life full of compulsion and no freedom leaves one with exasperation and discouragement, Albert Ellis believed that the answer to that was to take all of the "shoulds" away. Though God is a God who gives us freedom, He is also still a God of "oughts." Ellis made a valid observation when he concluded that some people take things too far, causing problems for themselves. But ridding ourselves entirely of all obligations and restraints is contrary to what the Bible teaches us. The best perspective seems to be somewhere in the middle.

Ellis, however, was very astute in realizing that irrational beliefs DO cause problems.

In Cognitive Therapy, instead of replacing irrational beliefs, therapists try to guide their patients by encouraging them to "just keep trying new ways of thinking, until you come up with a way that works for you." Of course, as Christians, our conviction that the Bible gives us the foundation on which to build our beliefs and thinking helps us to come up with those ways that work.

A person's attempts to make life work, stem from what he believes and what he thinks deep inside. That is true for all people -- Christians and non-Christians. It is how people evaluate life.

Proper thinking is important. The Bible acknowledges the importance of channeling our thinking in ways that benefit us, in passages such as Philippians 4:8 where it advises us to think on the things that are noble, pure, lovely, praiseworthy, etc., or in Colossians 3:2 where it tells us to set our minds "on things above, not on earthly things." Only then will we truly be able to live a contented life.

Rational Emotive Therapy and Cognitive Therapy have attempted to get at the same thing -- to change thinking. Clinicians who practice those forms of therapy have realized the truth that our thinking -- which comes from our beliefs -- is the key to understanding the problems that we have in life. Proverbs 20:5 describes that fact that "the purposes of the human heart are deep waters, but those who have insight draw them out." This is why just trying to change behavior without getting to the underlying beliefs (the "deep waters") is so hard for many people -- because many times an underlying belief contradicts the behavior change. That underlying belief says, "This behavior is essential to making my life work!"

Conclusion

Man's rational capacity is one of his "image-bearing" qualities that makes him like God and separates him from the animal kingdom. Man is capable of thinking deeply and existentially. He can reason. The word "evaluation" could summarize that rational ability. Man can think thoughts and form beliefs and then make an evaluation of those thoughts and beliefs. He can make an "evaluation" of himself and his world.

Our rationality is formed on the basis of our longings -- the longings for relationship and purpose. In our effort to "get" those longings met, we act in ways that attempt to attain pleasure or prevent pain. Met longings have to do with pleasure. Unmet longings have to do with pain. Those factors will determine our beliefs about how we "do" life, and we will keep living our lives according to those beliefs until those beliefs do not work for us anymore. Counselors must understand this (in their rational capacity) so that they can best help those they work with in counseling. It is a key capacity in regard to living life the way God intended, and thus, a key ingredient in good counseling.

CHAPTER 8

THE TELEOLOGICAL CAPACITY

Introduction

When the word *teleology* is used in this chapter, it is referring to being goal-directed and goal-oriented. Man is "intentional." He does things with an objective in mind.

The Teleological Capacity of man is that God-like capacity that we have for setting goals. So if we build on the previous chapters, the direction (Teleology) we choose to go is based on our thinking (Rationality) which is derived from our longings (for relationship/love and purpose – Social and Existential Capacities) and our need to get those longings met while protecting ourselves from the pain of their being unmet.

So while in the last chapter we summarized "rational" as "evaluation," "teleological" is "direction." So with "rational," we are evaluating the map. We are saying, "Here is the map. Here is how to make life work." The Teleological Capacity says, "Here is where I am going now. This is what I am going to do." The Teleological Capacity is for the purposes of direction.

Would you say it is true that everything we do has some sort of goal or objective in mind? Everything we do, no matter what it is -- whether we get up or not, whether we exercise, whether we study, whether we work, whether we play, whether we sing, whether we pray -- whatever we do, we have some goal in mind.

The idea that we do anything without some sort of purpose is hard to substantiate. It is hardly likely that we do anything for no reason -- that we can be "purposeless." It is much more probable to believe that there is always some goal behind everything that we do. Even if our goal is just to relax -- to do "nothing," we are still accomplishing a purpose. The idea that people do things in a vacuum with absolutely no goal is doubtful.

Everything we do has some sort of goal behind it. We have a motive. We do things with a purpose. We do things to get something.

Why is that important? Why is it crucial to understand that everything we do has some sort of goal, objective, motive? -- Because we cannot truly deal with our sin and make lasting and complete changes in our lives unless we understand and/or deal with the motive/s behind what we do.

Conscious Motives

Sometimes we understand what our motives are, yet when they cause us difficulties, we still feel compelled to hang on to them. One person's goal might be to "get everybody to like me." Is that a proper or "righteous" objective? It would be nice to live in a world where everybody liked everybody else. But do we NEED that to function in our world? No. Christ was perfect and not everybody liked Him! And is that something we can control? Rationally, we know we can't, yet sometimes people live as if they think they can. We can make ourselves miserable by having goals that we cannot control.

It is irrational to think that we can "get" everyone to like us. We may be able to "get" hundreds of people to like us, but there is nearly always one that just won't. And if you want to talk about a way of making your life miserable, just try to get everybody to like you for a year. Why will that make you miserable? -- Because you cannot do it. You do not have control of that. There is going to be somebody out there thinking, "I don't like you." Just the fact that you are such a "great" person will incite some people to dislike you. And sometimes the very fact that it seems that everybody likes you, will cause someone else to jealously think, "I hate you!"

And when you start wondering, "What did I do?" you will hopefully come to the realization that the answer is: nothing! You did nothing evil to them. And the more you try to get some of them to like you, the more they will hate you.

You simply cannot control the way someone feels about you!

Unconscious or Hidden Motives

Our motives can be deeply hidden inside of us. Sometimes we may know (on some level) what they are, but we purposely conceal them in order to cause others to view us in a particular way. Other times we do not even realize what they are and that they are there.

Look at Proverbs 20:5. "The purposes of a man's heart are like deep waters, but a man of understanding draws them out" (NIV). (*Man* can be male or female here -- as with most of Scripture. The passage could be rendered "a *person's* heart" and a "*person* of understanding.") "The purposes of a man's heart are like *deep waters*." What is it saying in this verse? It is telling us that people bury their motives deep inside themselves? Sometimes they are buried so deep that there is not even a conscious awareness of what the true motives are.

Proverbs 21:2 says, "All of man's ways seem right to him."

What is found in those passages is the assertion that sometimes the goals are not conscious. Sometimes the thing that a person THINKS he is after is not what he is really after at all. Sometimes people can deceive themselves. That is what the Bible talks about when it refers to "deep waters." And sometimes those deeply hidden motives are deceitful and wrong.

So beware of hidden goals in yourself and in others. There are things underneath that may be sinful that you are not even aware of. This is crucial to understand as we work with those we counsel.

Remember the discussion of the man who was still trying to please his father. He was living his whole life to make his father proud of him. He did not realize that was how he was living his life. All he thought he wanted to do was to work hard, provide for his family, and for everyone to be happy. He did not realize that underneath all of that, he was still trying to make his dad proud! He was still trying to live up to certain expectations. And it was not until a "man of understanding *drew it out*," that he came to the realization that most of the problems he needed help with were really about his dad and somehow being good enough.

And remember the discussions about those who are mistreated. Often they do not realize that they are living life with the motive, "I want to make sure this never happens to me again." They often do not realize that is what is driving them.

Scripture Concerning Motives

Scripture has much to say about motives.

John 6:64 -- God knows our thoughts and motives.

Philippians 1:15-18 talks about some preaching Christ "out of envy and rivalry" also out of "selfish ambition" and "false motives," but others out of "good will" and "out of love."

1 Thessalonians 2:3 says, "The appeal we make does not spring from error or impure motives, nor are we trying to trick you."

Proverbs 16:1, 2 -- "To man belongs the plans of the heart . . . All a man's ways seem innocent to him, but the motives are weighed by the Lord."

The author is talking about the PLANS of the heart. The motives are weighed by God! Motives are very important to God!

"Why are you doing this?" "What are you after?" "What are you trying to accomplish?" Those questions all address the idea of motives.

As was already stated, sometimes we do not know what our motives are. But it is important to God, and it should be important to us, to take some time to evaluate our motives and look at what we may be trying to accomplish.

Proverbs 24:12 -- ". . . does not he who weighs the heart, perceive it? Will he not repay each person for what he's done?" Again, He weighs the heart. God weighs what is really going on inside of us.

We already looked at Proverbs 21:2 -- ". . . all of man's ways seem right to him, but the Lord weighs the heart." A man's ways may seem right to him; yet there is a way that seems right, but ends in death (Prov. 14:12). And Proverbs 21:2 says that God WEIGHS what we think in terms of what is right and wrong concerning our motives, and at times we do not realize that underneath may be something that is not what He wants.

1 Corinthians 4:4-5 says, ". . . Wait until the Lord comes, who will bring to light what is hidden in darkness and will expose the motives of men's hearts. . . ." Again, here is the idea that part of judgment is weighing the motives. God knows why it is that you are doing what you are doing. He wants us as Christians to assess our motives.

James 4:3 says ". . . When you ask, you do not receive, because you ask with wrong motives, that you may spend what you get on your pleasures. . . ." It is clear that God wants us to do things with proper motives.

Prayer Motives

INAPPROPRIATE REQUESTS

Sometimes when we pray, we ask with wrong motives. Maybe we pray, "God, please help me win the sweepstakes" instead of, "God, please help us to have some financial relief" and/or "Help me find a good job."

"Help me get a date with that 'hot' guy or that beautiful girl" instead of, "God please help me find the man/woman that you have for me" and/or "Please help me to see behind what the guy/girl that I am interested in appears to be, and if I decide to date him/her, help me to trust in your sovereignty if he/she rejects me." We may pray, "Help our team win" instead of, "Help us all play our best, work together, and glorify you no matter what the end result is."

What might be a better prayer that summarizes all of the above ideas? "God, help me to accept whatever happens. Whatever You want to do, do it and help me to be okay with whatever that is, remembering that I have enough, no matter what other 'gifts' you give others."

Sometimes we ask with the wrong motives, with a sinful selfish goal; but it is not sinful to ask for things that we want that are appropriate, like, "God, please keep the plane up" (when I am flying) or "God please allow me to have a child" (as Hannah asked in 1 Samuel 1:11). Asking for our own desires for safety or enjoyment or comfort in life is not sinful -- as long as it assumes that God is in control and we are committed to being "content" in whatever He brings our way. But the problem comes when prayers start carrying a belief or demand that we *must* have those things -- that we *need* those things in order to be content in our lives.

Now, the inappropriateness of the previous examples may be obvious, but sometimes our motives are not as obvious. Can you think of a time when you have prayed for something that you wanted that could have come from evil motives? The Bible says that sometimes we ask with evil motives. So what is it that we ask for sometimes that could be illegitimate?

For an athlete it might be, "Lord, help me do well in the game/competition tonight." Is that a legitimate request? It could be, but it might not be. Why do I want to do well? Is it for His glory (which, of course, I would say it is!) or is it so that I can impress others and win more friends and admirers?

"I want another car." Is that okay? Well, maybe sometimes it is and sometimes it isn't. If one needs the car to get to work and the present car keeps breaking down, then maybe it is appropriate. But if a person wants the car to impress his or her friends, then it is probably not appropriate and comes from a sinful motive.

You might be asking, "Well, how do we know when it is from the wrong motive?" That may be hard to discern.

But are there times that you ask God for things with an improper motive? Most likely the answer to that is, "Yes." It probably happens. We all probably ask for some things that we really shouldn't be asking for, without regard for what God wants. If the Bible is talking about asking with wrong motives, then it is apparent that it does happen. It is good to take inventory, to discern for ourselves what those wrong motives would be for us.

PERFORMANCE PRAYERS

What else can be wrongly motivating us when we pray, other than what we are asking for? Could we ever pray with evil motives, in terms of what we are trying to get out of it? -- not just our *words*, but *the fact* that WE are praying? Do you know of anyone that ever prays to try to look good?

We may pray in order to sound spiritual. We may pray in order to have people look at us, respect us, to think, "Wow, what a godly person!" Do we have some biblical example that verifies that?

What does the Bible say in Matthew 6:1-18 about the Pharisees/hypocrites? That entire passage has built in it the whole idea of goals or motives.

The Pharisee and the Publican by Harold Copping
(Source: Copping, Public Domain)

Concerning prayer in verses 5-8 it says, "And when you pray, do not be like the hypocrites, for they love to pray standing in the synagogues and on the street corners, *to be seen by men.*"

Notice those last four words: "to be seen by men"/ by others. God is telling you, "Here is their goal. This is their motive, their intention."

The verses continue: "I tell you the truth. They have received their reward in full. But, when you pray, go into your room, close the door and pray to your Father, who is unseen. Then your Father, who sees what is done in secret, will reward you. And when you pray, do not keep on babbling like pagans, for they think they will be heard because of their many words. Do not be like them, for your Father knows what you need before you ask him."

When thinking about "babbling like pagans," it triggers the memory of an incident that happened years ago at a graduation ceremony. A mother and her two-year-old daughter were sitting together listening to the man on the stage who was offering the ceremonial prayer. The prayer continued to go on and on and on. Finally, amidst the somewhat monotone utterances, came a loud, childlike, "Amen!" But the child's hint to end the prayer did not meet her expectations, so as the prayer continued on, she said it again -- a little louder this time, "AMEN!" At that point, though the mother was trying to quiet her little girl, everyone around them started to laugh! The reason? They were all thinking the same thing -- that the prayer should be ending, but she was the only one who was brave enough to express that "It's time to be done now."

Now, that is not to say that he was definitely babbling like a pagan, but there are times when some people go on and on and on. Could it be that they are thinking more about impressing the people listening than thinking about God and what the prayer is about? It is easy sometimes to change our good goal of: "I want to pray for this person. I care for this person," to a goal of: "I hope this sounds good." "I hope I am using the right words." "I hope that people are, maybe a little, impressed with my prayer."

This is what Christ was saying about the Pharisees. He was talking about hypocrites that may appear to others as being "godly." They pray long, lofty, godly-sounding prayers "to be seen by men."

Ask yourself, "Could that be true of me? Am I sometimes more concerned about how I *perform* my spirituality? Do I *throw things in* my prayer, or even in casual conversation, to try to elicit acclaim from others? Am I sometimes more concerned about what impression I want to make on the audience?"

Have you ever interjected something like this when speaking with someone: "When I got up this morning, just before I read my Bible , . ."? Did you just want to "throw that in there" so the listeners knew that you read your Bible every morning? Are there times where you intentionally mention something because you want your audience to know what you do or did? It happens.

Sometimes we WANT to be seen by men. Sometimes we do it consciously. And sometimes we are not even aware that we are doing it. But the Bible says sometimes it happens and our real goal is to impress. Our real goal is to get people to like us and/or respect us.

This discussion does not, however, include the times when things are "thrown in" with a godly motive. An example given by a student was, "When I'm around an unbeliever, part of me wants to throw things into the conversation to give him something positive and help him understand my faith." That is not what is being discussed here. That would be a godly motive. If in essence one is saying to the guy, "I want you to hear this because this is something good for you," that is different than "I want you to think I'm godly." If information is suggested in order to *impress*, however, then obviously, the motive would not be proper.

That would be the distinction. "I want you to hear this because I think you have a need and I want you to find answers for that" is different from "I want you to think I'm godly and think I'm a great person," or even "I want you to become a Christian so I have another *notch* in my belt, of people I have led to the Lord." Philippians 1 says that even leading someone to the Lord can come from "selfish ambition." When the interest is to benefit me rather than you, then it is done with the wrong motive.

Quiet Godliness

Look at Matthew 6:1-4? It says,

> Be careful not to do your acts of righteousness before men, to be seen by them. If you do, you will have no reward from your Father in heaven. So when you give to the needy, do not announce it with trumpets, as the hypocrites do in the synagogues and on the streets, to be honored by men. I tell you the truth, they have received their reward in full. But when you give to the needy, do not let your left hand know what your right hand is doing, so that your giving may be in secret. Then your Father, who sees what is done in secret, will reward you.

He refers to impressing others twice in that passage: "to be seen by men," "to be honored by others." In other words, the desire should be to give in a way that is quiet and undisclosed.

How many times when a donation is made to someone or an organization is there a picture in the newspaper? Sometimes the check is huge -- several feet long -- having an amount like "$100,000" written on it, with a number of people holding the check. Now that doesn't always mean that the donation was given with the wrong motive. It can be a celebration shared with all who gave or an honoring of an unsuspecting giver or receiver but could it be that sometimes the gift is given to "be seen by men"? Could it sometimes be more for "self-enhancement" than pure motives? Maybe. It seems from the Matthew 6 passage that what God really likes is quiet godliness.

This passage is saying, "When you pray, go where nobody sees you. Close the door." Don't pray so that people say, "Wow, he/she is quite a pray-er!" Again, at times, public prayer is done with pure concern and allows all to unite in the words spoken. A public prayer can be a comfort and a true ministry. But God wants our intimate talks with Him to be personal, one-to-one, unobserved by others.

And when you give your money, do it quietly. Pull it out so that nobody sees. Give in a way that does not seek self-attention.

Milton Petrie was a wealthy man who loved to give what he had.[16] Petrie would take notice of events around the country and articles

---

[16] I first heard this story not long after Petrie's death on a TV program – I believe it was *Sixty Minutes*, but the story can also be verified in numerous internet articles such as : "A Real-life Santa Leaves A Big-hearted Will To Be Remembered," *Chicago Tribune News* (Nov. 24, 1999) posted story from *New York Daily News*.

in the newspaper and would give his money away to various causes -- much of it being donated anonymously. During his later years, he took note of news reporting a young woman who had been a model, Marla Hanson, whose face had been slashed in 1986. It was an act that was orchestrated by her former landlord after she rejected his sexual advances -- the injury attempting to end her career. Mr. Petrie heard about her plight and felt for her. Petrie donated money for her to have plastic surgery -- though he did not want it revealed that he donated the money. For a long time, she did not know who had donated the money to her and who continued to donate $20,000 a year to her. He revealed his identity to her just before his death in 1994. But after he died, it was revealed that he had generously given large sums of money to many people and causes where no one had ever known where the money had come from. It was his wife who revealed it, exposing him because she wanted people to know the wonderful things he had done. It was a beautiful story about how he gave his money and did not want others to know that it came from him. He loved to do all of this in secret, and his wife and the few who helped manage his financial affairs said that he got such a delight from knowing that others were helped and their lives were better. Milton Petrie was quoted as saying, "The more I make, the more I can give away. The good Lord has been good to me, and I'm trying to return the favor," and "I just want to do as much good in the world as I can" (cybernation.com, 2012).

That is the way the Christian life is supposed to be. The selfless Christian wants to see the effects of what is going on in others' lives and know that he could be a part of that. Yet, he does not want the affected party to know that he was a part of it. He has no *need* to make that known.

Nothing is wrong with feeling good about helping others, but sometimes it becomes easy to switch the goal to impressing people. "I want this act to convince others that I am a good person." God is saying, "Do not do that. Do not let your 'left hand' know what your 'right hand' is doing."

The last verses in this section -- Matthew 6:16-18 --say, "When you fast, do not look somber as the hypocrites do, for they disfigure their faces to show men they are fasting. I tell you the truth, they have received their reward in full. But when you fast, put oil on your head and wash your face, so that it will not be obvious to men that you are fasting, but only to your Father, who is unseen; and your Father, who sees what is done in secret, will reward you."

---

http://articles.chicagotribune.com/1994-11-22/news/9411230054_1_petrie-stores-milton-petrie-mr-petrie. Accessed on 7/28/12.

Most of us do not fast (especially around the holidays!), but if we do, what does the Bible say about how we should fast? It says, "Don't make it obvious"

The same idea is conveyed here. Do it secretly. Do it quietly. God wants us to practice "quiet" godliness. God says, "Don't get caught up in the glory. I know what you are doing and that is what is important. Do it quietly."

So the Bible gives us plenty of information on motives and how they can be good and evil. The evil can be apparent or it can be greatly disguised and come from very seemingly spiritual or religious people. God makes it clear that the goals of even religious people can be "to be seen by others" or "to be admired by others." Goals may be conscious and they may be unconscious.

Connections to Longings

So the Teleological Capacity refers to our goals and intentions. We are people of purpose. Therefore, we do things with an intention. We do things with a goal in mind. Behind everything that we do is a motive, even if we do not know what it is.

It is important to find out if it is a good motive. Ask yourself, "Am I driven by good things that fit with what God wants? Or am I driven by things that I alone want -- things that are more selfish?"

We have already looked at the fact that goals can be self-enhancing or self-protective. Goals can be all about our getting our own needs met apart from God. Our goals can be centered around protecting ourselves from pain in an illegitimate way.

So part of our objective should be to find out why we do what we do. "Why am I being so nice to that person right now?" "Why am I saying this right now?" "Why am I avoiding that?" "Is this for a good reason, or is this for a self-enhancing, self-protective kind of reason?"

How are they connected? Our goals spring from our beliefs and give direction to them with a purpose of getting longings met or protecting ourselves from pain. The teleological capacity is connected to the rational capacity. The rational capacity is connected to the social and existential capacities.

Goals and Desires

If we are to continue this discussion further, there needs to be a distinction made between "Goals" and "Desires." This is a concept that Dr. Larry Crabb (1982) devised that differentiates between something that can be controlled and something that cannot be controlled.

"Goals" in this section will be defined as "something I can control." For example: "I want to be a good sister." One can have control of that. "My goal is to be close to God." We have control of that as well. "I want to be a good student." Again, that is controllable. "I have decided to exercise to get my body in the best condition it can be in." That can be done.

"Desires" are things that we want, but DO NOT have control of. Examples: "I want my mate or roommate to change." "I want my boss to treat me better." Those may be good desires, but we do not have control of making those things happen.

We may think, "I don't like the way they are acting. I want them to be different." That may be a good desire, but it cannot be controlled. The problem comes *when we turn desires into "goals."* We try to control that which we cannot control. And when that happens, we resort to manipulative strategies.

We try to manipulate people to get what we want. We try to "guilt them" into it. We attempt to intimidate or we try to be really nice and sweet. Our intention is to do something to GET others to give us what we want, because we have turned a *desire* into a *goal*.

When we turn our desire into a *goal*, it is not a real goal because it doesn't fit the above definition. We do not have control of it; but we treat it like a goal. We put the pressure on ourselves (and others) to MAKE it happen.

"I want to get an 'A' on my research paper." Is that a goal or a desire? When this question is asked to students, many times they say it is a goal because, "I am the one who wrote the paper." But is that true?

What if the teacher thinks it is a "B" paper? Can you control that? Can you control your professor? Only the professor has control of the grade, right? So even if you did a fabulous job on the paper, you still might not get an "A." So getting an "A" on the research paper is really a *desire*, not a *goal*.

Sometimes husbands say that they just want to make their wives happy. Doesn't that sound like a nice goal? But should the husband in that situation make that a goal for himself?

What if the wife continues to reject him no matter what he does? What if she says that anything he does is never enough and she continues to complain, be dissatisfied, or be angry? Can he control that? The only thing he can control is the way he treats her. He can love her the best that he can. That can be his true goal. His wife being happy can be a legitimate desire, but he will only continue to make his life miserable if he makes it a goal -- because he may not be able to find a way to make her happy.

Our job is to love the best we can. If couples would get a hold of that concept, there would be less marital conflict.

Often goals (the REAL goals) are unconscious. A man may SAY his goal is to be a better husband and he may truly aspire to that; but he does not realize that, in reality, he is doing everything he can to MAKE his wife happy. As a result, when nothing "works" and she still is not happy with anything he does, he is miserable. Why? Because he cannot do it. He cannot MAKE HER happy.

Unconscious goals that are often revealed in counseling are, "I did not realize that I came to counseling so that you would team up with me to change my spouse," or "to think well of me," or "to blame my kid." But the counselor has to have the "ears" that can listen beneath the words and hear the underlying motives. If not, the counselor may reinforce wrong goals and wrong thinking.

Power Struggle

Sometimes our goal conflicts with another's goal. Then we can get into a "Power Struggle." A Power Struggle occurs when there are two incompatible goals. It goes something like this:

Coach: "I want you to be a role-player on the basketball team."

Player: "I want to be the leading scorer on the team."

Coach: "You need to do it my way, because this will make us the best team."

Player: "But I want to do it my way, because I get more glory."

Coach: "But my reputation as a coach depends on it."

Player: "But my reputation as a player depends on it."

Now, generally people do not come out and voice their goals that bluntly. These may not be words that are said, but they may be words that are thought and acted upon. The goals conflict, and if one person continues to push his belief on the other, the power struggle continues.

It is important to note that when anyone is involved in a power struggle, it is ALWAYS his or her fault. It takes "two to tango." If you are involved in a power struggle, it is your fault because you are making a choice to try to change the other person. If your goal is to change someone else, you do not have control of that! You do not have that kind of power. If you choose to refrain from trying to control the other person, then you are no longer in a power struggle.

That is so crucial to understand when it comes to counseling. We, as counselors, cannot change our clients. They will only change if they choose to. Counselors sometimes have the belief that they are smart enough, clever enough, or skilled enough to change people. Counselors cannot do that! If counselors can accept that truth, they will become less frustrated with their clients and have a better chance of not "burning out."

It is the same with parenting. If the parent thinks, "I'm going to change my kids," "I'm going to MAKE them godly!" "I'm going to MAKE them behave!" and then yells and screams at them, he is involved in a power struggle.

God does not want that. He does not want us involved in the power struggle. God does not say, "Make your kids godly." He does say, "Love them" and train them in a godly manner (Prov. 22:6). Give them good information (Deut. 6:7).

William Glasser (who was referred to in a previous section) says that there is one thing we can do. (This author would argue that there are probably at least two or three things we should or could do.) The one thing we can do with people, says Glasser, is to "give them information." In his mind, that is all we can do.

Though there are probably several things we can do, it is still up to the recipient to respond. He or she still has control of his or her actions. We can love them well, pray for them (prayer being a part of loving them well), AND give them information; but it is still up to them about what they want to do with that information.

If one gets involved in a power struggle, he or she needs to say, "This is my fault." He/She needs to pull back and say, "Lord, please forgive me for trying to control something that I cannot control. I am trying to change them. I am trying to play God. That is your job God, not mine. Help me to love them and give them good information. The rest is up to you."

We may cry for people who make bad choices. We may get angry for them because we care for them. That is different because we are not trying to "get them" to do something for us. There is a time to be sad and to be angry, and it can be legitimate because "I don't want you to do it for me, but I want you to do it for yourself." Yet, we still remember that only they are in charge of themselves and they are the only ones who can make their own choices.

This is where the "Tough Love" idea comes in. In parenting you say, "I love you too much to argue with you about this."

The parent may say, "Yeah, but she keeps following me around and she keeps yelling and screaming!"

"Well, what do you do?"

"I turn around and yell back!"

"That is the problem. Allow her to follow you around and/or keep yelling at you while you do your chores. Let her notice you acting the same way you would be acting if she weren't there. She will eventually lose her steam. After being ignored for awhile, she will conclude, 'This is no fun to play because you won't play!'"

"But she pushes my buttons!"

"Absolutely! And you react! That is what you are responsible for! You have to learn how to refrain from reacting -- to ignore and not reinforce that behavior."

It is very helpful for anyone to learn the difference between goals and desires. As counselors and parents, it is crucial!

Master Goal

Master goal: 1 Corinthians 10:31 -- "So whether you eat or drink or whatever you do, do it all for the glory of God."

The one goal we can control is godliness. Others cannot block that goal. Others can yell and scream at us. They can throw things at us. They can hate us. Our boss can fire us. Others can do all kinds of things to us. But you know what? We can choose to respond in a godly manner to them, no matter how nasty they are. We can be in control of our own godliness! It is not dependent on what others do.

Sometimes people say, "Well, I cannot do what is right because of what they are doing." That is not true! The idea that one cannot make good choices until the other person changes is simply wrong. We can make GOOD choices even if others are making poor ones.

Now sometimes it is not easy to make the choice to do what is right. The fact that it may be hard should not be minimized. But the idea that one has "no choice" (often heard from adolescents), is simply untrue. "I had no other choice! I had to punch him!" Is that right? If you have worked with kids, you have probably heard something like that. "He was provoking me. What else could I do? I had to punch him."

"No, there are some other choices. You could walk away."

"But if I walk away, I'm not a man!" Ah! Do you hear the belief? The belief is: "I cannot walk away because my reputation is too important!" The goal is: "I must look like a man"; therefore, *"I've got to punch him!"* That makes sense – according to that belief system.

So in reality, we always have choices even though sometimes it does not feel that way. And if the goal is, "I have got to prove my manhood," then sure, I am going to punch the other guy. It makes sense.

A better belief would be: "Maybe I do not need to prove I am a man or maybe the way I am choosing to demonstrate my manhood does not really demonstrate it. Maybe I would truly be proving my manhood if I walked away. Maybe that is not what my goal is all about. And maybe then, I CAN walk away."

(It should be noted here that the author is not implying that it is always appropriate to walk away. There is a time to demonstrate righteous anger to people, just as Christ did when He got out the whip at the temple and drove out the money changers. It appears that He used that whip in such a way that they were fearful of getting hit by it, because they "cleared out" of the temple -- Matt. 21:12 & Mark 11:15. However, Christ had a godly goal.)

We all have choices, but they may not always be the ones we think we have, and some of our choices may not be based on the right goals. Also, the same behavior can be godly or ungodly depending on the goal. But there is always a godly way to act, and we can always make a choice to please God.

Determine your goals and desires. Sometimes we have a wish list. "I wish my life would be different." We wish a lot of things would be different in our lives. We may wish we would inherit a large sum of money. We may wish we were handsome or pretty. We may wish we would be promoted or valued. We may wish we had different parents or siblings. We may wish we had a certain job. Are those things we can control?

Find a way to distinguish between goals and desires. That is very helpful when we find ourselves struggling with life's circumstances.

Take responsibility for your goals and pray for your desires. Often what we do is to reverse those. We pray, "Help me to be a better friend," and then we try to control our friends. We may pray, "Help me to be a better student," then we get angry when we don't get an "A." Or one may pray, "Lord, help me to be a better wife," and then try to control her husband.

The problem with these is they are bad "goals" (desires turned into goals.) You are going the wrong way. You are *praying for your goals* and *taking responsibility for your desires*. You need to reverse that. Take responsibility for your goals! Take control of proper goals by controlling what you can control. Do not try to control those things that are not under your control and that are your desires, like friends doing what you want and liking you or your desire to get an "A." (Remember, it is legitimate to pray for our desire that the world would be a better place, but we have to keep in mind that we cannot control anyone but ourselves.)

"I want to be a better student. Here are some things I can control today. I can put in an hour of study. I can begin my paper, etc. Here are some things I CAN DO today to make things different."

"Lord, here's how I would LIKE my roommate, my boss, my wife, my husband, my kids, my world, to respond to me. It would be SO GREAT if they would change! -- to be the kind of people that would be easier to get along with. But you know what, God? I am going to do what I can and try to make godly choices." And sometimes people will choose to act better when I choose not to try to control them. At least the potential grows!

Remember, goals are often unconscious. Often we are not aware that we are trying to control something that we cannot control. So if you perceive a wrong goal in someone that you care about, there may be times where it is appropriate to give soft, loving confrontation. And there are times for heavy, strong confrontation when done in love for the good of another.

But start by looking into your own life. Take control of what you can and leave the rest to God. You can always do what is right and godly in any situation. As counselors you can practice this in your counseling and model this for your clients.

Summary

All people do things with a motive. That motive may or may not be realized. Sometimes it takes others to "draw it out." Anger and frustration may indicate improper motives. In understanding those improper motives, distinguish between goals and desires. Then avoid the power struggle and take responsibility for what can be controlled. In essence, set godly goals.

This is vitally important for counselors. We cannot control our clients. We cannot change them. If we think we can (belief) and try to (goal), then anger and "burn out" may follow. We can only control ourselves. We can love our clients, give them good information, and pray for them, but the rest is up to them. There are those that will make the choice NOT to change. If we get into power struggles with our clients, it is our fault. That is when we need to humbly ask for forgiveness and then enter their lives again -- doing only what we can control. This is the secret to a long ministry in counseling!

CHAPTER 9

THE VOLITIONAL CAPACITY

The next topic to consider when looking at how we were made in God's image is the idea of choices. God created us to be choice-makers, just as God is also a choice-maker. We will call this aspect of personhood the "Volitional Capacity."

The Volitional Capacity is for the purposes of deliberation and determination. We make choices. We have looked at the Rational Capacity where evaluation takes place and the Teleological Capacity which involves direction. The next capacity involves deliberation and determination. That is a very academic way of saying, "We are 'choice-makers.'"

In other words, man has a capacity to CHOOSE his goals, CHOOSE his desires, CHOOSE his thinking, and CHOOSE how he is going to meet his needs. It all works together. We are choice-makers, which is based on our goals, which are based on our thinking, which is based on how we are trying to get our needs met. We have a capacity to choose a certain course in life. We have a capacity to choose our goals and our thinking about how to get our needs met. We have a WILL. When the Bible talks about a "will," this is what it is talking about -- the Volitional Capacity.

Biblical Data

The Greek language used in the Bible shows that there is an exercise of volition. Several words in the Greek talk about our volitional capacity. "Boulomai" -- expresses the deliberate exercise of volition.

God as subject:
Matt. 11:27, Luke 10:22 -- ". . . those whom/to whom the Son *chooses* to reveal him."

Man as subject:
James 3:4 -- ". . . Ships . . . are steered . . . wherever the pilot *wants to go*."
James 4:4 -- "Anyone who *chooses* to be a friend of the world becomes an enemy of God."

In Erickson's *Christian Theology* (1985), he wrote about Irenaeus and his view of the image of God and man. Irenaeus (n.d.) believed Adam, in God's image, had reason and free will. Other theologians, such as Hodge (1979), Chafer (1978), and Knox (1982) include "will" as part of what it means to be in the image and likeness of God. This is how God can hold people responsible. We are free agents who can choose.

The whole idea of "agency" is the idea of choice-making. We have freedom to choose whatever we want. That does not negate God's sovereignty. God is sovereign and in control, but we are still free, moral agents who have the freedom to choose good or bad. How God's sovereignty and man's volitionality come together is a mystery. That will be one of the questions we can ask when we get to heaven. But Scripture teaches both. The following are a few verses that demonstrate those concepts.

GOD'S SOVEREIGNTY

Isa. 46:10 – "I make known the end from the beginning, from ancient times, what is still to come. I say: My purpose will stand and I will do all that I please."

Dan. 4:35 – "All the peoples of the earth are regarded as nothing. He does as he pleases with the powers of heaven and the peoples of the earth. No one can hold back his hand or say to him: 'What have you done?'"

Eph. 1:11 – In him we were also chosen, having been predestined according to the plan of him who works out everything in conformity with the purpose of his will."

Ps. 115:3 – "Our God in heaven; he does whatever pleases him."

Rom. 9:18 – "Therefore God has mercy on whom he wants to have mercy, and he hardens whom he wants to harden."

Ps. 135:6 – "The Lord does whatever pleases him, in the heavens and on the earth, in the seas and all their depths."

Acts 15:17b-18 – ". . . the Lord, who does these things that have been knows for ages."

MAN'S FREEDOM

Rom. 1:24-28 – "Therefore God gave them over in the sinful desires of their hearts to sexual impurity for the degrading of their bodies with one another. They exchanged the truth of God for a lie, and worshipped and served created things rather than the Creator – who is praised forever. Amen. Because of this, God gave them over to shameful lusts. Even their women exchanged natural relations for unnatural ones. In the same way the men also abandoned natural relations with women and were inflamed with lust for one another. Men committed indecent acts with other men, and received in themselves the due penalty for their perversion."

I Cor. 10:27 – "If some unbeliever invites you to a meal and you want to go, eat whatever is put before you without raising questions of conscience." Verse 30 – "If I take part in the meal with thankfulness, why am I denounced because of something I thank God for?"

Philemon 14 – "But I did not want to do anything without your consent, so that any favor you do will be spontaneous and not forced."

John 1:13 – ". . . children born not of natural descent, nor of human decision or a husband's will, but born of God."

John 3:16 – "For God so loved the world that he gave his one and only Son, that whoever believes in him shall not perish but have eternal life."

Compare Rev. 17:13 (choice) with 17:17 (sovereignty).

Rev. 17:13 – "They have one purpose and will give their power and authority to the beast."

Rev. 17:17 – "For God has put it into their hearts to accomplish his purpose by agreeing to give the beast their power to rule, until God's words are fulfilled."

But though God is sovereign and knows the future, we are unrestrained choice-makers. We can make choices about our lives and what we want to do with them.

Our ability to choose is why God can hold us responsible. He could not hold us responsible if we were not free agents.

B. F. Skinner

There are secularists, though, who have argued with that idea of man being a choice-maker. B. F. Skinner asserted that we are trainable -- much like animals -- responding to positive and negative consequences, being in essence only mere products of our environment. Following an evolutionary model (presuppositions), we are simply higher functioning animals. And as animals, we respond to our environment in terms of the reinforcement we receive.

Although Skinner did not deny the presence of internal forces, he did deny their place in scientific psychology. And following a deterministic view, he did not believe in free will. He wrote a book entitled, *Beyond Freedom and Dignity* (1971), implying that man has no real freedom. We are "empty organisms" that are programmable and controlled by our environment.

The idea of humans being image bearers with the capacity for free choice contradicts his teachings. We are simply higher-functioning animals and psychology is simply the science of learning how to reinforce desired behavior and eliminating unwanted behavior. In doing so, we can better cope and adapt to our environment.

A few things from his life demonstrate how consistently he followed his theory. He built an enclosed crib (labeled an "air crib") for his daughter to provide a controlled environment and alleviate some difficulties with early childcare. Pictures of it show it to be quite comfortable and it appears that he and his wife were very loving toward her. His daughter seemed to have functioned quite well, apparently having no ill effects from it.

He remained consistent with his theory throughout his life. "Well into his 80s, Skinner continued to work with enthusiasm and dedication. He regulated his habits -- recording his daily work output and the average time spent per published word (in minutes). Thus, he became a living example of his definition of humans as complex systems behaving in lawful ways" (Schultz & Schultz, 2013, p. 376).

Skinner's techniques of reinforcement are not much different from strategies implemented by Christian parents. Even most programs that have to do with delinquency are based on reinforcement – token economy and reward systems. So there is truth to what Skinner was saying in regard to our behaviors as products of our training. (Proverbs 22:6 substantiates that belief when it says, "Train a child in the way he should go, and when he is old, he will not turn from it.") Behavior modification and token economy are techniques used in schools and businesses and Skinner's theories/techniques are helpful in counseling.

So how was Skinner wrong? He was wrong in that he did not believe that we are image-bearers with the capacity for choice. His presuppositions were faulty – he started at the wrong point. He did not begin with God and God's Word and therefore rejected the notion of man having a free will.

Connecting the Capacities

So how does one's capacity for making choices connect to his or her longings, rationality, and teleology? We choose a course of life based upon our goals, based upon our beliefs about what will fulfill longings, or protect us from longings not being met (pain of rejection).

Through his years on Earth, man chooses a certain path in life. His goal is to "get" something. He believes that in getting that particular thing, his needs will be met and he will protect himself from pain.

Do you see how it all fits together? We are breaking it into parts, but there is a holistic picture that exists at the same time.

Morality

When considering morality, one can find supporters of the idea that morality is a separate capacity. And some may say that morality is a part of this capacity, the Volitional Capacity, only. This author believes, however, that morality is a part of EVERY capacity. Morality is the outworking of the capacities. It is the direction of each particular capacity.

We can think the right way. We can think the wrong way. We can choose the right way. We can choose the wrong way. We can have a good goal. We can have a sinful goal. We can emote in a way that God wants us to emote. (We will talk about that in Chapter 11 – The Emotional Capacity). Or we can emote in ways that are wrong. There is a righteous anger and there is an unrighteous anger.

Scripture teaches that "directional" quality of sin. It means to "miss the mark" (Rom. 3:23), to "transgress" the law of God (1 John 3:4), to "rebel against" or "disobey" God (Deut 9:7) and to "trespass" (Col. 2:13). The directional tone is apparent as opposed to a separate capacity. Are we moving toward God or away from Him?

Recognizing That I Am a Choice-Maker

People need to know they are choice-makers. This is especially true in counseling and a point our clients need to understand. Sometimes we talk like victims: "I *have to*," or "She *made me* mad." But it is important to know we are choice-makers. We do not "have to" do anything and no one can "make" us mad.

Some people do not realize that, however. Who are the people that might grow up without realizing they are choice-makers? Choice-making may be hard to understand for those who have grown up with authoritative parents that have taught them, in essence, "I have made all of the choices for you; therefore, simply follow what I have told you to do."

Who are the other people that would not see themselves as choice-makers? Very dependent people and very needy people may not see themselves that way. They say, "Oh, I don't make any choices. I always let 'so-and-so' make them for me. I depend on them to make the choices for me.

But is that really true? Who is making the choice to let someone else choose for them?

Giving one's choice away is a choice. Letting other people make choices for oneself is a choice. Letting people run our lives is a choice. We are no less choice-makers simply because we give our choices away. We just made choices that we were not aware of and now we are choosing to let someone else make our choices/decisions by complying with what they want.

Hypnosis

This is true with hypnosis. "The subject's sense of safety and morality remain entrenched throughout the experience. . . A hypnotist can't get you to do anything you don't want to do" (Harris, 2010).

But some exclaim, "I saw them get up there and act like chickens on stage!" or "They barked like dogs." Well, on some level, that is what the hypnotized subject *wanted* to do.

Sometimes they continue, "But you don't know this person. They are so introverted. They're very quiet and they would never. . ." You know what? Something in them said, "I want to. I will enjoy this, on some level."

This was dramatically confirmed for this author years ago when a campground worker dressed in a costume before doing his "job" which involved interacting with the campers. One extremely introverted man that put on a costume every day, immediately transformed into an outgoing entertainer the minute he had donned the "protective" wear! The change was remarkable!

Hypnosis could be something like that. It may give a sense of "freedom" to some who may not otherwise feel the freedom in a typical setting.

And if you watch the hypnotist, you may note that he will often enter into the audience – going right to the front row. (That is where most of the people sit who are thinking, "I want to be involved with this.") And he might be thinking that the ones in the closest rows are probably the more suggestible ones.

He will pick a few -- bringing them up on stage with him. And being trained to look into their eyes and to perform a few "tests," the hypnotists can usually discern who is more susceptible to being put into a trance and who is not. He then chooses to keep some of the volunteers and send others back to their seats. The remaining ones will be used for the demonstration.

There are people out there on the "given-to-trance" scale that are very, very suggestible people. And then, there are other people that one could try to hypnotize until they are blue and they are still going to respond, "I will not be hypnotized!" The person who is doing the hypnotism demonstration can often tell the difference when choosing his volunteers.

The hypnotist starts talking in a very slow, soft manner and says something like, "You are now feeling more relaxed." And the volunteer starts relaxing. In time, the volunteer does what is being asked of him – even barking like a dog or acting like a chicken.

But those hypnotized still do not go against their convictions or do things they morally oppose. People do not do what they don't want to do. What the hypnotists are doing is simply suggesting things to suggestible people.

It is amazing. But the subjects are merely responding to what the hypnotist suggests to them to do. They have not lost their volitionality. They are still choice-makers -- even under hypnosis.

Conformity

God wants us to make godly choices as strong choice-makers, not simply as compliant conformists. He gave us the freedom to choose, and it is important to use that ability in a way that is honoring to Him and to recognize that we alone are in charge of ourselves.

Konrad Lorenz (1970) is famous for his experiments that verified the phenomenon of "Imprinting." Imprinting is a term used to describe what happens with newborn animals (primarily in the bird family). The first being they see is "Mama." They hatch, see a moving being, and that moving being then becomes their leader.

(Source: 34696971 clipart.com, 2011)

Lorenz (1970) did experiments making himself the first one they saw. Lorenz would walk and newborn goslings would follow him. He played in the water. They played in the water with him. He was really the forerunner in ethology – the scientific study of animal behavior. In his studies, he found that he could actually be "Papa" to many animals.

Some look at the Christian life like that. They think that godliness is like "imprinting." -- You just blindly follow the leader. They think their response to Christian leaders should be, "I will do whatever you tell me to do."

They do not realize that they are still making choices. They may have given away their choice-making ability by saying, "I'll do whatever you tell me to do" (almost like that hypnotic trance), but they are still making choices.

It is doubtful that is what God wants. And when we get into the habit of just accepting others' choices and they turn out to be wrong, we are wrong too. If their "ship" is going down, we are going down with them. If we do not exercise our choice-making ability and allow it to become strong, we are easily "blown around" by the "winds" of life. Something inborn in all of us just feels good when we contemplate the options and make our own choices. Being strong, godly choice-makers is what God wants of all of us. He designed us that way.

But when you give someone the freedom to choose, he may not always choose the godly path. Yet, God gave Adam and Eve the freedom to choose what trees to eat from (Gen. 2:16, 17), even though He knew they were going to eventually eat of the forbidden tree. Theirs was a true choice. So when we, as sinners, choose Christ, the choice is real because we have evaluated the other options and made a free choice.

Those who do not feel a sense of freedom to choose either find a way to "rebel" at some point in their lives or they spend their lives looking for an authority figure who can tell them how to live their lives. Neither is what God desires for us.

One thing that is true about the rebellious ones is: at least they know they are strong choice-makers. And when they do CHOOSE Christ and/or CHOOSE to "repent," it is heart-felt and is more real to them than to those who merely conform. It seems harder to reach the conformists or to see change in them compared to the rebellious because one never knows where the conformists really stand.

The conformist is often unable to view himself as, and respond as, a choice-maker -- which in turn means that though his choices may seem godly, he is not really making godly choices. He is just doing what he was told to do. Conformists are often the ones who suffer from depression in their teenage or adult lives.

And so even though many parents dread the teenage "testing" of boundaries and authority, there is something good in that independent spirit. In that stage of "testing," teens are exercising and developing their ability to choose. They are saying, "I want to be sure that I understand and actively choose whether to obey the rules or not." There is something good in that, where at least they are finding out they can make their own choices. What is better is when they choose to make *godly* choices.

Parents can respond, "Yes, you can make your own choices. I want to reinforce that. I'm glad you're making your own choices. But you need to know you just made a bad choice. And there are consequences for that." But the most important thing is that if they can really "own" their choices, then when they "own" Christianity, it's theirs.

Some Amish have a tradition called "rumspringa." Rumspringa is the time when they turn sixteen years old and have the freedom to go out and experience the ways of the world. They are "turned loose" to go out and "sow their 'wild oats.'" If they then choose the worldly life, they make that choice on their own with their parents saying, in essence, "We give you the freedom to make that choice. We will not put our stamp of approval on that. But you know what? If and when you come back, you come back saying, 'I want this.' Then you will be 'owning' it. It will be your own decision." And many of them do come back and become Amish. They exercise their volition to choose their own way of life.

The Amish may be on to something. They are respecting their children's ability to choose. They are saying, "You go and find out that you are a choice-maker. And we will pray that you will make good choices."

We need to find a way to reinforce BOTH – the ability to choose and the need to make godly choices. As Christians, let's encourage and exercise volition in ourselves and others. As counselors, let's encourage that in our clients as well.

Recognizing Choices

Sometimes people will say, "I cannot make any choices. There are no choices to make."

Is that ever true? Is there ever a time when there are NO choices to make? Probably not, though sometimes our choices are very limited. If you have ever seen the movie, *Cast Away*, starring Tom Hanks, you will understand how it illustrates the reality of limited, yet available, choices.

In the movie, Tom Hanks plays a man who is stranded on a deserted island. His dialogue concerning his choices goes like this.

> . . . I knew she had to let me go, that I had lost her -- because I was never going to get off that island. I was going to die there, totally alone. And the only thing I could control was when, and where, and how. So I made a rope to hang myself and I had to test it and the limb snapped. And I couldn't even kill myself. I had control over NOTHING!
>
> And that's when the feeling came over me, that somehow, I knew I had to face life, alone. I had to keep breathing, even though there was no reason to go on. And that's what I did. I stayed alive. I kept breathing.
>
> And then one day the tide came in and brought me a sail. And now I'm back. And I'm talking to you. And I have ice in my glass. And I've lost her all over again!
>
> But I know what I have to do now. I've got to keep breathing. Because who knows what the tide could bring? (Broyles, *Castaway*, 2000).

Sometimes our choices are very, very limited. All we can do is choose to keep breathing. When a person is depressed, sometimes all he or she can do is get out of bed. All he can do is get dressed. All she/he can do is get herself to the appointment or get himself to the doctor. But we have choices. We are NEVER without choices! As limited as they might be, they are there.

And when someone says, "It was tough, but I got myself to the appointment today," as a friend you can respond, "Praise God. You made a good choice! You found a way to do something that was very difficult!"

Hopefully you will not say, "You mean that is all you did today? You got ready and came to the appointment? That is nothing!"

Sometimes even those little things need to be encouraged. Saying "Good for you!" may be what that person needs to hear because when someone is really depressed, it is tough to make good choices! And when someone makes a good choice, we want to encourage that because no matter what state we are in, we always have choices and can always make good choices. Counselors need to remember that. Encouragement goes a long way with our clients!

Sometimes all a person can manage to do is to put one foot in front of the other. But if that is true, then that is where to start and one can build on those choices. Encourage your client (or yourself if difficulties come your way) to do just that, and remind them that "one day you might find yourself out of the depression or moving past the unfortunate or disappointing situation. Then you are going to be glad that you made a choice back there to keep doing the things you needed to do."

Sometimes we can be surprised by how strong we have become, but the more we practice making choices, we strengthen our ability to make more choices in the future. Practicing making good choices can lead to more good choices in the future.

We don't know what God is going to bring "with the tide." God gave Tom Hanks a sail and he had no idea, after having been on that island for a number of years, that was going to happen.

Now, it was still up to him. He still had to make the choice to use it. He had to put it on a raft and tie it together. He had some work to do. But GOD gave him the sail. He then had choices to make regarding how he was going to work out all of the details.

Each of us has control of our own lives. We can pray for a sail, but it is up to God to bring it. In the meantime, we can keep breathing. We can choose to control what we are able. That is choice-making at its best.

So help your clients become aware of the fact that each of us is a choice-maker and we need to recognize our choices. We all need to look for those choices, because even though our choices may be limited or may not provide the alternative that we would really like, they are still there. And we can choose the godly way to go.

As counselors, help clients strengthen this capacity. Do not do for them what they can do for themselves. Start with small steps. Encourage them along the way. Help them develop volitional strength. Help them own their own progress or recovery. We want them to be strong and able to handle life because of what they choose, not because they are dependent on us. Help them become strong choice-makers and reinforce and pray for godly choices.

CHAPTER 10

THE BEHAVIORIAL CAPACITY

Introduction

The Behavioral Capacity is for the purposes of action and locomotion. God is a God who acts. We are creatures who act . . . behave . . . do things. This is an aspect of what it means to be in God's image.

Many verses in the Bible pertain to behavior. Romans 13:13 is one that summarizes the way that God would like us to behave. It says, "Let us behave decently, as in the daytime, not in orgies and drunkenness, not in sexual immorality and debauchery, not in dissension and jealousy."

Paul is saying, "Let's act like good people!" "Behave decently."

God is a behavioral creature. He made us like Himself in that way.

Reviewing the other capacities, we see how our being continues to reflect God in whose image we have been created.

God is a volitional creature. He made us to be choice-makers.

God is teleological. He made us goal-oriented.

God is rational. He made us to be thinking creatures.

God is existential. He designed us with a capacity for meaning and purpose.

God is social. He designed us with a capacity for relationships and love.

All of those capacities are God-like capacities that demonstrate how we are made in the image and likeness of God.

So what is the difference between our God-like capacities and God's capacities? Answer: We are trying to get our needs met. God doesn't have any needs. We are dependent. He is self-sufficient. Look at how those capacities connect in a practical way. One behaves in a manner consistent with his choices, which are based on his goals, which come from his beliefs about how to fulfill his longings and avoid the pain of longings not being met. They all work together.

When you behave or see others' behaviors, what you are seeing is the outworking of what is underneath -- that is, a set of choices. Beneath that, there is a reason for doing it. There is a motive or a goal. Beneath that, there is a belief system. What is the belief system about? It is about how to get needs met -- how to make life work. It is about how to get love and meaningful purpose and have impact in the world.

A Practical Example

Consider this example from the author's own life:
When I was growing up, I would practice basketball every day in the summer. As a high school student I would practice four to five hours a day. In fact, my high school yearbook has a picture of the fieldhouse when it was first built and my car was parked in front of it -- all alone with no other vehicle. I was in the fieldhouse gym every time I could get in there, to practice and play basketball.

Why would someone do that? I was acting out a set of *behaviors*. I was always practicing. Why?

I made a *choice* (volition) to practice four to five hours a day because my *goal* (teleology) was to be a great basketball player based upon my *belief* (rationality) that being good at basketball would fulfill my longings or in other words, get my needs met. It was a belief that said, "When I am a great basketball player, people will like me, accept me, and respect me. They will meet my *needs* (longings). My name will be in the paper. I will be well-known. I will be well-liked. Life will work well!" When you see a set of behaviors, realize that what the person is doing is telling you something about what is on the inside.

The behaviors you see are telling you, "These behaviors are coming out of choices." Is that a direct choice the person is making? Or is that something that is an indirect choice -- one feels like he *has to* do it but did not realize that it was a choice?

When basketball ended for me, what do you think I felt? (Though we will talk about the Emotional Capacity in the next chapter, we will touch on the subject here.) I had practiced hard. I went to college. I got a scholarship to play basketball, and yet, my sophomore year I got cut from the team. What do you think I felt when I got cut from the team?

If it was my goal to be a great basketball player and somebody said, "Not only are you not a great basketball player, but you are not good enough to play on our team," what do you think I felt? Disappointment? Sadness? Self-contempt? Contempt for others? I may have felt all of those things, and more!

Overlooking the emotional aspect for now, consider the behavior "change" that followed. When I realized that I could not play basketball anymore, I remember thinking (and it was almost a conscious thought), "I am going to take all of this energy that I had used for basketball and pour it into my academic major." It was my sophomore year of college and I was in my second year of Greek, so I thought, "I know what I can do. I am going to be a *Biblical Languages* major. I am going to take all of this energy and put it into a new set of behaviors." But the part you need to understand from this example is this: The goal had not changed! Only the behaviors had changed.

I still wanted to be well liked and respected. I still wanted to be well thought of. I still wanted to be somebody important. But I could not do it through basketball, so I decided to do it through theology . . . spirituality. What I did not realize was that I was doing the same thing!

But in my mind, I was thinking, "This goal is a lot better. God is smiling on me now because I am putting all of my energy into His Word. And I am going to do it well. I am going to practice hours a day!"

And I did -- parsing and conjugating, and reading and studying. I put all of my energy into it. It was not until I was working on my master's degree in counseling that I realized that the reasons why I was doing what I was doing were the same. They had not changed!

Now did coming to that realization mean that I needed to stop studying theology or throw my Bible away? No. It just meant that I needed to do some of those things with a different motive and maybe I did not have to be so demanding of myself. Maybe I did not need to put so much pressure on myself. If I really believed my needs were already met, I could study hard without being driven.

I had been doing all of those things because my thinking was, "I am not good enough." The compensation or attempt to meet the need to feel good enough had previously taken place with basketball, but when basketball ended, then the compensatory behavior was transferred to studying theology.

The point is this: sometimes we change behaviors, but we have not changed the internal mechanisms that are guiding those behaviors. A person may have the same beliefs about how to get his needs met; he may just be attempting to meet those perceived needs a different way now.

Consistent behaviors will tell us something about what is going on inside. Merely changing behaviors may not change the internal realities (behavioral substitution). But changing behavior is *a key element* when working with internal realities because changing behaviors can reinforce the correct internals (Eph. 4:17-32).

And one may look better. One may look more godly and more spiritual. But the behaviors that can be seen may not be more godly or more spiritual.

So ask yourself, "What drives me?" or "What drives them?" Why do I do what I do? It may be for good and godly reasons or it may not. It could be driven by sinful or selfish reasons -- even if it looks to others as if it is spiritual. It is good to challenge yourself and ask God to help you see what is underneath and what is driving you.

Nothing is wrong with attempting to do good behaviors even when you are not sure what may be motivating you. None of us is always going to have flawless motives, and having to be totally sure that our motives are always one hundred percent pure, could lead us to avoid attempting anything. In Philippians 1, Paul tells us that the Gospel can be furthered even when those propagating it have wrong motives. You may not always be able to be aware of every motive. We can be blind to ourselves. Yet, we can always choose to do good works while at the same time asking God to convict us of sin that is deep in our being.

Changing Behavior

Understanding hidden beliefs can be imperative to making some behavioral changes. Yet, at times changing behavior first is a good starting point. Attempting behavior change can REVEAL the motive more quickly and clearly. This sometimes happens in counseling situations.

Behavioral homework is often part of the counseling process. It reinforces what has been dealt with in the session -- in terms of beliefs and goals. If a husband says that he loves his wife and wants to be a good husband, a good question for the counselor to ask is: "What do you want to DO this week to love her?"

The question builds on the previous chapter's discussion of choices, using "collaborative homework." The idea is "I want US to come up with an 'assignment' together, because if I tell you (the client), 'Here is what you ought to do,' then I am making the choice for you and your response can be, 'Well, okay. I will do it because it is what the counselor told me to do' which usually does not promote lasting behavior change." The client needs to make a conscious *choice* in regard to his "homework" assignment.

Why would it be initially helpful to practice in tangible ways some of the things that have been discussed in the counseling session? Maybe it will help the husband discover the answer to this question, "Do you REALLY want to love your wife?"

By practicing a behavior that should demonstrate love, the client may come to the realization himself that he really does not want to do that particular behavior and maybe his real goal (whether conscious or unconscious) is more to get his needs met than really loving his wife. It can allow the client to discover on his own what his real goals and beliefs are.

Secondly, this is done because sometimes people start looking inside themselves during the counseling process and become so intrigued with that inner aspect that they forget that the new knowledge gained needs to be used in practical ways. They may get caught up in thinking,

"Wow! Am I an interesting creature! Look at my thoughts and desires and goals and how I am getting my needs met. This is fascinating! But please don't ask me to DO anything." Behavior change is a necessary component of inner change (Eph. 4:17-32).

Yet, we have demonstrated that at some point, discussion of the inner reality is necessary. This comes more to the forefront when a person is earnestly seeking behavioral choices. That may be a time to look at the goals and thinking that are connected to those choices from the very beginning. When people want a simple "formula" to practice in order to make life work better for them -- to make their husband or wife act the way they want, to gain some kind of acclaim, etc. -- those are times when it is most important to look into the goals and beliefs. Otherwise, they may be misled into thinking they are receiving some method that will meet all of their desires of making life "work" for them. If one does not understand the goals and beliefs that are driving him, then "prescribing" behavior without understanding can cause problems.

It is just like painting over rust. If you do not get rid of the rust underneath, eventually it will penetrate right through the new coat of paint. But once you have taken care of the "rust" (the inside), the outer "paint" (behavior) has a better chance of lasting. At that time (when the rust has been dealt with -- beliefs), it is more effective to put one's energy into the outer aspects of the material – the behavior.

So consistent behaviors demonstrate what is going on, on the inside – choices, goals, thinking. Merely changing those behaviors may not change the internal realities. But "tracking" those behaviors is important because those behaviors reveal the realities on the inside -- allowing the discovery of the true problems and the possibility of true change.

Earlier in this chapter, the term "Behavioral Substitution" was used. Behavioral Substitution is the name some assign to that phenomenon of changing that outer manifestation without changing the inner core of what is driving a person. When someone just switches one behavior for another without changing the foundation, it is like switching an addiction. He or she may not be addicted to alcohol anymore. He or she may be addicted to painkillers, or smoking, or eating, or sex, or something else.

Though changing behaviors may not change internal realities, changing behavior IS a key element when dealing with internal realities. Each affects the other. Both must be dealt with in counseling.

Example of Behavior Identifying a Belief

COMPULSIVE BEHAVIOR

NEATNESS

Take the following example of behavior signifying an underlying belief. A number of people in our world engage in compulsive behaviors. (It should be noted here that obsessions are uncontrollable thoughts and compulsions are behaviors that people feel driven to act out over and over again.) One such compulsion is a compulsion for neatness. (This is not just a desire for things to be neat, but a demand that everything in the person's life be neat, orderly, and tidy in a way that satisfies his/her obsessive thoughts.)

Assume for this example, that a husband has a compulsive need for order in his home. After his wife puts things away, he goes through and lines things up in an order that seems proper to him. Maybe he starts by reorganizing the cups in the cupboard, turning the handles so they are all on the right side. He might proceed to arrange the fringe on the rugs so that the strings are all straight and none are overlapping. He may confirm that the entries written in the checkbook ledger are all written in a particular way. (Maybe the dates are all written with slashes instead of dashes or the first letters in the entries are all capital.) His closets are perfectly arranged – shirts and pants washed and crisply ironed. His mail is placed in perfectly labeled organizational slots. If someone would try to "mess up" anything in his house or in his life, he would feel as if he was not able to cope with the alterations.

When people who struggle with this kind of compulsive behavior are asked to change the way they do things, their typical response is, "I CAN'T!" But is that true? In reality, can't they rearrange their closets? Obviously, Yes! And on one level, even the most compulsive person knows that it is true. He CAN! It is just very difficult!

The compulsive person's response indicates what is deep down and how he is lying to himself. He wants to believe that is not possible. What he is really saying is, "I don't want to do it."

Many times the underlying belief is, "If these things are not perfect, then I won't be able to deal with it or something bad will happen." If the person could truly believe that if something bad does happen, that it is okay because his needs are met in Christ, then the compulsive drive diminishes. Behavior can change when inner beliefs change! It is also true that practicing behavior change can help the inner beliefs change as well. That is why behavioral homework is so important in counseling.

For the client suffering from this kind of compulsive behavior, a counselor may ask him about his closet. The sufferer might tell the counselor that his pants and shirts are all neatly placed in his closet, with a week's worth of clothing sets planned in advance. In other words, Monday's pants and shirt are together, followed by Tuesday's pants and shirt, etc. Given what has been previously discussed with the client in counseling regarding what is driving his behavior (the internal realities of beliefs, goals, and choices that lead to needs being met), the counselor may ask him to purposefully "mess up" his closet. The counselor may say, "Please put Monday's pants with Tuesday's shirt."

When such a behavior change is recommended to this type of client, the counselor will usually see immediate terror appear in his client's eyes. But after a discussion about why the behavior is important, if and when the client agrees to carry through with the behavior, then real change has begun to take place. The client struggling with the compulsive behavior is beginning to believe that God is enough, even if he feels out of control.

The key to knowing if change has genuinely occurred is when the client returns and reports that he successfully completed the "homework." He may say it was difficult, but that life went on and all of the dreadful things that he feared would happen, did not happen. He has learned something! The internal work and insight led to behavior change. The behavior change helped reinforce the internal work. Hopefully he will continue to practice the new behaviors and as he does, he will find more freedom from the disabling symptoms. In doing so, he will also learn to trust more in God to meet his deepest longings.

But even good behaviors can be "empty." And though they may not be done obsessively, having no idea what is going on inside can leave one prone to "drifting" away from what is right. As Christians, we are taught to center our beliefs on what the Bible teaches. Our beliefs – whether correctly formed through biblical teaching and understanding or incorrectly formed to selfishly meet unnecessary or inappropriate desires -- are the *foundation* on which we build the story of our lives -- our behaviors. When there is no *rock* or foundation to stand on, one could be left prone to being misled by others to abandon his/her behaviors for a more seemingly "worthy" or "exciting" cause.

HAND-WASHING EXAMPLE

Another type of compulsive behavior is excessive hand-washing. What could be the belief behind the behavior of a compulsive hand-washer (or someone who constantly checks and rechecks things, or any other of a number of compulsive behaviors)? What makes someone wash his hands 30, 40, or even 50 or more times in a day? The thinking may go something like this, "If I don't wash my hands, the germs will get from my hands into my food."

If you have ever seen the movie, *The Aviator*, you may remember what one of Howard Hughes's girlfriends told him when he was concerned about cleanliness. She responded, "Nothing's clean Howard. We just do the best we can" (*Aviator*, 2004).

The compulsive hand-washer may play out that belief a little further and think, "It will contaminate the food. It will get in my children's food. They will get sick. And I will be responsible."

That is highly unlikely. But even if it did happen and the obsessed person was responsible for his child's illness, if the belief is, "That is catastrophic and must not happen," then the one with the faulty thinking becomes BOUND to the obsessive behavior. If he could somehow come to the realization that all of those bad things COULD happen, yet it would still be "okay" (God would still be in control and he would be forgivable, that his imperfect being would be viewed as perfect in God's eyes), then, again, the compulsion would minimize. Sometimes we can do our best and bad things still happen. That is something no human can absolutely control all of the time. You ARE GOING TO BE RESPONSIBLE for mistakes whether you are trying to do your best or not. Sometimes we can even think we have done everything right and bad things still happen.

Now take a look at your hands. If you were asked right now, "Are your hands clean?" what would you say? Yes?

But are your hands really clean? How do you know they are clean? You might say that you just washed them. But couldn't they be a little dirty? They have touched your clothing recently. Couldn't your clothing be just a little dirty? Wouldn't it make sense to go wash your hands to make sure that they really are clean? -- Maybe. But there is a time when continuing to wash your hands defies all reason.

It is true that "I never know if they are clean enough!" That is a reasonable thought. But the belief system that supports that statement is not based on God's ultimate control. True behavioral change involves faith. Do I have faith in God's control of things and am I able to deal with whatever He brings my way -- even if it is a germ? If I have done all that I can do (a *reasonable* number of times), that is where I need to trust God to take care of the rest.

Compulsive behaviors come from obsessions -- which are uncontrollable thoughts that drive the person to engage in particular behaviors. The beliefs go something like this: "If my hands aren't clean enough, then I could give germs to other people that could cause harm to them for which I am ultimately responsible."

So compulsions are belief-driven. If one can really believe that 1) "If germs get into the food and hurt someone and *I'm responsible, it is not catastrophic and life can go on,*" and 2) if one realizes, "God understands and will take care of me and my family in the way that He seems fit, and supply all of my needs," then he or she can quit washing so much. Whatever happens, it is not the end of the world. (It may be heartbreaking, but not devastating -- in the absolute sense. Life can still go on.) God knows, understands, and forgives if necessary. The same is true for obsessive checking or any other compulsive behavior. The beliefs HAVE TO be altered for lasting change to take place.

Behavior Chapter Summary

As Christians, God asks us to act. And yet, the Bible acknowledges that we are full of sin and cannot do enough deeds to earn our relationship with God or to be found righteous before Him. So we make choices to DO what we believe is right -- based on our understanding of what the Bible teaches. It is important to understand the depth of our sin and motives; but having that knowledge or seeking that knowledge should not keep us from moving out and behaving in ways that further God's kingdom. We can show love to others -- allowing God to accomplish His purpose through us. BEHAVIOR is important. But behavior by itself is hollow. Behavioral change is important, but internal change is necessary as well. Both are needed and both need to work in tandem. Otherwise, we simply paint over the rust, and the rust will emerge again.

As counselors, remember to deal with both. Too many counselors get caught up in providing insight for their clients, but insight alone will not change anyone. They must *practice* what they learned from their insight. If not, they will be in danger of being like the person in James 1:22-24. They look at themselves in the mirror and then walk away. That whole section in James is about reflecting and doing. Yes, God wants us to reflect, but He also wants us to act. "Faith without works is dead" (James 2:26). If we simply help our clients be intrigued with themselves as we focus solely on insight and internal realities, we may be reinforcing a different form of sin. Let's deal with the whole person – inside and outside.

CHAPTER 11

THE EMOTIONAL CAPACITY

The last capacity in our list of God-like capabilities is the "Emotional Capacity." The Emotional Capacity is "for the purposes of indication" (especially regarding goals and beliefs). Emotions are indicators. Think of them as the lights on the dashboard of a car. When the light says, "Service engine soon," "Battery," "Oil," or whatever, the problem is not usually the light. The problem is something under the hood or deep within the car. It is not the light, but what has caused the light to go on.

Sometimes, however, we attack the light. "Oh, the light came on! I need to fix that light!"

If one attacks what he sees -- the light -- will that help the car? What if someone finds a way to make the light go off? Is that a good thing?

A friend of the authors actually did that very thing. He found a way to keep the light in his car from coming on. He continued to drive the vehicle until his car overheated. In fact, the motor was damaged. Attacking the light caused problems for him.

Sometimes people ignore the light. They see the light, but they just do not want to take the time to think about why it is on. They may say, "Oh, don't worry about it. It's just the light. Maybe it will go off on its own." What can happen if we ignore the light?

Another option would be to completely cover the light. Some may put a piece of duct tape over it. Then individuals would not have to even see that the light is on. One could pretend that everything is fine and not be bothered by any reminder that something may be wrong.

But the light is trying to tell us something. It might be something deep within the car that needs to be addressed. The same is true with emotions.

Some people attack emotions. They attempt to "snuff out" emotions in themselves or others. "You shouldn't feel that way!" "Stop being angry!" "What are you crying about?" They try to stop emotions from showing up. But attacking emotions is like attacking the light. When one attacks a negative emotion, it does not help. Attacking a negative emotion will often even intensify that emotion!

Others ignore emotions. They pay little attention to what they are feeling on the inside. They know that their emotions seem out of place, but they just do not want to take the time to figure out what is wrong or do not know how. They may think that somehow the problem will go away on its own and everything will be fine.

Then there are those people who try to completely "cover up" their emotions. Those people are known to deny them -- in essence, repress emotions. They think that if they deny them, their emotions will not be there. They pretend that nothing is wrong and can become so adept in their pretending that they ultimately convince themselves (and often others) that everything is as it should be.

But we cannot totally obliterate our true feelings. They are always there somewhere. We can disguise them or deny them, but they are still there -- indicating what we are thinking on the inside.

God gave us emotions as a way of saying, "There's something inside that I want you to look at" -- especially as it pertains to goals and beliefs. That does not just mean "bad" emotions. That includes "good" emotions too. Emotions indicate that we are thinking something. That "something" involves a goal and a belief. Our emotions indicate both positive and negative beliefs -- appropriate and inappropriate, helpful and detrimental, both the good and the bad.

If one is having "happy" emotions, that means he believes something -- that he is thinking something. A belief is behind those "happy" emotions. That belief involves a goal that has not been blocked. A goal or a desire has been achieved. (Though having "happy" emotions does not necessarily mean that what he is happy about is a good thing. It just means that the goal he was hoping for was achieved. It was not blocked.)

But we can rejoice in the Lord (Phil 4:4) and be feeling good for godly reasons. Rejoicing is a "happy" emotion that comes from a godly goal. Yet, even sadness or anger can be godly. God is both sad and angry at times.

Our emotions indicate both the good and the bad; however, in this chapter the focus will be more on the negative aspects of our emotions. Remember as you continue reading though, that the emotional indicators are not just negative; they can be positive as well.

Godlike Capacities – Negative and Positive

This final capacity, the "Emotional Capacity," again corresponds to a capacity found in God. Look at these passages in the Bible: Judges 10:16 (anger), Psalm 103:13 (compassion), Psalm 145:8 (gracious, compassionate, slow to anger, rich in love), Matthew 26:38 (overwhelmed with sorrow to the point of death), John 11:33-35 (deeply moved, wept),

Ephesians 4:30 (grief), and Philippians 1:8 (affection). The passages reveal to us that God is emotional. God is a persistently emoting being! In fact, the Bible tells us that He gets angry every day! (Ps. 7:11).

Some read Psalm 7:11 and presume God to be entirely full of anger and merciless, brutal judgment. But imagine running the universe. Think of all of the information that would be coming to you! Think about what is happening in the life of just one person – in his world alone! Though God feels joy and contentment, it is understandable why the Bible says that God "expresses his wrath every day."

The movie, *Bruce Almighty*, demonstrates that concept pretty well. There is a scene where Bruce is on the computer and prayers continue to come pouring in. The actor, Jim Carrey, is so inundated with needs and requests that he frantically wonders, "What do I do?"

Try being God for awhile. Imagine the kind of information He is getting. It only makes sense that God would get angry every day, given what sinful people do in a fallen world.

But God also feels joy every day. He has the whole gamut of emotions. Obviously in our fallen world, He sees many things that are sad, so He becomes saddened. We can grieve the Holy Spirit (Eph. 4:30), so He is disappointed. But it seems from Scripture that God has and feels a whole range of emotions. He is not some kind of "stoic" blank. He is emotional and created us to be emotional as well.

Theologians Attest to God's Emotions

Numerous theologians have written about emotion in God. McClain (1983) reported that God has a capacity for emotion. In his discussion on the image of God in the human, Erickson (1995) includes emotions. Chafer and Walvoord (1974) specified a "capacity for feeling" (p. 167) in God. Laidlaw (1879) stated that "we feel after Him" (p. 180). Thiessen (1949) described God's "affections" (p. 222). Man's capacity for feeling emotions reflects that of God's.

Emotions Are Universal

What does the picture to the left portray? What emotion do you see? Obviously, that's happy.

It is interesting to note that facial expressions are universal emotional indicators. Every culture has the same facial expressions for the same emotions. Have you ever thought about that? People from all cultures smile when they are happy and cry or frown when they are sad or angry.

Babies seem to know inherently which facial expression applies to which emotion. God created them that way. Which emotion is the baby to the right exhibiting? We can tell by looking at the baby that something is wrong. No one seems to have to teach babies how to express sadness and discomfort.

Even those with disabilities understand the difference (unless damage to the brain has hindered the thinking process). On October 27, 2008, the *Today Show* interviewed twenty-year-old Patrick Henry Hughes. He was a young man who was born with abnormal arms and legs (which kept him from walking) and no eyes; yet he was an accomplished vocalist and instrumentalist --playing the piano and the trumpet (in the University of Louisville marching band where his father pushed his wheelchair).

At the end of the segment, he sang while accompanying himself on the piano and was admiringly thanked by Meredith Vieira. At that point, his face lit up with a smile. This was from a man who had never seen anyone smile before! How could he know what it looked like or how to do it? Yet he did. All of mankind possesses that God-like capacity to feel.

That is the wonder of God's creation of man. It is amazing that God built something in us that is consistently found in every culture and in every human being. Now it can be "tweaked" a little bit differently. A raised eyebrow might mean one thing in one culture and be different in another. Or certain hand signals may be different. But facial expressions are universal.

Connections to the Other Capacities

Connecting all of the capacities goes something like this: We feel or emote based upon the outcomes of our behaviors, choices, goals, beliefs, and longings being met or not being met.

So if our longings are met, we are happy. We are satisfied. We are content.

If our longings are unmet, we feel the negative emotions. We are sad. We are angry. We are disappointed. We are confused. We are frustrated.

Emotions are observed with the realization that they are indicating something. Your anger reveals something about what is inside. Your happiness divulges something about your belief system. Each emotion is telling specifically about your beliefs and your goals in regard to longings being met or not. The emotional capacity works together with all of the other capacities to explain what is going on inside of you.

Three Types of Inappropriate Goals

ANGER -- BLOCKED GOAL

Dr. Larry Crabb (1982) deems unrighteous anger as the result of a blocked "goal." (*Goal*, in this section, will be defined as an objective that can be controlled.) *Goal* is in quotation marks in the previous sentence because it is a *perceived* goal -- a desire that the person has mentally changed into a goal. *Desires* are sometimes viewed as *goals*. When a person attempts to assume control of something where that control is not guaranteed and that control fails, anger is often the result.

Unrighteous or inappropriate anger comes from a blocked "goal." As sinful beings, our anger is many times inappropriate -- meaning we are trying to get something for ourselves. We are trying to get our needs met and someone or something is getting in the way. Now this "goal" is really a "desire," because we are holding on to a belief that we MUST have something that we really do not need. Many times we are trying to try to control something we cannot control, and we are being blocked.

An anger problem consists of wrong expectations. Inappropriate anger happens when we try to control something that we have no control over. We feel that we NEED something that we really do not need.
Remember this author's story about being "cut" from the basketball team? I was not only disappointed and sad; I was angry with the coach and I was angry with me. Why? My goal was blocked!

For others, getting cut was "no big deal" and life "moved on." For me, it was a big deal! My goal of being a great basketball player was blocked. I had based my life on that goal. My emotions made sense if you knew what was underneath.

When you are dealing with anger problems (and we are talking about unrighteous anger, not the good kind of anger) -- temper problems, you are dealing with blocked goals. So when you see that type of anger in yourself or others, ask yourself, "What goal is being blocked? What am I after? What are they after? What is not happening that is being relied upon to get needs met? How am I/are they trying to MAKE IT happen? What is it that I am/they are trying to control?

Sometimes we are angry for legitimate reasons – like when someone is abused by another, when we see blatant sin, etc. We have already mentioned the fact that God gets angry every day. If we think as God does, we are never happy about sin. Anger over such things is legitimate. Unrighteous anger stems from a belief that we must have something that we really do not need. It is a perceived need, not a real one. Our desire has become too important and has turned into a goal.

ANXIETY -- UNCERTAIN GOAL

Anxiety comes from an uncertain goal. It might not happen. On test day, a student may be thinking, "I want to get an 'A' in this class. Now the professor is passing out the test. I'm feeling anxious." Why? -- Because his goal is to get an "A." That is a wrong goal. Getting an "A" should be a desire. As a "goal" it is going to cause anxiety.

Many scriptures talk about anxiety. Philippians 4:6 is one of them. It says, "Be anxious for nothing." How can one do that? How can a person avoid being anxious? What are appropriate goals that cannot be blocked?

A good goal for a student may be: "I'm going to do my best today and whatever grade I get will be okay." Now of course, the student would love an "A," but the things he has control over are how much he studies and what type of effort he puts into his test-taking. The best way of thinking is, "I'm going to do the best I can. I can control that. I will strive to get an 'A,' but the final outcome is in the hands of the professor."

If a student did that, he would not have as much anxiety. Why? He does not HAVE TO have an "A." An "A" is not hooked to his identity anymore.

And that is the real key when you are a student. You do not have to have certain grades. They are grades and do not reflect who you are as a person. They only reflect your work in the class and how that was evaluated by the teacher.

Some students have activities and employment added to their class load. To put the expectation of having to receive an "A" to be "okay," could be very unrealistic It makes sense that that type of load combined with an obsession for "A's" could make a person feel anxious, and in time, miserable -- and for some people, "burnt out." But if one has the idea: "I'm going to do the best I can, given I'm working forty hours a week, given the activities or responsibilities that I have, and given that I only have so much time to study this material," then there will be less anxiety – at least the disabling kind of anxiety.

Did you catch that? -- The "disabling" kind of anxiety. Is there such thing as an "abling" kind of anxiety? Can anxiety ever be helpful or good? That might depend on how you define "anxiety."

If you have taken a course in research and/or statistics, you may be familiar with the term "curvilinear relationship." Researchers have found that there is a curvilinear relationship between "anxiety" and performance. What the research (Humara, 2001) is telling us is that one needs an appropriate level of "anxiety" (or "arousal" – another term associated with low level "anxiety").

Some people talk about a good kind of anxiety and a bad kind of anxiety. When referring to the "good" kind of anxiety, the author prefers the term, *concern*. The "good" kind of anxiety is not what is being referred to when the Bible warns against "anxiousness."

It is sometimes helpful to have a level of concern. Sometimes a level of inner energy and determination gives one the intensity to accomplish more and often in a shorter amount of time. Sometimes that focus helps a person perform better. The following diagram illustrates the curvilinear relationship of anxiety to performance.

Curvilinear Relationship of Anxiety and Performance[17]

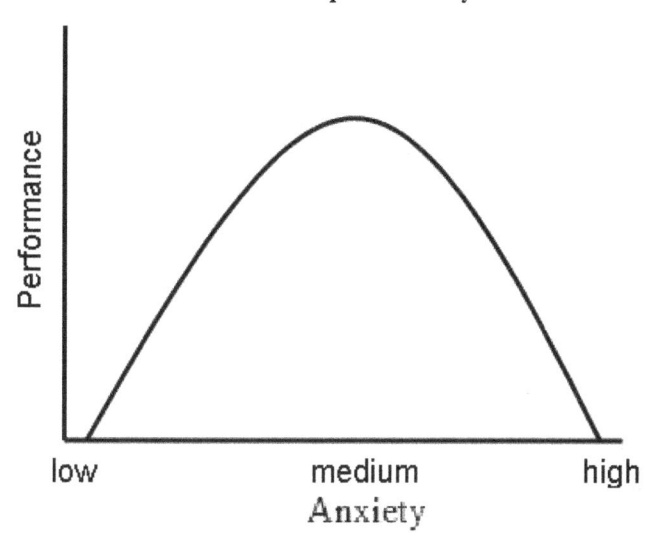

(Public Domain)

    You will notice in the illustration that a certain level of anxiety is good. This is the type of anxiety that would fit more into the category of focus, concern, and anticipation. Some researchers refer to the low to moderate level of anxiety as "Arousal Anxiety" (Cuncic, 2009) Performance levels continue to rise.

    But too much pressure focused on the situation impairs performance. This is when it changes from concern to true anxiety – the type that we typically refer to -- the disabling anxiety.

    So when there is a test coming up, if you have a "healthy concern" (what the diagram refers to as low to moderate anxiety), then you are going to want to study and be as prepared as possible. If the bills need to be paid, then you show up to your job and put in the time that is required of you in order to earn the wages that will pay the bills. And if you can get that concern to a peak point -- like an athlete who gets "psyched up" for an event -- getting that adrenaline pumping in an anticipatory way -- then that can actually help you perform better. That is what the research is saying. However, if you go too far with that pressure or concern -- now turning it into inappropriate anxiety (the type of anxiety that Philippians 4:6 refers to) -- then performance goes down (Brehm, Kassin, & Fein, 2005).

17

Everyone has at least one story of performing well in practice, but when performing in the game/meet/contest, anxiousness prevented the performance from being top notch (or at least, as practiced). Sometimes a basketball player is so anxious that he cannot hit the foul shot that is automatic any other time. Sometimes an instrumentalist squeaks or misses notes that are otherwise not missed. Sometimes a speaker forgets what he was planning to say. Sometimes an interview for a job can go much worse than hoped for because the interviewee was so anxious. Whatever it was, the problem was caused by anxiety.

So some anticipatory energy or concern is good. But too much? That becomes unhealthy anxiety and impairs performance. That type of unproductive anxiety comes from an uncertain goal -- "I've got to stay on the balance beam, because it's hooked to my identity." And though the belief is that it MUST happen, the realization that it might not happen fuels the anxiety.

For this author, as a basketball player, when I was standing at the foul line and someone would yell, "Relax!" what do you think happened? Remember what happens when you attack an emotion? It intensifies! Yelling "Relax!" did not help.

If you are a basketball player, you understand the term "concrete elbow." That is where one gets so nervous that instead of having a nice follow through, the arm stops and there is no nice wrist motion after the ball is released from the hand. And do you know what happens to the ball when your arm and elbow get "stuck"? The ball does not get to the rim.

So imagine that taking place at a basketball game you are attending. What happens when the player shoots a foul shot and the ball does not even get to the rim? What does the crowd chant? "Air ball! Air ball!"

Now if my goal as a player had been to do what I was able to do at that time, if my goal was to honor God no matter what my performance, if I had not needed to be the star athlete so much, then it would not have mattered how I performed or what the crowd yelled. And if I had really believed that, the ironic thing is that I would have actually performed better! And the other ironic fact is that even if I had become the star player, as time passed most people would not remember me or my performance anyway, and even if they did, there would be a new generation that would not really care about it that much. So the lie that Satan deceives us with -- that being a "celebrity" is important -- just is not true and it will not truly satisfy.

But even if a mistake was remembered by others, it is still not crucial. It is not hooked to my identity. It has no influence on my standing or acceptance with God. In fact, mistakes help me realize my humanity and dependency on a perfect God.

Society says, "Performance is your identity and if you perform well, then you are okay. We'll love you. You're accepted. You have meaning and purpose. But if you don't perform well, then please don't show up because we have no use for you." And if you "buy" that, if you believe it, then you feel anxious and it affects your performance and can even affect your health.

Here is the key. The concept that is important to embrace is: "This has NOTHING to do with you as a person." Your performance is just that -- a performance. Sometimes you succeed. Sometimes you don't -- you fail. Welcome to humanity! But you are still you -- a person that God loves and accepts just as you are and that God wants to use for His work.

Sometimes you look good. Sometimes you look bad. Sometimes you are pretty. Sometimes you are ugly. Sometimes you are fat. Sometimes you are thin. Sometimes you get what you are hoping for. Sometimes you don't. That is life, but it is not who you are as a person.

And sometimes bad things happen that have nothing to do with our performance or our presentation to our world. Sometimes things are totally out of our control. But ultimately, God is in control. Putting our faith and trust in a loving God who has our best interests in mind, minimizes or eliminates the anxiety. And putting our faith there reminds us that we do not NEED what we think we need to be complete and content.

INADEQUACY -- UNREACHABLE GOAL

Inadequacy comes from an unreachable goal. Perfectionism fits in here. A 94% grade on a test -- even if it is an "A" -- isn't enough. The thinking is: "I've got to have 100s. I've GOT to be the best!" So what happens when we set our standards so high? We make ourselves miserable trying to get there.

And what if one day we somehow manage to get there? What if we have a whole semester where we have nothing but 100s (if that could happen)? The result of success with this type of perfectionism is (if we were able to meet that standard), we then RAISE the standard!

Why do we do that? Talk to people who have met their goal. Dorothy Hamill won a gold medal in the 1976 Olympics. After her accomplishment, she was asked, "How does it feel?"

She responded something like this: "Well, it feels good, but I've worked my whole life -- since I was a little girl -- to get here. Now I don't know what to do."[18] She seemed uncertain about herself and her life. What she seemed to be communicating was, "Where do I go from here?"

As viewers of the Olympics, we often watch the TV and think how wonderful it would be to attain that. We think the winner should be elated. And sometimes the winners are.

But life still goes on. They still have to figure out what they are going to do from there. And sometimes professional athletes have a real "identity crisis" when they leave their sport – whether by choice, accomplishment, or injury. Part of the reason is: how do you raise that bar?

Sometimes it is hard to grasp the idea that sport or that accomplishment is not who we are. The gold medal was a great accomplishment for Dorothy Hamill, but it is not who she is. That gold medal is not Dorothy Hamill.

Bill Russell was a famous basketball player who played for the Celtics in the 1960s. He was once introduced as "Bill Russell, the basketball player." When he got to the podium to speak, he started with a correction -- that he was not "Bill Russell, the basketball player." He was "Bill Russell, who used to play basketball." Then he proceeded to tell the difference -- that that was not WHO he was. He was a person first.

What he was saying was, "This is not who I am as a person. I have numerous attributes and characteristics. Having been a basketball player is only one aspect."

Proper Goals Lead to Peace

When you become aware of your blocked goals, your uncertain goals, or your unreachable goals and you change them to appropriate goals, you feel less angry, less anxious, and less inadequate. Then you are able to experience peace and joy because you do not have to try to control what you cannot control. Then it is not about getting your needs met. What you really need is already met. If you get what you want, that might be great! But if it doesn't happen, you are still okay. And even if you do find success, it does not define you. You are much more than that.

---

[18] I heard Dorothy Hamill say this in a TV interview many years ago after the 1976 Olympics, but can't identify the program. The fact is verified, however, on various internet sites, one being http://www.achievement.org – specifically: http://www.achievement.org/autodoc/printmember/ham1int-1. *Academy of Achievement* (Scottsdale, AZ, June 17, 2000), "Dorothy Hamill Interview." Paragraph 38 under heading: What were the rewards for you? *". . . when that actually happens, it's disconcerting. I mean, now what? What happens now? We didn't plan for that."*

Isn't it nice to realize that if you, as a Christian, fail your class and/or if you never make any money and/or if you are out on the street and destitute, you are still going to heaven? Even if the worst imaginable things happen to us or are initiated by us, we are still loved by God, and He still allows us to go to heaven.

And when it comes to anxiety, most of the time, "what ifs" do not even happen. The fact of the matter is, even IF they did happen, they would still not be the worst things we could experience. The worst thing that could happen would be to end up in Hell. Yet, as Christians, we are on our way to heaven. That is pretty amazing. If we could get a hold of that, we could relax much more with life.

I once watched a movie (the title I cannot recall) that followed the life of a man who was kidnapped by terrorists. At one point, after he had been in captivity for many months, he said to his cellmate, "You know, I used to worry about the 'stupidest' things."

When we get to heaven that is probably what most of us will think. "I worried about some of the 'stupidest' things!" And if we could just get a glimpse of that here, that would help us keep our priorities focused on things that truly matter.

The well-known author, Donald Miller, talked about that to a group of people gathered at a church in Indiana. He said, "I arrived at the post office one minute later because somebody pulled out in front of me. Can you believe I got upset about that?" His intention was to communicate to his audience the absurdity of our anger when we are delayed for a matter of a few seconds because of a red light or someone pulling out in front of us.

If we could get a glimpse of the big picture, we would be saying something like, "Hey! Relax! It's not a big deal!"

Why do we get angry about those things sometimes? -- Because we are trying to control things that we cannot control. When we do that, we can make ourselves miserable!

So if you understand your goals and make appropriate changes, you can find a sense of peace in your world. And if you pay attention to emotions, if you understand that they communicate something more than just what may be observed, then you have a way of looking inside the soul.

What Should We Do With Emotions?

So what should we do with our emotions? Do we express them? Should we suppress them? What is the appropriate approach for the Christian?

Sometimes in Christian settings there is a sense that showing emotion is inappropriate. People sometimes seem to convey, "Hey! Put a 'lid' on it!" In fact, some people think that as good Christians, we are supposed to look like the character, Spock, on *Star Trek* -- just **stoic** all the time.

"Hey, we just found out we are going to have a baby!"

"Well, that happens."

"My mother just died!"

"Well, death is a part of life." And if they are "spiritual," they may add, "But, 'all things work together for good for those who love God'" (Rom. 8:28).

For some, expressions do not seem to waver. Their voices sound monotone. And many Christians equate that lack of emotional expression with something good.

After the death of a husband, sometimes those observing the widow say things like, "Oh, she's handling things really well," or "I know his death was tragic, but at the funeral she was really doing well." Why? -- Because she was not crying. And obviously, she is more spiritual and godly if she is doing "okay" and not crying. -- That is what some may think.

Now, a widow who acts that way could be a very godly person and what you see may be truly what is being felt on the inside. She may already have some level of "resolve" regarding the death. But be careful about saying that suppressing emotions is more godly and more Christian. If suppression is what is happening, it might not be the godly choice and could lead to more emotional problems.

Some also put on the "plastic" smiles. They plaster smiles on their faces, even when things get difficult, and they pretend to be happy and content.

This has happened at times when a Christian leader has been found to have committed sinful acts. Why would someone in that situation be smiling? You know that he could not be happy about the accusations and the media attention on his failures, yet he wears an odd sort of smile on his face. Former President Richard Nixon was a good example of that type of response when he smiled and acknowledged the crowd before boarding the helicopter, leaving the presidency.

Sometimes people appear to be happy all the time -- or at least when others see them. (The Beatles sang about "the face that she keeps in the jar by the door." Even the Beatles were aware of the pretense of happiness that people sometimes feel compelled to convey. Yet, the "smiler" may or may not be consciously aware of "bad" feelings.) They always have a smile on their faces. But if a smile is inappropriate and doesn't correspond to the situation, it is probable that it is a façade, and the fake smile is an attempt to hide or deny what is being felt inside. The Bible does not instruct us to "always suppress."

Yet it does not teach, "Always express," either. The "always express" concept seems to be more evident in the secular world. "Hey, you've got emotions? Get them out! Catharsis! If you bottle them up, they'll hurt you."

Research has been done on anger in an attempt to find out if expressing anger makes a person feel better. The findings were that for some people the answer is, "Yes." Expressing their anger makes them feel better. For other people, it increases the level of anger! (Bushman, 2002; Geen & Quanty, 1997).

So what is the right way for the Christian to deal with emotions? Express? Refrain from expressing? Repress? The key appears to be the situation, how it affects oneself and others, and BALANCE.

Ecclesiastes 3:1-8 says, "There is a time . . . to weep and there is a time to laugh . . . a time to embrace and a time to refrain . . . a time to be silent and a time to speak. . . ." In other words: There is a time to express and a time to refrain from expressing.

If you are wise in dealing with your relationships, then you have learned that there is a time to "put a lid" on it. Good counsel for married couples or anyone who deals consistently with others is to learn how to "put a lid" on the argument sometimes. Does that mean suppressing emotions? You still need to understand that emotional feeling exists. But sometimes you need to suppress the expression of the emotion.

There is a time to bite your lip. Don't say what you are thinking. If you need to get away, that is fine. Always expressing what you feel can be detrimental. It is not always wise. You can do damage to another person.

But always suppressing emotions, pushing them down, putting a smile on your face and acting like things are okay when they are not, can also be detrimental. Pretending isn't the answer.

What is the answer? The most important thing is to acknowledge your emotions. Acknowledge your feelings, and use that acknowledgement to learn about yourself. Endeavor to discover what is happening inside you and work on making changes if needed. Sometimes we are sad or angry about legitimate things that are results of living in a fallen world, but our emotions may also be indicating illegitimate beliefs. Ask yourself, "What am I afraid of or what goal is being blocked." "Is there a problem with me?" "Is there a problem with them?" "If I AM going to express, what is my purpose for expressing?" "Why am I telling them that?" "Is this really helping them?" "Is it helping me?"

Always acknowledge emotions, but then decide whether to express or refrain from expressing based on the motive to love and minister. The purpose is the key. What is your goal?

In Ezekiel 24:15-17, God tells Ezekiel to "groan quietly." (The NASB says, "Groan silently.) God wanted to communicate a message to His people through Ezekiel's quiet grief; yet, we know that Christ wept openly (John 11:35). The Bible does not teach that it is good to express all emotions all the time -- especially when it may "damage" the hearer, or when avoiding that expression is helpful to accomplishing God's purposes. If we do choose to express our emotions, our prayer should be, "Lord, help me have a good purpose for sharing this with them. I hope it's for their benefit."

Sometimes we need to say, "I'm angry with you!" Sometimes that is the godly way to deal with a situation and is the very thing that will demonstrate love.

I remember saying that to my children when they were growing up -- "I'm angry with you right now!" Why did I tell them that? In one case, I wanted my child to hear loud and clear that when you throw rocks at people, it hurts them! I wanted that child to know that I did not want him to do that anymore. I remember saying to that child, "See this angry face? Don't forget this!" I wanted him to see my anger!

I think God does that sometimes. "I want you to see my angry face! I'm not happy with you right now." Why would God want us to experience His anger? -- Because He loves us enough that He wants to teach us right from wrong and teach us that we will have a better life if we follow His guidelines.

But we should always acknowledge our emotions: "Hey, I'm angry." "I'm disappointed." "I'm sad." "I'm ashamed." Whatever it is, acknowledge that emotion and then say, "Is this a time that I need to bite my lip, or is this a time that I need to let them know? Should I express outwardly or acknowledge inwardly only?"

Sometimes you might acknowledge that emotion, refrain from expressing it, yet "file the information." Sometimes if you see a pattern, then it is helpful to say, "You know, I've seen this four or five times and I want to talk to you about it. Each time I was angry and I am angry now, so I want to discuss it with you."

Why would you be doing that? Hopefully, it would be for the other's good.

Ezekiel was told to "groan silently." When his wife died, God said, "I don't want you to put on sackcloth and ashes. I don't want you to go out and publicly lament and grieve. I want you to do it quietly. In fact, I want you to put on your regular clothes, wash your face, and don't do the normal grieving that the Jews do."

"Why?"

"It's going to be a sign to my people."

Now remember, his wife died! That was a tremendously sad event for him! But God said, "I want this to be a sign to my people."

God didn't say, "Don't groan!" He said, "WHEN you groan, do it quietly." "Don't suppress. Acknowledge. Then groan quietly."

The Christian author, C.S. Lewis (1961), describes his grief over his wife's illness and death in the book, *A Grief Observed*. The movie, *Shadowlands*, also tells the story -- depicting his emotional distress and giving an account of the natural human response to grief.

God does not say, "Push it down." He does not want us to repress our emotions. He does not want us to deny them either. He wants us to be honest about our emotions and make a choice as to whether we should express our emotional pain or pleasure outwardly, or acknowledge it inwardly. Ask yourself, "What is my PURPOSE for expressing or remaining quiet?" If it is time for the latter, then groan, but do it silently. Do not repress it or deny it -- just do not draw attention to it at this time.

WHAT DID CHRIST DO WITH HIS EMOTIONS?

What did Christ do with His emotions? In John 2:15-16, the Bible gives us an example of Christ aggressively demonstrating some intense anger. He made a whip out of cords and "drove all from the temple area . . . he scattered the coins of the money changers and overturned the tables." He then told the ones who sold doves to "Get these out of here! How dare you turn my Father's house into a market!"

At that moment, He was an angry man! He obviously communicated that anger and they got the message because he "drove them out"! They must have acknowledged his authority on some level or at least His ability to hurt them. It sounds like when he swung that whip, they moved. They responded by getting out of there!

John then quotes Psalm 69:9, describing that event from Christ's perspective saying, "Zeal for your house will consume me" (John 2:17).

Does that mean it is okay to be "destructive" sometimes? Christ scattered coins and overturned tables. Does that affirm that some forms of aggression are legitimate? -- Good question.

John 11:35 describes another demonstration of Christ's emotions. It says that "He wept." When Lazarus died, Jesus cried.

Now the rational part of us may want to say, "Wait a minute now! You are the son of God. You KNOW Lazarus is going to be raised. You KNOW what is going to happen. What are you sad about? If anybody has a reason to say, 'Let me explain this to you all; we don't need to cry here,' it would be you."

Yet Jesus wept. He allowed Himself to feel life in a fallen world! Maybe Christ's tears resulted from thinking about what Lazarus went through when he died -- the experience of being ill and dying. Or maybe it was His sympathy for what Lazarus's sisters were feeling -- loss and dealing with the fact that Lazarus was gone. It could be He was thinking about the basic concept of death -- that we all have to experience it – the physical separation from others and the death of our bodies that we must all face as a penalty for sin. Or maybe he was just feeling his own personal grief and loss at that time. The Bible does not tell us, but if we are to be imitators of Christ, we know that it is legitimate to feel sad and cry.

Be willing to cry for yourself, but also be willing to be sad and to weep for others. Laugh with them. Joke with them. But also be sad with them. In counseling, our clients need this.

Remember that we are also models of Christ – imperfect, yes, but we are His representatives. When others see us "bottling up" our emotions or expressing our emotions, they develop an image. That image may be the only thing they have to draw from when choosing what to do with their own emotions. Sometimes modeling teaches better than speaking.

When you say, "Oh yeah, it's okay to cry," but you never do, others do not believe it is really okay to cry. They may feel like you are saying, "It's okay for *you* to be 'weak' because that may be who you are, but it's not okay for *me* because I am 'stronger' and really in a sense, 'better.' God is the only true strong one, and He wept! Showing emotion is not a sign of weakness or deficiency. Expressing feelings is not saying there are problems. It is a sign that we are functioning the way God intended us to function – to feel a whole gamut of emotions.

I remember asking a terminating client once, "What helped? What didn't help?" I expected him to give me an account of what I had said, or homework I had given, or something about the Scriptures we had discussed. But he said nothing of those things. He responded, "I remember the time you cried with me. That made the most impact. The time that really helped was when you just wept with me and you didn't say anything because I knew you cared. I knew you understood. And it sort of gave me hope."

To me, I was simply feeling what he was feeling. It wasn't a technique. I didn't tell myself, "Okay now, at 11:15 today, cry -- as part of the treatment plan."

No. I was being human. Sometimes being human with people helps because it allows *them* to be human and it gives them permission to feel and express that. They get a sense that, "I can be human too." (And incidentally, sometimes *modeling* the Bible is the best way to communicate God's Word. Sometimes you can give the Gospel without reading a word!)

Christ did that. He wept.

Remember Gethsemane (Matt 26:37-38)? Jesus said, "Will you come with me, you three? Will you walk with me because I'm in agony right now?" He was communicating His anguish over what was to come. It seems that He didn't want to be alone when He went up to pray.

And yet, why did Jesus go a little farther and fall with His face to the ground? In the end, emotions are something you have to do on our own. As much as you can share them with others, ultimately, you have to feel them yourself.

Jesus went on a little ways and He fell to His knees and said, "If there's ANY WAY I can get out of this, 'take this cup from me.'" He wept. His sweat was "like great drops of blood," the Bible says (Luke 22:44). He was feeling and emoting and expressing everything that was tormenting him. The Bible tells us what He was going through.

And again, as Christians we could think, "Wait a minute. You're going to die and you're going to rise again. This is all part of an eternal plan. Why the emotions?"

Christ was telling us, "Because I'm real!" He gave us a model. Godliness sometimes looks like agony because it is, at times.

Imagine going to the cross, knowing what the soldiers and the people are going to do, knowing that the Father is going to turn His back, knowing the sin of the world is going to be on your shoulders. Imagine looking into your future and seeing that! Christ was human and He said what most of us would say, "If there's ANY way, PLEASE, take this cup from me! I don't want to go through this!" However, He followed that with, "But your will be done. I'll do whatever you want."

That is what godliness looks like. It means we may say, "I don't want to go through this! I don't WANT to do it." But we trust God and add, "But your will be done."

Isaiah 53:3 tells us that Christ was called a "Man of sorrows." If that is the case, then people must have seen tears and sadness. He lived in a fallen world. He felt the presence of sin more heavily than we do because He was tempted, but never sinned.

It is hard to imagine how He must have felt with all of that! And if we think about all of the times that we do not let our sin affect us, that we do not feel angry or sad about it -- just letting it "roll off" of us, or we are not even aware of it, to be aware of all temptation and to feel all of the human sorrows that accompany life would have been a lot to deal with.

Emotions Are Complex

So which emotions are appropriate when? That is a hard question because of the complexity of emotions. Sometimes there isn't a right or wrong emotion. The cartoon demonstrates the complexity of emotions. It is one example of how complex emotions can get.

This illustration shows a family hugging their son after his long-awaited return. Typically, when you think of someone coming home to a loving family, you assume that they are going to be what? -- Happy. But why are there so many tears?

The same reactions have taken place at many "happy" events – such as the rescue of the Chilean miners in October of 2010. Many of the "happy" miners, their families, rescuers, and onlookers had tears in their eyes. Why? It was a happy time!

(Public Domain)

Emotions are complex. Why did some family members of the Chilean miners start weeping when they were reunited with their loved one? What makes that emotion complex? Yes, they did spend many days underground, and they were separated -- fearing that they may not survive, but okay, they DID survive! They were rescued! Everyone ought to be happy! So why were there tears?

Remember the election of Barack Obama in November of 2008? When TV cameras scanned the crowds gathered in Chicago (Obama's home town), there were a number of people with tears in their eyes -- especially African-American people. Why would they have tears?

Proverbs 14:13 says, "Even in laughter, the heart may ache and joy may end in grief." In the case of the Chilean miners, the families were remembering their fear of losing their loved one and empathizing with the pain that one may have suffered underground. In the second case, people were remembering a time when prejudice was so widespread in America that no black person could have ever received enough votes to win. They were remembering all of the suffering that had to take place for people to "blaze the trail" to Barack Obama's victory. Sometimes the happiest moments bring tears. And sometimes emotions are just unpredictable.

How many times have you thought, "If that ever happened to me, I would be so happy/angry/sad/elated/worried . . ," and then it happens and you think, "I'm not feeling what I thought I was going to feel." Sometimes we cannot predict the way we are going to feel, so it is probably not best to try to predict emotions. You do not know how you will feel when something happens until you get there.

I thought when my children left home that I was going to have trouble dealing with it because years ago when we watched home movies of our children much younger, I was "distraught." At that time, I did not know that I was going to get "teary" and feel that "tug" on my heart. We were thinking, "Let's watch these old home movies. That will be fun." As I felt myself "tearing up," all I could think about was, "Where did those ten years go? And five years from now they are going to start moving out of the house!" I even had trouble teaching class the next day! So I assumed that when our children moved out, I would really struggle.

But when the kids did start moving out, I thought, "This is okay. I can handle this. In fact, it's kind of nice in some ways."

Now does that mean I love them any less or that I do not miss them? No! But God allowed it to be gradual enough -- they became more independent when they started to drive, and they had their friends and their jobs and college and apartments -- that I was okay with it. I would have never guessed that would be my reaction. Emotions are often unpredictable. They certainly can be complex.

EMOTIONAL PACKAGES

Emotions come as a package. Do you want the good ones? You have got to take the bad ones too. It seems that you cannot have one without the other.

We tend to want to place an order with God: "Could you just give me the good ones please and keep the bad ones out?" It does not work that way. Do you want to feel intense joy? You are going to feel deep pain. Do you want to feel contentment? You are going to have sadness. Do you want to feel peace? You are going to have sorrow. It is just the way it works. Do you want to know what real love is? Do you want to know what passion is all about? You are going to be hurt at your deepest level. If you want to love well, you are going to be hurt -- and maybe hurt deeply.

But you know what? We should not want to trade it in – not if we want to love well. Because the opposite is becoming stoic, and while trying to protect ourselves from deep pain, we miss out on knowing deep joy, intense love, and profound gratitude to God for His love, His acceptance, and His blessing.

When the tears of the African-American people flowed after Obama was elected, emotions were clearly more evident among the older people who had "borne the most scars" of prejudice. Congressman John Lewis told of sobbing when he went to the poll to vote, yet it was an indication of the intense joy he was feeling (NBC Today Show, 2011). He could have never felt that same level of joy if he had not felt that depth of pain. He would not have appreciated what had transpired had he not experienced the opposite and could compare the difference.

Some work so hard to avoid pain that, in a sense, they "shut off" their emotions. When people deny and do not allow themselves to consciously "feel," they limit their deep joy. When repressing emotions as a way of protecting themselves from pain, they rob themselves of the chance of enjoying the "up" times and experiencing all that God gives them. So some choose to "constrict" their emotions. One can have "constricted emotions," "restricted emotions," or "flat affect."

But what if you are just an optimist? Obviously, being an optimist is a positive trait; but if you are an optimist, you are still going to feel. There will still be times of sadness and testing; however, though you feel it, you can still carry on. The optimistic part is, "I can go on." The glass may be half empty, but you know what? It is also half full.

Now, being a "Pollyanna" is different. Some people are optimistic to a fault, where they will not let themselves feel sadness and they will always find a silver lining. If you never let yourself acknowledge the realities of life in a fallen world, there is a problem. If you are always Pollyanna, then you are denying something and/or repressing. You are not being honest with others and possibly with yourself. Some day it may catch up with you. You may "break." And then, the "fall" will be much harder.

Remember, God has given us a gamut of emotions -- a capacity to feel. Do not expect your emotions always to tickle. But do feel them, because it is part of being like God.

Sorrow

GODLY SORROW VERSUS UNGODLY SORROW

The Bible makes a distinction between godly sorrow and ungodly sorrow. Second Corinthians 7:10 says, "Godly sorrow brings repentance that leads to salvation and leaves no regret." In other words, it is a good kind of sadness.

An incident with Peter is a good example of godly sorrow. The Bible says Peter went off and "wept bitterly" (Matt 26:75). Why? He had denied the Lord three times.

There is a time to weep bitterly. There is a time to feel that kind of sorrow. When Peter felt that kind of sorrow, it led him to want to be a different person. He did not want to selfishly protect himself in that way anymore. He did not want to do the damage that he did. He may have looked into the Lord's eyes and thought, "I see the hurt that I've caused. I don't ever want to do that again." Remorse is a good thing. Remorse leads to repentance.

A problem that sometimes exists in secular psychology and secular counseling is a lack of remorse. Many times, a perpetrator of sexual or physical abuse feels no remorse. The author has observed some types of "group counseling" for perpetrators of abuse. The counselors "dig" into their pasts to find where they have been hurt. They look at their beliefs and their behaviors. But sometimes the counselors do not move into the realm of vividly showing the damage that the perpetrator has inflicted on the victim or seek remorse for those actions.

There is a time for remorse. There is a time to take responsibility, to feel the impact of what has been done. There is a time to "feel" it, to take it in, because good, godly sorrow leads to remorse. (Remember David's reaction in 2 Samuel 12 when he was confronted by Nathan?) Until the perpetrator looks at the damage and sees what he has caused, the counselor probably will not have much success in helping the perpetrator break the habit/cycle of perpetration. Godly remorse leads to repentance.

If the response is "Yeah, Yeah, I've learned my lesson, Yeah, I won't do that, Yeah, I know," then you don't get it! That attitude says, "I know I got caught. I'll be smarter next time." Not until it hits you deeply and you feel sorrow and remorse will you really strive to make lasting changes. It is not real unless you feel it deeply and you think "This is what I've caused and I don't ever, ever want another human being to feel that again." If that happens, then you are there. That was Peter.

Judas felt sorrow and he went out and hanged himself (Matt 27:5). That is "ungodly" or "worldly" sorrow. Second Corinthians says, "Worldly sorrow brings death" (2 Cor. 7:10). Worldly sorrow says, "I didn't get what I wanted. Therefore, there's no reason to go on."

Godly sorrow says, "I messed up royally, yet there's still hope." In godly sorrow there is still the hope of forgiveness and a sense of purpose. I can go on.

Whatever Judas's goal was, whether it was to bring Christ into His kingdom -- sort of a "forcing of His hand" as the Messiah to overthrow the Roman government -- or not, Christ said, "You don't get it. It's not about what you want. It's about what God wants. This isn't about a political kingdom. This is about a spiritual kingdom." Whatever Judas's goal was, it did not happen. He felt there was no hope. He did weep bitterly. But then he hanged himself.

If one were observing Peter and Judas weep at that time, they may not have looked that much different. The intensity of the emotion is not necessarily an indicator of what is going on. It has to do with what is happening inside. It has to do with the beliefs. Are you sad because someone hurt you or because you hurt them? Are you sad because you didn't get what you wanted? Are you sad because you got "caught"? Or are you sad because you are feeling remorse related to guilt? The facial expressions in response to any of those reasons may look the same, but it is what is going on inside that truly indicates the heart of the person

THREE CATEGORIES OF TEARS

Sorrow often demonstrates itself through tears. That is the means that God has given us to express our sadness. While some people express their tears at appropriate times or from congruent feelings, others find a way to "create" tears intended to deceptively lead those around them to assume their sadness. There are basically three types of tears: Illegitimate Tears, Legitimate Tears, and Mature Tears.

1) Illegitimate Tears. When people cry to get their way, they are "manufacturing" *illegitimate tears*. A good example of that is the technique that Marie implemented on the show, *Everybody Loves Raymond*. She would make a sad face, get out her tissue, and seem to be able to "create" real tears.

That happens sometimes. Illegitimate tears come from our selfishness. We think, "I didn't get what I wanted so I am going to try to manipulate and get it." Sometimes the tears are saying, "Feel sorry for me. Give me what I want. Be manipulated by me." Obviously, those are illegitimate.

2) Legitimate Tears. These tears can happen when we weep over someone who has died. *Legitimate tears* come from unmet, legitimate longings or an empathic response (John 11:35). When things do not go

well, when things do not work out, there is a time to cry. It is legitimate to want things to go well. It is okay to cry when we lose something that we desire or someone we love. Tears are appropriate in those circumstances, even though some think they are not.

3) Mature Tears. We cry *mature tears* when we cry over our sinfulness. It may or may not relate to damage that we have caused to someone else, but it always relates to the recognition of our own sin. That takes a level of maturity where one is willing to "own" what he or she has done and "feel" it. Mature tears come from a realization of one's own sinfulness often coupled with the damage it does or has done to others. It penetrates one's being enough that one thinks, "I don't ever want to do that again."

If you see tears coupled with someone expressing, "I didn't win the lottery and they did! That's not fair!" Those probably aren't legitimate tears. It could be sadness that the tearful one does not have enough money. But, many times, tears happen because one's own selfishness has been upset.

So illegitimate tears are "forced" with the intention of "getting" something from others. Legitimate and mature tears come from the acknowledgement of a loss or lack of something that is/was legitimately longed for or legitimately recognized as sinful.

Anger

APPROPRIATE AND INAPPROPRIATE ANGER

The validity of anger as being one of God's emotions has already been discussed. Scripture makes numerous references to God's anger. For that very reason, we know that anger is not a bad emotion in itself. A number of verses talk about God's anger and Christ's anger. We already looked at Psalm 7:11 that tells us that God "expresses his wrath every day." Mark 3:1-6 discusses Christ being angry and "deeply distressed at their stubborn hearts."

Appropriate Anger. So when is anger appropriate for man? Ephesians 4:26 says, "Be angry, yet do not sin" (NASB). The New International Version says, "In your anger, do not sin." This Scripture is saying that being angry is legitimate. Not only is anger legitimate, at times it is necessary. But sinning while angry is not legitimate.

James 1:19, 20, says we should be "quick to hear, slow to speak, and slow to anger; for the anger of man does not achieve the righteousness of God" (NASB). The story of the Prodigal Son demonstrates a father who was "slow" to anger and eventually saw his son return to him with a changed heart. We could probably categorize Christ as being slow to anger when he responded to the Jews, especially the Pharisees by saying that He wished He could gather them together "as a hen gathers her chicks under her wings" (Matthew 23:37). Numerous times, when Christ was compassionate and did not condemn the sinner.

Proverbs 29:11 says, "A fool gives full vent to his anger, but a wise man keeps himself under control." Notice that the Bible does not say that a wise person never gets angry. The wisdom of the wise man is demonstrated by how he manages his anger -- he keeps himself under control.

In the previous verses, it seems from Scripture that anger is a valid emotion -- even though it is often discarded as inappropriate in some Christian circles. The Bible advises, however, to regulate the expression of anger. When we are angry, we are told not to sin. Anger should be something that "comes slowly." -- It is important that we have a "long fuse." And anger is something that should be kept under control.

The New Living Translation of the Bible is more specific in its rendering of Ephesians 4:26. It says, "Don't sin by letting anger gain control over you." The idea of having a level of control over our expression of anger seems to be an element that separates appropriate anger from inappropriate anger.

There is a good and godly anger. There are times when it is appropriate to be angry. It was probably appropriate to be angry with Ted Haggard, the former evangelical preacher who was in the news in November 2006 for violating laws (along with violating Christian principles) by purchasing methamphetamine and soliciting a male prostitute. For what he did and for how it damaged God's work, it is probably legitimate to feel anger. So what makes that anger appropriate?

Could anger toward Ted Haggard be inappropriate? What would make it inappropriate? Could one person be angry at him and that be appropriate and another person be angry at him and it be inappropriate? Yes. It depends on what is going on, on the inside.

Appropriate anger has to do with the response to sinfulness. Remember the discussion about my son throwing a rock that hit someone's head? I looked at that as WRONG, sinful behavior. I wanted to be angry at that. The message I felt and wanted to convey was, "That was wrong and I don't want you damaging people like that!" It would have also been appropriate anger even if he hadn't hit someone because he had disobeyed Dad's rule that was meant to promote correct behavior. He was thinking of what he wanted to do and disregarded what he had been taught was right. As a father, if I get angry about that, that is appropriate. Knowledge of disobedience of God's laws (in this case,

"Children, obey your parents" Eph. 6:1) is an appropriate time for anger. Anger over *blatant sin* and in the case of Ted Haggard, *hypocrisy*, is appropriate anger.

But if I am mad at my son because he made me look bad when he threw that stone, then that would be inappropriate anger. Now it has to do with his blocking my "goal" of looking good in the community. It would have been blocking my ambition to promote myself to others, placing the importance on myself and disregarding what was best for my son. "You made me look bad!" "You embarrassed me!" "I didn't get what I wanted and I'm mad!" That is not appropriate anger.

Inappropriate anger has to do with selfishness. And quite often, people do not even realize that the anger they feel is because of their embarrassment or other form of selfishness. A father may think he is punishing the behavior, but is really punishing because he looks bad.

"I am angry and will discipline you because you damaged somebody or you disobeyed," is different from "I'm mad because you embarrassed me!" The first would be appropriate. The second would be inappropriate.

So if we go back to the example of Ted Haggard, it is appropriate to be angry at the fact that he *damaged the Gospel* in some ways! He did not represent God. He sinned! He hurt many people. It is appropriate for us to be angry about that.

What would be the inappropriate side of anger directed against Haggard? What type of anger would involve selfish internals? "I had expectations for you." "You ruined my plans for the church." "You ruined my ambition to be on TV with you, etc." Now we are getting into selfishness.

So, two people could be angry at him -- one for appropriate reasons and one for inappropriate reasons. We are looking at an internal reality and external manifestations.

Cautions regarding inappropriate anger are given or implied in the next few verses.

Inappropriate Anger. Proverbs 22:24 says, "Do not make friends with a hot-tempered man, do not associate with one easily angered" (NIV). "Keep away from angry, short-tempered people" (New Living Translation). Someone who is "hot-tempered" or "short-tempered" is demonstrating inappropriate anger. We are cautioned to avoid easily angered people because associating with them could cause us to be influenced and "stirred up" in ways that are not godly. But here again, there is a distinction between slow, thoughtful, controlled anger and quick, easy, uncontrolled anger. We are not to spend a great deal of time with people who have a habit of demonstrating inappropriate, sinful anger.

Job 5:2 explains the results of inappropriate anger. "Vexation slays the foolish man, and anger kills the simple" (NASB). "Resentment [anger] kills a fool and envy [anger] slays the simple" (NIV). "Surely resentment [anger] destroys the fool, and jealousy [anger] kills the simple" (New Living Translation). Anger can come from a number of improper beliefs. Resentment, envy, and jealousy are all descriptive words for forms of inappropriate anger.

Proverbs 15:18 cautions that, "A hot-tempered man stirs up strife, But the slow to anger pacifies contention" (NASB). "A hot-tempered man stirs up dissension, but a patient man calms a quarrel" (NIV). "A hothead starts fights; a cool-tempered person tries to stop them" (New Living Translation). The word "hot-tempered" here, is talking about a "hot," thoughtless, intensity that is not controlled or driven by a godly purpose. Again, the Bible does not say NOT to get angry, but it does advise careful evaluation of the situation and tolerance (not judging too quickly, since you also are a sinner), before "lashing out."

HOT ANGER

The previous verses refer to a type of "hot anger." There is a type of "hot" anger that the Bible talks about, that is sinful. If I am losing my temper and/or yelling, throwing things, hitting things or people and/or causing *unwarranted* damage to satisfy my need for selfish desires; then, something is wrong. The type of "hot" anger or "hot-temper" that is referred to by biblical translators (as in Prov. 15:18) is an ungodly type of anger and demonstrates a selfish lack of control. The word "hot" is a good translation of the Hebrew word that comes from the root "to be hot, to conceive" and can be used of animals in "heat" (the heat involved in breeding). The word itself means "burning anger, rage" that has the element of heat with it (Brown, Driver, & Briggs, 1968, p. 404).

But one kind of "intense" anger still maintains godly control, even though it is demonstrated with forcefulness. That type of anger can be propelled by intense energy and raise the angered person's body temperature so that he/she feels a strong sense of "warmth" (We may say he was "hot."), yet still have a controlled and godly purpose. Though a person may feel "hot" while experiencing that type of anger, it is not what the Bible is referring to when it uses the term "hot" in association with anger.

When the Bible talks about the "wrath of God," it is usually talking about an anger that can destroy people and things, yet it was not an anger that had lost control. (God always has control, and strong anger demonstrated by Him is always for a good purpose.) It could be that the godly person has already demonstrated a "long fuse" and has patiently renounced the sin ("slow to anger") and/or tolerated it in hopes of change until finally it is clear that more intensity is needed. Or maybe it was only the first exposure to the sin which was seen as so blatantly disrespectful of God and/or others or hurtful to others, that anger is strongly expressed in confrontation. That appears to be the type of intense anger that Christ demonstrated when he entered the temple courts.

The book of John says that He "made a whip out of cords, and drove (out) all from the temple area . . . he scattered the coins . . . and overturned their tables" (John 2:15).

(Public Domain)

The picture on this page shows a demonstration of what it must have looked like. When Christ grabbed the whip, He was probably feeling something! It says that He made a whip and DROVE the money changers out of the temple! And He was very energized! We might say He was "hot"! But it was a sinless type of energized anger. He was angry because of how God and people were being sinned against. He was angry over their selfishness and disregard for the pain they caused others. Remember, this is righteous anger. He was tempted in all ways like us, yet without sin. He was saying, "Get out! And get out now!"

Some people have said, "Yeah, but he didn't hit anybody with the whip."

Do we know that? Maybe He just hit tables. But it seems clear that the money changers thought that if they were not going to move, He might "help" them move. It is this author's opinion that He allowed His intense anger to be demonstrated with such fierce and forceful action and strong passion, that it caused fear in those who experienced it. It seems clear that most of the people/money changers were thinking, "I don't want to wait and see if He's going to hit me or not. I'm going to get out." They must have been afraid of being hit. And Christ "overturned the tables"! He "damaged" the setup and possibly the tables. He probably made a big mess! But He did it with a godly objective of getting their attention and exposing their sin. That is righteous anger.

There is a time to demonstrate that level of anger – to make it well known. Of course, as with anything, we have to be careful not to take that too far. It needs to be demonstrated with care for the other person. It should not be just for revenge or just taking out on them how we feel.

In Deuteronomy 32:35 and Romans 12:19 the Lord says, "Vengeance is mine, I will repay" (NASB). "It is mine to avenge." Vengeful anger is not the type of anger that is godly. God, says, "Let me do it. Don't you pay them back!"

Be angry. Tell them, "I'm angry about this. I'd like your behavior to change. But it's not my job to make you pay." Do not get caught up in the vengeful "pleasure" of "payback." (This is not referring to appropriate consequences that help the sinner learn and with his best interests in mind.) If you are thinking, "Given they hurt me, I want to hurt them a little bit," that is not God's way. Vengeful behavior may feel good temporarily, but it's not how God wants us to respond. "Revenge is mine," says God. "Let ME handle it."

COLD ANGER

There is another type of anger that Christians can be "good" at. It does not show itself in the same forceful way and, for that reason, is not as apt to carry the same "sinful" label, but it is another type of unrighteous anger. It is a "cold" anger and it is not always minor. It has potential to be a lot more sinful than "hot" anger.

So maybe I say, "I don't feel like talking."

And you say, "Why? Are you angry with me?"

"No. Everything's fine. "

"Well, it seems like you're angry."

Inside the person is thinking, "I . . . I'm not going to talk to you. I'm not going to look at you. And I'm going to give you the 'cold' shoulder for the next few days." (This is usually communicated through actions). Or sometimes a sinister smile accompanies the "cold anger." Some Christians may say that way of being angry is legitimate because it does not come out with intensity. Is it more "Christian" if it does not appear to be "hot"?

Yet, the internal realities of unrighteous anger are still the same. In this case, "You blocked my goal and now I'm going to make you pay." That could be just as bad as, or worse than, "hot" anger.

FOREBEARANCE

Though there is a time to show forceful anger, there are also times to remain calm and show forbearance. For the most part, it is usually best to be composed.

The Bible mentions "long-suffering" many times as it relates to mankind being forbearing with each other. Ephesians 4:2 talks about "showing forbearance to one another in love" (NASB). Ephesians 5:22 mentions "longsuffering" (NASB) – also sometimes translated as "patience." Colossians 3:12, 13 appeals to Christians to show "patience [long-suffering/ forbearance]: bearing with one another, and forgiving each other" (NASB) and identifies how that relates to *the Lord*'s "long-suffering"/ forbearance/patience with us.

It is like having a long fuse. We should be "slow to anger" -- withholding a demonstration of anger until a necessary point is reached when it is time to express it, sometimes with a level of intensity.

The first time a parent may ask one of his kids to hang up his/her coat, he should say it calmly. If he reminds the child again, he can assume that there may be a good reason for forgetting or not doing it. If it gets to the third or fourth time, it is time to get angry and show him or her that this is the consequence for not obeying. Even if the child "forgot" again, it is time to make it a priority to teach the child to write himself or herself a note, tie a string around his/her finger, etc., and make it a POINT to remember.

We see this many times in our judicial system. The penalty for a "first time" offense is usually less than it is for people who habitually commit the same crime. There is a time for "forbearance." Since none of us is perfect, we need to allow for imperfections in others and give them a "second chance." When that "second chance" is ignored or abused, a stiffer penalty should be applied in order to help them take more seriously the implications of the crime they have committed and its effects on themselves and others.

DENIED ANGER

Denied anger is not helpful. Sometimes people use the terms "bothered," "aggravated," or "frustrated" to minimize what may really be a more intensely felt emotion. Sometimes they deny any sort of negative feeling at all. Denied anger is often suppressed until it finally "boils over" and words are said without control or thought about how those words may impact the other person. Denied anger can implode upon the "denier" and his audience. God does not want us to deny our anger. He gave us the emotion of anger for a reason. That is why it is important to acknowledge anger, yet be controlled in how the feeling is demonstrated.

PROVOKED ANGER

We can provoke anger. Such is what the Bible tells us can happen in the raising of children. Colossians 3:21 says, "Don't embitter children." In other words, "Don't make them mad." The New American Standard Bible says, "Fathers, do not exasperate your children, that they may not lose heart." The New International Version translates it: "Fathers, do not embitter your children, or they will become discouraged." The New Living Translation says: "Fathers, don't aggravate your children. If you do, they will become discouraged and quit trying."

Each of those versions tries to communicate to us the danger of doing things that will exasperate those whose charge we have been given. What are the ways children can be embittered? (Embitter means to provoke someone to the point that they feel bitter, disrespected, in essence -- angry.)

We can do that by not affirming their God-given capacities to think for themselves, behave for themselves, show proper emotions, etc. Parents who avoid affirming positive behaviors and efforts or who treat their children like they cannot make decisions for themselves can cause their children to become discouraged and angry. Not keeping promises and inconsistency can cause anger in children. Obviously, abuse and neglect can cause anger. Improper shaming, such as for a mistake like spilling the milk, can eventually lead to anger.

WHATEVER IS IN ACCORDANCE WITH LOVE

A typical (usually unspoken, though understood) belief of many Christians is: "Keep your anger in. Always suppress." A typical belief of some secular counselors is, "Get your anger out! Always express." Which is better, "clam up" or "blow up"?

What is the balance? How do we know whether to "express" or "suppress"? What is the measuring stick for whether anger that we feel is appropriate or inappropriate?

The Bible teaches that whatever we do toward another should be *in accordance with love* ("Love your neighbor as yourself," Matthew 22:39 -- NASB). When dealing with appropriate anger, there is a time to retain the feeling and there is a time to express our anger. When anger is inappropriate, we need to acknowledge our sinful goals/desires and selfishness and replace the wrong desires with good ones.

What does it mean to love? If love means that I need to say, "You know what? I'm angry with you right now; I need to share that with you," then that is what I need to do. I need to express that anger. If love means I need to bite my lip and hold off; "The timing's not right; you're not ready for it . . ." or whatever the reason, then I need to wait. Love is the key.

SEVEN A'S OF ANGER

This next section is intended to give guidelines for how to deal with anger -- whether appropriate anger or inappropriate anger. The following are seven "A" words that describe a process that can be helpful to manage the anger that is inevitable for any of us who live in this fallen world.

1. **Accept** the fact that you are going to feel angry from time to time. Anger is a part of the human experience. We are emotional and feel angry because we are like God (image-bearers), who is emotional and feels angry sometimes. It is not possible, if we are feeling healthy emotions (or even if we are not) for us to live in this sinful world and not get angry sometimes.

Anger is a method of response to sinfulness and/or living in an imperfect world. The Bible does not say, "Don't be angry." It says, "In your anger, don't sin" (Eph. 4:26). There is a big difference! You are going to get angry, but when you do, do not sin with it. It is the way that you deal with that anger that matters.

2. **Acknowledge** your anger when it is present. Unacknowledged or denied anger is a dangerous thing. (Not only is it dangerous, it is unbiblical -- as we have already demonstrated.) You are a volcano waiting to go off and/or are a "depression" waiting to happen. Denied anger can only be pushed down and pressured for so long. Then it explodes with tremendous outward or inward damage taking place. (Outward would be yelling and physically damaging people and property. Inward would be depression and/or other mental disorders).

If you "push" anger down -- forcing smiles and pretending it is not there, it will most likely eventually leak out. When that happens, it is telling you that you have got to do something about the repressed anger. Your body tells you, "I can't do this anymore." It implodes. Sometimes that means you get depressed.

Or if the anger builds and builds and builds, one day the bomb will go off – either literally or figuratively! One comment from someone can set off uncontrolled anger. It can take just one little thing and it erupts. Why? Because one keeps pushing the anger down and down until the body finally says, "I can't take it anymore!"

Unacknowledged or denied anger is a dangerous thing! Anger has more power when unacknowledged. Christians can become especially adept at "covering" their anger through looking "spiritual," through pretending, and saying things like, "Oh, I'm a Christian; I don't get angry" or "You're a Christian; you shouldn't get angry." That's dangerous! Acknowledging your anger is the first step to dealing with it in a truly godly way.

3. **Allow** some time before responding. In regard to anger, the Bible does talk about a correlation between "quickness" and "foolishness" (Prov. 14:17, 29; Ecc. 7:9). If you are "quick" with your angry response, there is more likelihood that your response will lack good judgment and/or cause some type of damage. Sometimes it is helpful to count to ten or take a walk before responding. Though sometimes it is necessary to react quickly, most of the time it helps to give yourself time to think about your choice of words or actions and evaluate more efficiently what would be best. If you do not give yourself that time, there is a far greater chance of saying or doing things that cause damage and/or you later regret.

4. **Address** the internal issues. While giving yourself time before responding, you need to look inside to see if you are experiencing righteous anger (anger at sin) or unrighteous anger (selfish anger as a result of not getting what you wanted or thought you needed). Determine how much of this is YOU and your blocked goal and how much of this is THEM and their sinfulness. If it is unrighteous anger, you need to go to God and confess your sin and follow that with choosing to pursue godly goals and behaviors (1 Cor. 10:31).

If you have given it some thought and you reach the conclusion that most of the problem is truly the other person's sin, then the next step is to determine the best way of dealing with your anger while demonstrating love. "Should I bring this up and discuss it with them? Or do I need to just keep this one to myself for awhile." "How should I respond to them?" "What is the best way to love them?" You may even need to enlist the ear of a supportive person where you can, in confidence, "vent" your feelings without unnecessarily hurting the person with whom you are angry.

5. **Ask** God for help. Prayer acknowledges our dependence on God and softens our spirit. This will help in our response.

Ask God to help you know how best to address the other person. Then just pray for that person. It is tough to pray for somebody you are angry with, and not soften. Pray, "Lord soften my spirit, and help me know how best to address this issue regarding them." Sometimes prayer helps take your anger down a "few notches."

6. **Align** yourself with love. Our goal is not to "always express" or to "always suppress" our anger. Our goal is to do what is best for the other person (the essence of "love"). That may involve expressing appropriate anger at times or refraining from expressing that anger for godly purposes. We need to look at the best way to deal with that anger without sinning (Eph. 4:26).

7. **Alleviate** the energy behind the anger. You need to remember that there can be tremendous energy in anger. Converting your anger into energetic, useful activities (i.e., exercising, cleaning, mowing, chopping wood, raking leaves, etc.) will aid in the process and accomplish some good objectives as well. Sometimes you may need to do this before responding, and maybe even before looking inward (as a way of releasing some of the tension and pressure).

If you are feeling that burst of energy that can accompany anger, and especially if you have had problems with anger (temper problems) in the past, get away from the situation. Then think through, "How much of this is me? How much of this is them?" But if you cannot even think because you are so mad, then do something constructive with that energy. Mow the lawn. Lift weights. Clean the house. Chop wood. Run. Take a walk.

Some suggest "beating the bed with a bat" to release angry energy. That may not be the best idea – especially if you happen to damage the furniture. But if hitting a punching bag is exercise for you, then maybe that is legitimate. However, if you can find an energetic activity that also accomplishes something constructive like running or cleaning, the resulting positive feeling of accomplishment can also help to temper the angry energy.

Then if and when the relief valve is released, it is more of a gentle release rather than a strong explosion. At that point, hopefully, you will surmise, "Now I can think a little more clearly. How much of this is me? How much of this is her/him? How do I want to respond to her/him?"

Now did Christ take time before expressing his anger? He did take time to get away from the crowds and rest, but the Bible doesn't say or even suggest that it was because He wanted to give Himself time before responding to His anger. There is a difference with Christ in that He was perfect. Being perfect, He wouldn't have to think through His beliefs and goals because they would also be perfect. He did demonstrate patience and love and that God is slow to anger. For God, "going with the moment" was obviously the proper choice; but for us as sinners, we may need time to process things and alleviate some of the stress before we respond.

Anxiety

When we are dealing with anxiety, we are dealing with "uncertain goals." Anxiety involves fears. Four common fears are: fear of failure, fear of rejection, fear of new situations, and fear of people. (Two others often commonly included are: fear of death and/or fear of serious physical ailments.) When we talk about how to deal with anxiety, we want to find goals that we can control. As a student, rather than "I've got to get A's," my goal could be to study hard and put appropriate time into projects and papers. "I've got to succeed" or "I've got to be the best" or "I've got to have everybody like me," could be replaced with goals that can be achieved. What is causing the anxiety is that the "goals" set are not controllable. If I change my goal to that which I can control, the anxiety will dissipate.

If I realize that I am already loved and I do not have to get everybody to love me, I can relax and move forward with confidence. What removes fear? "Perfect love casts out all fear" (1 John 4:18). When I KNOW I am loved, I do not have to be afraid. Why? -- Because I am no longer worried about you rejecting me. I know God is going to love me no matter what, so I do not have to be thinking, "Oh no! What's going to happen here?" There is no condemnation (Romans 8:1).

Correct thinking is the key (2 Kings 6:8-17, Phil. 4:4-7). Change your beliefs. Change your goals. Have goals that you can control. Have a belief that says, "This is the way I'm going to go. I'm going to do the best I can do in this class, on this report, on this speech, in this interaction with this important person, and if it doesn't go well, it is not the end of the world." If one can truly believe that, it will lessen the anxiety.

Conclusion of the Emotional Capacity

Emotions are indicators. They tell us what is going on inside of us. For us as counselors, they help us to know what might be going on in our clients. Let's acknowledge emotions and use them in constructive ways. That is so much better than denying them, attacking them, or ignoring them. Looking spiritual does not mean that we ARE spiritual. This is especially true when it comes to emotions.

CONCLUSION

If we want to help people in counseling, we need to understand what constitutes proper and improper functioning. How are we supposed to function? Or another way of saying it would be: What is "right" functioning? How can we determine what is "wrong" (psychopathology) if we do not know what is right? To understand what is "right," we need a "theory of personality" or in biblical terms, a "biblical anthropology." This author labels that "The Seven Capacities."

The Seven Capacities (social, existential, rational, teleological, volitional, behavioral, and emotional) make up a theory of personality that can lead to a model of counseling. These seven capacities can be "categories of thought" for the counselor. As we work with clients, we are asking, "Which capacity is central to what is happening in the client?" We may be observing different emotions that point to blocked or uncertain goals. We may be seeing patterns of behavior that follow certain beliefs. We may be noticing choices that are conscious or unconscious. And we may be hearing deep longings for relationship and/or meaning and purpose.

This "model of counseling" or these "categories of thought" do not work in a linear fashion. Conceptually, emotions point to behaviors, behaviors to choices, choices to goals, goals to beliefs, and beliefs to longings. But counseling is messier than that. One client may start with goals, another with behaviors, and still another with longings. Emotions will emerge at different times and unconscious goals may "leak out," then disappear. Every client will be different and even the same client will show different aspects at different times.

The counselor may choose to focus on beliefs at one time and choices another. It may depend on the day or what is happening in the counselor or the client. And sometimes what is being shown is appropriate and needs to be reinforced. At another time, it is illegitimate and needs to be gently confronted.

But whatever is there and however we as counselors choose to deal with it, a unified whole is present. A person with personality is displaying all of these capacities, even if that display is in a form of denial. This "unified whole" is how God made us. This is how we are like Him. We are image bearers.

Yet sometimes some of these capacities are moving in the wrong direction as the result of sin. We all have "irrational beliefs" or as some say, "stinking thinking," at times. Our clients may be making bad choices, engaging in hurtful behaviors, and have improper goals. Our job as counselors is to uncover what is wrong and help our clients get back on the right track. We are uncovering the sin and attempting to lead people back to God's design. Why? Because God's design works!

This is where our presuppositions come into play. If our theology is correct -- God being the creator and making us like Himself -- then He has a design. His design is what we are after whether it be in how we live our lives or in how we counsel. That is why the Bible is so important in this discussion. It gives us a biblical anthropology, a theology of personality, a "blueprint" for the soul. With this guide, a model of counseling can emerge that stays within biblical parameters and is relevant to a hurting world.

And if our counseling is truly biblical (not just name only), then the Holy Spirit (the Great Counselor) can take over where we are lacking. He is the great change agent; we are only instruments. Therefore, our counseling needs to be bathed in prayer, dependent on the Spirit, theologically driven, and clothed in humility. When this happens, real change can take place -- which is what counseling is all about.

SCRIPTURAL INDEX ACCORDING TO PAGE NUMBER

Page	Scripture Reference
13	Heb. 11:1
15	Eccl. 3:11; Gen. 1:1; Exod. 3:14
18	Prov. 15:13, 17:22; Psalms -- entire book; 2 Sam. 6:14; Luke 2:11; 2 Cor. 2:7; Isa. 53:3; Phil. 4:11
19	2 Cor. 12:9
23	Ps. 111:2
24	Ps. 19:1
25	John 11; John 2; Exod. 3, 4; Gen. 17; Acts 9
26	2 Tim. 3:16; Exod. 3, 4
27	2 Tim. 3:16
28	Gen. 1:26, 27
29	Prov. 14:16
30	Eph. 2:1; Rom. 6:23; Jer. 17:9; Rom. 3:23
31	Isa. 64:6; Rom. 1; Matt. 23; Prov. 20:5
32	Eph. 6:10-18; Mark 8:15; Ezek.18; Jer. 31:30
34	1 John 1:9
35	Rom. 5:6-8; John 3:16; 1 Cor. 6:11
36	Gen. 50:20
37	1 Cor. 10:31
43	1 Cor. 10:31
45	Prov. 29:13; 1 Cor. 15:33; Prov. 23:7
46	Prov. 29:13; 1 Cor. 15:33; Heb. 10:25; Phil. 4: 8; Ps. 1; 1 Cor. 15:3; Eph. 6; Phil. 4:1; 2 Tim. 2:15
56	Exod. 18;.18:23
58	Phil. 4:6; Matt. 6:34; Luke 2:8-9,
59	Luke 2:10-20
62	Isa. 55:8-9; Prov. 3:5; Ps. 19:1
63	2 Tim. 3:16
64	James 1:8; Dan. 4:28-33; John 8:44
65	Isa. 55:8-9
67	Ps. 111:2; Gen. 1:28
68	Phil. 2:10
69	Prov. 23:7
76	James 2:1-4
80	Prov. 22:2; Prov. 29:13; Matt. 5:45
81	Ps. 14:1; 1 Cor. 15:33; Titus 1:12, 13
82	Heb. 5:14
83	Phil. 1:9-10; 2 Pet. 1:3; Gen. 1:28
86	Gen. 1:26, 1:27, 5:1; 9:6; 1 Cor. 11:7; James 3:9

87	John 4:24; Gen. 1:26-28
90	Matt. 17:5; John 17:1, 16:28, 16:13
91	John 3:35, 15:10, 16:10, 16:14, 14:16, 17:5, 8:16, 17:3, 17:18; Matt. 10:40; Acts 10:38; John 14:26, 16:7
93	John 3:16; Rom. 5:8, 8:39; Eph. 5:2; Gen. 3:8
95	2 Cor. 5:19; Rom. 5:10; Col. 1:21-22
96	Eph. 1:5
97	1 John 3:1
100	Rom. 8:28, 9:11; Eph. 1:11; 2 Tim. 1:9, 3:10; Acts 11:23; 1 Pet. 4:3; Acts 27:43; Rom. 9:19
101	1 Cor. 10:31
102	Gen. 3:8; 2 Cor. 5:19, 20; Matt. 5:16; Isa. 43:7; 1 Cor. 10:31
104	Gen. 1:26, 28; 2:15
111	Rom. 1:18
114	1 Pet. 3:3; Job 42:15
116	1 John 2:16
117	Ps. 42; 42:1; 63; John 4:10-13; 7:37, 38;
118	John 13; Ps. 42:1-2; Ps. 63
119	Eph. 4:1-32; 1 Cor. 4:2
120	Eccl. 3:11; Gen. 2:18;
121	Matt. 26:36ff; Heb. 10:25; Gal. 6:2
122	Eccl. 3:11; Matt. 11:28 - 30
123	Mark 4:38
124	Prov. 13:24;
125	Matt. 19:16-22; Mark 10:17-23; Matt. 22:37-39; Mark 12:30-31; John 3:16; Matt. 10:17, 22; Matt. 26:39; Mark 14:36; Luke 22:42; Matt. 14:23; Mark 14:17; Matt. 26:37; Luke 8:2; Mark 4:38
126	Ps. 63:3
127	Matt. 14:15-22, Matt. 15:36; Mark 8:1-8
129	Prov. 29:13
132	John 6:35; John 7:37; Eccl. 2:24-25; Exod. 18
133	Ps. 1:3; Exod. 18:13-27; Mark 1:35, 4:38,6:30, 6:45, 14:32, Luke 4:28-30; 4:42; 6:12; 8:22,23; 21:3; John 11:53,54; Luke 21:37
135	John 7:37; Rom. 1:18
137	Jer. 2:13; Prov. 27:20
138	1 John 2:15-17
141	Jer. 2:13
142	Eccl. 3:11
143	Prov. 17:22
144	Ps. 14:1; Gen. 9:6
145	Gen. 3:6
149	Eph. 6:2, Gen. 2:24;
150	Deut. 24:5

153	1 Sam. 15:30
155	Mark 4:38; Matt. 26:39; 2 Cor. 4:7-9, Rom. 8:38
156	Luke 4:28-30; Matt. 2:13; John 11:54; Mark 6:30
157	Gen. 3:8-10
160	2 Cor. 5:20
161	1 Sam. 15:3; 1 Sam. 15: 13, 14, 15, 19, 20-21
162	1 Sam. 17:28
164	Gen. 29, 30; Prov. 20:29
165	Prov. 26:18-19
167	Gen. 18:12
176	Eccl. 3; Prov. 17:22; Exod. 4:10; 2 Cor. 4:7-9
177	2 Cor. 4:7-9; Rom. 8:38
178	Jer. 2:13; 1 John 4:19; John 4:13
179	Ps. 23:5; 1 John 4:18, 19; Ps. 118:6; Matt. 7:11
181	Phil. 4:6; Eccl. 3:11
182	Ps. 94:11
183	Eph. 4:23; Prov. 23:7; Gen. 2:19; Rom. 8:16
184	Col 3:10; Matt. 3:9; John 5:39, 13:12, 15:18; 1 Cor. 13:7; 1 John 4:16; John 21:17, 10:15; Luke 16:15
195	Ps. 1; Phil. 4:8
200	Phil. 4:8; Col. 3:2; Prov. 20:5
203	Prov. 20:5
204	Prov. 21:2; John 6:64; Phil. 1:15-18; 1 Thes. 2:3; Prov. 16: 1, 2
205	Prov. 24:12; Prov. 21:2; Prov. 14:12; 1 Cor. 4:4-5; James 4:3
206	1 Sam. 1:11
207	Matt. 6:1-18; Matt. 6:5-8
208	Phil. 1
209	Matt. 6, 6:1-4
210	Matt. 6:16-18
214	Prov. 22:6, Deut. 6:7
215	1 Cor. 10:31
216	Matt. 21:12, Mark 11: 15
218	Matt. 11:27, Luke 10:22; James 3:4, 4:4
219	Isa. 46:10; Dan. 4:35; Eph. 1:11; Ps 115:3; Rom. 9:18; Ps. 135:6; Acts 15:18;
220	Rom. 1:24-28; I Cor. 10:27, 30; Philem. 14; John 1:13; John 3:16 Rev. 17:13; Rev. 17:17
221	Prov. 22:6
222	Rom. 3:23; 1 John 3:4; Deut. 9:7; Col. 2:13
225	Gen. 2:16, 17
230	Rom. 13:13
232	Eph. 4:17-32
233	Phil. 1

234	Eph. 4:17-32
238	James 1:22-24; James 2:26
241	Phil. 4:4; Judg. 10:16; Ps. 103:13, 145:8; Matt. 26:38; John 11:33-35
242	Eph. 4:30; Phil. 1:8; Ps. 7:11
248	Phil. 4:6
252	Rom. 8:28
253	Eccl. 3:1-8
254	Ezek. 24:15-17; John 11:35
255	John 2:15, 16; Ps. 69:9; John 2:17; John 11:35
257	Matt. 26:37-38; Luke 22:44; Isa. 53:3
258	Prov. 14:13
260	2 Cor. 7:10; Matt. 26:75
261	2 Sam. 12; Matt. 27:5; 2 Cor. 7:10
262	John 11:35
263	Ps. 7:11; Mark 3:1-6; Eph. 4:26; James 1:19, 20; Matt. 23:37; Prov. 29:11
264	Eph. 4:26; Eph. 6:1
265	Prov. 22:24; Job 5:2
266	Prov. 15:18
267	John 2:15
268	Deut. 32:35; Rom. 12:19; Eph 4:2
269	Eph. 5:22; Col 3:12,13,21
270	Col. 3:21; Matt. 22:39
271	Eph. 4:26
272	Prov. 14:7, 29; Ecc. 7:9; 1 Cor. 10:31; Eph. 4:26
274	1 John 4:18; Rom. 8:1; 2 Kings 6:8-17; Phil. 4:4-7

SCRIPTURAL INDEX IN BIBLICAL ORDER

Genesis
1:1	p. 15
1:26	pp. 28, 86, 87, 104
1:27	pp. 28, 86, 87
1:28	pp. 67, 83, 87, 104
2:15	p. 104
2:16	p. 225
2:17	p. 225
2:18	p. 120
2:19	p. 183
2:24	p. 149
3:6	p. 145
3:8	pp. 93, 102, 157
3:9	p. 157
3:10	p. 157
5:1	p. 86
9:6	pp. 86, 144
17	p. 25
18:12	p. 167
29	p. 164
30	p. 164
50:20	p. 36

Exodus
3	p. 25, 26
3:14	p. 15
4	p. 25, 26
4:10	p. 176
18	pp. 56, 132
18:13-27	pp. 56, 133

Deuteronomy
6:7	p. 214
9:7	p. 222
24:5	p. 150
32:35	p. 268

Judges
10:16	p. 241

1 Samuel
1:11	p. 200
15:3	p. 154
15:13	p. 161
15:14	p. 161
15:15	p. 161
15:19	p. 161
15:20	p. 161
15:21	p. 161
15:30	p. 153
17:28	p. 162

2 Samuel
6:14	p. 18
12	p. 261

2 Kings
6:8-17	p. 274

Ecclesiastes
2:24	p. 132
2:25	p. 132
3	p. 176
3:11	pp. 15, 120, 122, 142, 181
7:9	p. 272

Ezekiel
3:1-8	p. 253
18	p. 32
24:15	p. 254
24:16	p. 254
24:17	p. 254

Daniel
4:28-33	p. 64
4:35	p. 219

Job
5:2	p. 265
42:15	p. 114

Psalms
Entire book	p. 18
1	pp. 46, 195
1:3	p. 133
7:11	pp. 242, 263
14:1	pp. 81, 144
15:18	pp. 259, 260
19:1	pp. 24, 62
22:24	p. 259
23:5	p. 179
29:11	p. 257
42	p. 117
42:1	p. 117
42:1-2	p. 118
63	pp. 117, 118, 126
69:9	p. 255
94:11	p. 182
103:13	p. 241
111:2	pp. 23, 67
115:3	p. 219
118:6	p. 179
135:6	p. 219
145:8	p. 241

Proverbs
3:5	p. 62
13:24	p. 124
14:7	p. 272
14:12	p. 205
14:13	p. 258
14:16	p. 29
14:29	p. 272
15:13	p. 18
15:18	p. 266
16:1	p. 204
16:2	p. 204
17:22	pp. 18, 143, 176
20:5	pp. 31, 200, 203
20:29	p. 164
21:2	p. 204, 205
22:2	p.80
22:6	pp. 214, 221
22:24	p. 265
23:7	pp. 45, 69, 183
24:12	p. 205
26:18	p. 165
26:19	p. 165
27:20	p. 137
29:11	p. 263
29:13	pp. 45, 46, 80, 129

Isaiah
43:7	p. 102
46:10	p. 219
53:3	pp. 18, 257
55:8	pp. 62, 65
55:9	pp. 62, 65
64:6	p. 31

Jeremiah
2:13	pp. 137, 141, 178
17:9	p. 30
31:30	p. 32

Matthew

2:13	p. 156
3:9	p. 184
5:16	p. 102
5:45	p. 80
6	p. 209
6:1-4	p. 209
6:1-18	p. 207
6:5-8	p. 207
6:16	p. 210
6:17	p. 210
6:18	p. 210
6:34	p. 58
7:11	p. 179
10: 17	p. 125
10: 22	p. 125
10:40	p. 91
11:28	p. 122
11:29	p. 122
11:30	p. 122
14:15-22	p. 127
14:23	p. 125
15:36	p. 127
17:5	p. 90
19:16:22	p. 125
21:12	p. 216
22:37	p. 125
22:38	p. 125
22:39	pp. 125, 270
23	p. 31
23:37	p. 263
26:36ff	p. 121
26:37	pp. 125, 257
26:38	pp. 234, 241, 257
26:39	pp. 125, 155
26:75	p. 260
27:5	p. 261

Mark

1:35	p. 133
3:1-6	p. 263
4:38	pp. 133, 123, 133, 155
6:30	pp. 133, 156
6:45	p. 133
8:1-8	p. 127
8:15	p. 32
10:17-23	p. 125
11:15	p. 216
11:27	p. 218
12:30-31	p. 125
14:17	p. 125
14:32	p. 133
14:36	p. 125

Luke

2:8	p. 58
2:9	p. 58
2:10-20	pp. 59
2:11	p. 18
4:28	pp. 133, 156
4:29	pp. 133, 156
4:30	pp. 133, 156
4:42	p. 133
6:12	p. 133
8:2	p. 125
8:22-23	p. 133
10:22	p. 218
16:15	p. 184
21:3	p. 133
21:37	p. 133
22:42	p: 125
22:44	p. 257

John

1:13	p. 220
2	p. 25
2:15	pp. 255, 267
2:16	p. 255
2:17	p. 255
3:16	pp. 35, 93, 125, 220
3:35	p. 91
4:10	p. 117
4:11	p. 117
4:12	p. 117
4:13	pp. 117, 178
4:24	p. 87
5:39	p. 184
6:35	p. 132
6:64	p. 204
7:37	pp. 117, 132, 135
7:38	p. 117
8:16	p. 91
8:44	p. 64
10:15	p. 184
11	p. 25
11:33	p. 241
11:34	p. 241
11:35	pp. 241, 247, 254, 255, 262
11:53	p. 133
11:54	pp. 133, 156
13	p. 118
13:12	p. 184
14:16	p. 91
14:26	p. 91
15:10	p. 91
15:18	p. 184
16:7	p. 91
16:10	p. 91
16:13	p. 90
16:14	p. 91
16:28	p. 90
17:1	p. 90
17:3	p. 91
17:5	p. 91
17:18	p. 91
21:17	p. 184

Acts

9	p. 25
10:38	p. 91
11:23	p. 100
15:18	p. 219
27:43	p. 100

Romans

1	p. 31
1:18	pp. 111, 135
1:24-28	p. 220
3:23	pp. 30, 222
5:6	p. 35
5:7	p. 35
5:8	p. 35, 93
5:10	p. 95
6:23	p. 30
8:1	p. 274
8:16	p. 183
8:28	pp. 100, 252
8:38	pp. 155, 177
8:39	p. 93
9:11	p. 100
9:18	p. 219
9:19	p. 100
12:19	p. 268
13:13	p. 230

1 Corinthians

4:2	p. 119
4:4	p. 205
4:5	p. 205
6:11	p. 35
10:27	p. 220
10:30	p. 220
10:31	pp. 37, 43, 100, 101, 209, 215, 265, 272
11:7	p. 86
13:7	p. 184
15:3	p. 46
15:33	pp. 45, 46, 81

2 Corinthians
2:7	p. 18
4:7	pp. 155, 176, 177
4:8	pp. 155, 176, 177
4:9	pp. 155, 176, 177
5:19	pp. 95, 102
5:20	pp. 102, 160
7:10	pp. 260, 261
12:9	p. 19

Galatians
6:2	p. 121

Ephesians
1:5	p. 96
1:11	pp. 100, 219
2:1	p. 30
4:1-32	p. 119
4:2	p. 268
4:17-32	pp. 232, 234
4:23	p. 183
4:26	pp. 263, 264, 271, 272
4:30	p. 242
5:2	p. 93
5:22	p. 269
6	p. 46
6:1	p. 264
6:2	p. 149
6:10-18	p. 32

Philippians
1	pp. 208, 233
1:8	p. 242
1:9	p. 83
1:10	p. 83
1:15-18	p. 1204
2:10	p. 68
4:1	p. 46
4:4	pp. 241. 274
4:5	p. 274

Philippians cont.
4:4-7	p. 274
4:6	pp. 58, 181, 248, 274
4:7	p. 274
4:8	pp. 46, 195, 200
4:11	p. 18

Colossians
1:21	p. 95
1:22	p. 95
2:13	p. 222
3:2	p. 200
3:10	p. 184
3:12	p. 269
3:13	p. 269
3:21	pp. 269, 270

1 Thessalonians
2:3	p. 204

2 Timothy
1:9	p. 100
2:15	p. 46
3:10	p. 100
3:16	pp. 26, 27, 63

Titus
1:12	p. 81
1:13	p. 81

Philemon
14	p. 220

Hebrews
5:14	p. 82
10:25	pp. 46, 121
11:1	p. 13

James
1:8	p. 64
1:19	p. 263
1:20	p. 263
1:22	p. 238
1:23	p. 238
1:24	p. 238
2:1-4	p. 76
2:26	p. 238
3:4	p. 218
3:9	p. 86
4:3	p. 205
4:4	p. 218

1 Peter
3:3	p. 114
4:3	p. 100

2 Peter
1:3	p. 83

1 John
1:9	p. 34
2:15	p. 138
2:16	pp. 116, 138
2:17	p. 138
3:1	p. 97
3:4	p. 222
4:16	p. 184
4:18	pp. 179, 274
4:19	p. 178, 179

Revelations
17:13	p. 220
17:17	p. 220

REFERENCES

Adams, J.E. (1973). *The Christian counselor's manual.* Phillipsburg, New Jersey: Presbyterian and Reformed Publishing Company.

Adams, J.E. (1978). *Competent to counsel.* Phillipsburg: The Presbyterian and Reformed Publishing Company.

Allport, G. (1954). *The nature of prejudice.* Cambridge, Massachusetts: Addison-Wesley Publishing Co., Inc.

Bauer, W., Arndt, W.F., & Gingrich, F.W. (1979). *A Greek-English lexicon of the New Testament and other early Christian literature (2nd ed.).* Chicago: The University of Chicago Press.

Boettner, L. (1974). *Studies in theology.* Phillipsburg, NJ: The Presbyterian and Reformed Publishing Company.

Bono, D. (1991). The impact of cooperative learning on Suzy and Janie's attitudes about math. Retrieved from http://mathforum.org/~sarah/Discussion.Sessions/biblio.attitudes.html.

Brown, F., Driver, S.R., & Briggs, C.A. (Eds.) (1968). *A Hebrew and English Lexicon of the Old Testament.* Oxford: Clarendon Press.

Calvin, J. (1979). Commentary on genesis. In J. King (Ed.), *Calvin's commentaries (Vol. 1).* Grand Rapids, MI: Baker Book House.

Chaddha, R. (2008). *Talking with Kanzi the Bonobo.* Retrieved from www.pbs.org

Chafer, L.S. (1974). *Major Bible themes.* Grand Rapids, MI: Zondervan Publishing House.

Changing Minds. (2002). *Reaction formation.* Retrieved February 3, 2009 from http://changingminds.org/explanations/behaviors/coping/reaction_formation.htm

Cook, R. (2004). Kohler's research on the mentality of apes. In J.L. Gould & C.G. Gould, *The animal mind.* New York: W.H. Freeman & Company.

Crabb, L.J. (1982). *Core I.* [Lecture Notes]. Winona Lake, IN: Grace Theological Seminary.

Crabb, L. (1987). *Understanding people.* Winona Lake, IN: BMH Books.

Cutler, B.L., Penrod, S.D. (1988). Juror decision making in eyewitness identification cases. *Law and Human Behavior, 12,* 41-55.

Dehaene, S. (1997). *The number sense: how the mind creates mathematics.* New York: Oxford University Press.

Davis, J. J. (1975). *Paradise to prison.* Winona Lake: BMH Books.

Diamond, J. (1994). Sex differences in science museums; a review. *Curator, 37(1),* 17-24.

Edgington, T.J. (1985). *An evaluation of the motivational constructs of the human heart —and a defense of the concepts of the "personal circle."* [Unpublished doctoral dissertation]. Grace Theological Seminary, Winona Lake, IN.

Edgington, T.J. (1988). *Fundamentalism viewed as a single dimension and multi-variety in predicting a level of cognitive complexity among fundamentalist seminary students.* (Unpublished doctoral dissertation). Ball State University, Muncie, IN.

Edgington, T.J. & Hutchinson, R.L. (1990). Fundamentalism as a predictor of cognitive complexity. *Journal of Psychology and Christianity, 9(1),* 47.

Edgington, T.J. (1995). *Healing helps from the Bible.* Winona Lake: Evangel Press.

Edgington, T.J. (2006). *Theological foundations.* [Lecture Notes]. Grace College, Winona Lake, IN.

Edgington, T.J. & Edgington, L.K. (2013). *Biblical psychology.* Leesburg, IN: Edgington Publications.

Ellis, A. (2004). *Rational emotive behavior therapy: it works for me, it can work for you.* New York: Prometheus Books.

Encarta. (1998-2004). *World English dictionary.* Mountain View, CA: Microsoft Corporation.

Erikson, M.J. (1995). *Christian theology*. Grand Rapids, Michigan: Baker Book House.

Farnsworth, K.E. (1975). Psychology and Christianity: a substantial integration. *Journal of the American Scientific Affiliation, Science in Christian Perspective, JASA 27*, 60-66.

Flat Earth Society Inc. (1998). *The Flat earth society*. Retrieved from http://www.alaska.net/~clund/e_djublonskopf/Flatearthsociety.htm.

Frankl, V.E. (1959). *Man's search for meaning*. New York: Washington Square Press.

Frazier, D. & Forward, S. (1997). *Emotional blackmail*. New York: HarperCollins Publishers.

Freud, S. (1913). *Totem and taboo*. Mineola, New York: Dover Publications, Inc.

Freud, S. (1927a). *Civilization and its discontents*. London: Hogarth Press.

Freud, S. (1927b). *The future of an illusion*. London: Hogarth Press.

Freud, S. (1939). *Moses and monotheism*. Letchworth, Hertfordshire: Hogarth Press.

Freud, S. (2002). *Civilization and its discontents*. London: Penguin.

Friedrich, S.L. (2007). Denial. *Encyclopedia of mental disorders: del-fi*. Retrieved from http://www.minddisorders.com/Del-Fi/Denial.html.

Gentry, R. (2005). *Tad Lincoln*. Retrieved from http://www.everythinglincoln.com/articles/TadLincoln.html.

Getz, G. (2002). *Building up one another*. Colorado Springs: David C. Cook Publishing.

Glasser, W. (1998). *Choice theory*. New York: HarperCollins Publishers.

Harder, A.F. (2002). The developmental stages of Erik Erikson. Retrieved from http://www.learningplaceonline.com/stages/organize/Erikson.htm.

Harris, T. (2010). *How hypnosis works*. HowStuffWorks, Inc. Retrieved from http://science.howstuffworks.com/hypnosis.htm.

Hill, R.B. (2009). Historical context of the work ethic. *History of work ethic*. Retrieved from http://www.coe.uga.edu/~rhill/workethic/hist.htm.

Hodge, C. (1979). *Systematic theology* (Vol. 2). Grand Rapids, Michigan: Wm. B. Eerdmans Publishing Company.

Hovind, K. (1999). The Hovind Theory. In K. Hovind, *Unmasking the false religion of evolution*. Retrieved from http://www.cs.joensuu.fi/~vtenhu/hovind/CHP-5.htm.

Hutchinson, J.C. (1998). The design argument in scientific discourse: historical-theological perspective from the seventeenth century. *Journal of evangelical theological society*. Retrieved from http://www.etsjets.org/ files/JETS-PDFs/41/41-1/41-1-pp085-105 JETS.pdf.

Joy, D. (1969). *The effects of value-oriented instruction in the church and in the home.* (Unpublished doctoral dissertation). Indiana University, Bloomington, IN.

Keil, C.F. & Delitzsche, F. (1975). *Commentary on the Old Testament (Vol 7).* Grand Rapids, Michigan: William B. Eerdmans Publishing Company.

Kittel, G. & Mromiley, G.W. (1964). *Theological dictionary of the New Testament (Vol. 1).* Grand Rapids, Michigan: William B. Eerdmans Publishing Company.

Knox, D.B. (1982). *The everlasting God.* Hertfordshire: Evangelical Press.

Kulikovsky, A.S. (2005). Scripture and general revelation. *Journal of Creation, 19(2),* 23-28.

Laidlaw, R.A. (1879). *Bible doctrine of man.* Edinburgh: T. and T. Clark.

Lamont, A. (1997). *Great Christian scientists: Blaise Pascal (1623-1662): outstanding scientist and committed Christian.* Retrieved from http://www.answersingenesis.org/articles/cm/v20/n1/pascal

Lewis, C.S. (1955). *Surprised by joy.* New York: Harcourt, Inc.

Lewis, C.S. (1980). *Mere Christianity*. New York: HarperCollins Publishers.

Li, A. & Adamson, G. (1992). Gifted secondary students' preferred learning style: cooperative, competitive, or individualistic? *Journal of Education of the Gifted, 16(1),* 46-54. Retrieved from http://mathforum.org/~sarah/Discussion.Sessions/biblio.attitudes.html

Lorenz, K. (1970). *Studies in animal and human behavior*. Cambridge, MA: Harvard University Press.

MacArthur, J. (2009). The Josiah Grauman story. [Video file]. Retrieved from http://billsbible.blogspot.com/2009/09/josiah-grauman-story-john-macarthur.html

McClain, A.J. & Whitcomb, J.C. (1981). *God and revelation*. [Unpublished syllabus]. Winona Lake: Grace Theological Seminary.

Oehler, G.F. (1883). *Old Testament theology* (Vol. 1). New York: Funk and Wagnalls Company.

Plaster, D. (2003). *Systematic theology*. [PowerPoint slides]. Grace Theological Seminary, Winona Lake, IN.

Raffaele, P. (2006). Speaking Bonobo. *Smithsonian Magazine*. Retrieved from http://www.smithsonianmag.com.

Randall, R.P. (1955). *Lincoln's sons*. Little, Brown & Co. Retrieved from http://www.abrahamlincolnsclassroom.org/Library/newsletter.asp?ID=35&CRLI=115.

Rogers, C. (1961). *On becoming a person.* Boston: Houghton Mifflin Company.

Rogers, C. (1977). *Carl Rogers on personal power: inner strength and its revolutionary impact.* New York: Delacorte Press.

Ryrie, C.C. (1978). *The Ryrie study Bible.* Chicago: Moody Press.

Seaman, R. (n.d.) RNZAF A-4 skyhawk team tricks. Retrieved January 5, 2009 from http://www.richard seaman.com/Aircraft/AirShows/RNZAF/Skyhawks/TeamTricks/index.html

Schultz, D.P. & Schultz, S.E. (2013). *Theories of personality.* Belmont, CA: Wadsworth Cengage Learning.

Skinner, B.F. (1976). *Beyond freedom and dignity.* Indianapolis: Hackett Publishing Company Inc.

Sporer, S.L., Malpass, R.S., & Koehnken, G. (1996). *Psychological issues in eyewitness identification.* Mahwah, New Jersey: Erlbaum.

Stephen, W. (1986). The effects of school desegregation: an evaluation 30 years after brown. In M.J. Saks & L. Saxe (Eds.), *Advances in Applied Social Psychology* (Vol. 3) (181-206). Hillsdale, NJ: Erlbaum.

Taxidermy4Cash (2004). John Edmondstone. In *Charles Darwin.* Retrieved from http://www.taxidermy4cash.com/darwin.html

Theissen (1949). *Lectures in systematic theology.* Grand Rapids, Michigan: Wm. B. Eerdmans Publishing Company.

Topinka, L. (1984). *Mount St. Helens: a general slide set.* Vancouver, WA: USGS/Cascades Volcano Observatory. Retrieved from http://www.nt.ntnu.no/users/ystenes/div/bilder/sidesp/helene/slideset.html

Webster, M. (1983). *Webster's ninth new collegiate dictionary.* Springfield, MA: Merriam Webster Inc.

Wells, G.L. & Olson, E.A. (2003). Eyewitness testimony. *Annual Review of Psychology, 54,* 277-295.

Westminster Assembly. (1646). *Westminster confession: article 12.* London.

Wikipedia. *Kanzi.* Retrieved August 10, 2012 from http://en.wikipedia.org/wiki/Kanzi.

Williams, R.J. (1976). *Hebrew syntax.* Toronto: University of Toronto Press.

Yancy, P. (1988). *Disappointment with God.* Grand Rapids, Michigan: Zondervan.

CPSIA information can be obtained
at www.ICGtesting.com
Printed in the USA
BVHW041703100523
663940BV00005B/51

9 781304 545787